Helping Battered Wo

Helping Battered Women

New Perspectives and Remedies

Edited by

Albert R. Roberts

New York   Oxford
OXFORD UNIVERSITY PRESS
1996

Oxford University Press

Oxford   New York
Athens   Aukland   Bangkok   Bombay
Calcutta   Cape Town   Dar es Salaam   Delhi
Florence   Hong Kong   Istanbul   Karachi
Kuala Lumpur   Madras   Madrid   Melbourne
Mexico City   Nairobi   Paris   Singapore
Taipei   Tokyo   Toronto

and associated companies in
Berlin   Ibadan

Library of Congress Cataloging-in-Publication Data
Helping battered women : new perspectives and remedies /
edited by Albert R. Roberts.
p. cm.   Includes bibliographical references (p.   ) and index.
ISBN 0-19-509586-3 ISBN 0-19-509587-1 (pbk).
1. Abused wives—Services for—United States.   2. Abused women—
Services for—United States.   3. Social work with women—United
States.   4. Wife abuse—United States—Prevention.
I. Roberts, Albert R.
HV1445.H387   1996
362.82'928'0973—dc20   95-2158
1 3 5 7 9 8 6 4 2

Printed in the United States of America
on acid-free paper

Preface

Since the publication of two of my earlier books, *Sheltering Battered Women* (1981) and *Battered Women and Their Families* (1984), the policies and programs for battered women have changed dramatically. Professional and public interest in reform legislation, advocacy efforts, and services developed on behalf of battered women and their children has grown tremendously in the past decade. Each year, hundreds of thousands of battered women in acute crisis situations seek help from battered women's shelters, hospital emergency rooms, police departments, the courts, and community mental health centers. This book examines the latest legal remedies, emergency adult abuse protocols, treatment approaches, intervention strategies, and advocacy and programs for battered women and their children.

This book will present major policy reforms and recent program developments. It is the first book to examine major criminal justice and social work issues from both a macropolicy and a microclinical perspective. It is a collaborative work, with original chapters written by prominent social workers, clinical psychologists, policy analysts, and criminal justice educators. The contributors have extensive experience gained over many years of working on behalf of women living in violent relationships. Each chapter documents the tremendous effort to develop policies, programs, and services to meet the needs of battered women. Today, legal remedies, twenty-four-hour hotlines and shelters, proarrest policies, and victim advocacy services are widely supported by both federal and state funding.

Part I of this book, consisting of five chapters, explores the latest policy issues, empirical research, social change efforts, and case management strategies. Chapter 1 identifies and shatters the nine most common myths regarding battered women. It then provides a selection of case illustrations, the 1994 legislation, and clinical issues to be discussed throughout the book. Chapter 2 examines the summary findings of a national survey of the objectives, advocacy and social change mission, and services provided by 622 battered women's organizations throughout the United States. Chapter 3 reports the summary findings of an important research study comparing incarcerated battered women who killed their abusive partner with a community sample of battered women who did not kill their partner. Chapter 4 examines criminal justice and case management strategies recently implemented in New York City on behalf of abused senior citizens, particularly elderly battered women. Chapter 5 reviews the major theories of the causes of domestic violence, the dearth of longitudinal studies, and the treatment methods appropriate for battered women.

Part II, consisting of four chapters, provides detailed information on police responses to abused women in the 1990s; the latest civil and criminal remedies that magistrates can order on behalf of battered women; the changing legal remedies; the recognition of women battering as a crime; expert testimony; and the battered woman syndrome (BWS). The areas highlighted in Chapters 6 through 9 include the purposes of restraining orders, class action suits, consent decrees against two police departments that led to improved police responses, and the benefits of introducing expert testimony on the battered woman syndrome to support the self-defense claims of battered women charged with the homicide of their abusers.

Part III has five chapters, on crisis-oriented responses, mental health assessment and interventions, services for battered women and their children and the false connection between alcoholism and domestic violence. The first chapter in this section offers insights into the ways in which Roberts's seven-stage crisis intervention model can be effectively used with emergency shelter residents to resolve their acute crisis situation. Chapter 11, the second chapter in this section, provides a comprehensive analysis of the issues, research, and programs for children of battered women. Chapter 12 discusses a variety of empirically based strategies for assessment and intervention designed specifically for battered women (e.g., self-report measures, posttraumatic stress disorder (PTSD) and other abuse-related symptoms, and specific treatment goals for short-term treatment). The assessment strategies and therapeutic approaches described in Chapter 12 address presenting problems experienced as the result of actual beatings and as a reaction to the battered woman's environment. Chapter 13 focuses on two common false assumptions: Alcohol use and/or alcoholism causes men to batter, and alcoholism treatment alone will end the abuse. Chapter 14 emphasizes the cultural barriers and obstacles to delivering services to battered Latina women.

The focus of this book is on the most effective policies and programs currently available for eliminating battering by spouses as well as cohabiting partners. This interdisciplinary volume should become a valuable aid to social workers, psychologists, criminal justice professors, family physicians, judges, legislators and policy analysts, reference librarians, and family violence scholars.

New Brunswick, N.J.   A.R.R.
April 1995

Acknowledgments

First and foremost, I would like to express my gratitude to all the members of my author team who made this book possible. Second, I appreciate the sage advice and guidance of Senior Editor Gioia Stevens. Third, I would like to thank Michael J. Smith, one of the diligent reviewers of the manuscript, for his thorough comments on an earlier draft. Finally, I would like to acknowledge the editorial and production staff at Oxford University Press, particularly Irene Pavitt, Assistant Managing Editor. She was responsible for keeping the book on schedule while coordinating numerous details related to copyediting, production, and design.

Special thanks go to a cadre of former honor students in the Administration of Justice program at Rutgers University who served as interviewers between 1990 and 1992, including Mark Boyer, Lisa Cassa, Pat Dahl, Patricia Cassidy, Patrice Paldino, Gina Pisano, Joann Gonsalez, Jeannine Saracino, and Lisa Trembly.

My appreciation also goes to Stephanie M. Ingersoll for preparing a thorough author index, and to Carolyn S. Stoltman for assisting me in preparing the subject index.

I have interviewed hundreds of battered women over the past sixteen years. This book grew out of my in-depth interviews with incarcerated battered women as well as former college students and graduate students at C. W. Post College, Brooklyn College, Indiana University, and Rutgers University. Finally, I would like to dedicate this book to the many survivors of woman battering who have taught us all about resiliency and coping with crisis.

I was fortunate to have had several professors in graduate school whose advice and insights brought out the best in me, including Paul Ephross, Joe Grau, Peter P. Lejins, and Daniel Thursz. These dedicated and brilliant educators freely shared their ideas and knowledge with me. Dean Mary Davidson deserves special appreciation for her encouragement and recognition of my publications. Finally, I want to express my gratitude to my wife, Beverly, for her support and understanding, not only in the publication of this book, but with all my previous publications.

Contents

Foreword

I have been involved with woman-battering cases for twenty-three years. In my work as a judge in the Bronx, New York State Family Court, and previously as a legal services attorney, I have seen thousands of battered women who have been subjected to prolonged, serious physical violence and psychological terror.

Effective help for victims of family violence requires cooperation among the various helping professionals. Those of us in this field found that counseling and treatment alone cannot end the danger that victims encounter from the people with whom they live and on whom they may be economically dependent. Legal action alone cannot turn their fear of harm into a successful plan for safety. For women to escape the violence in their lives, the counselors, psychologists, nurses, doctors, social workers, advocates, and lawyers treating and assisting them must work together, offering resources and viable alternatives.

Wife beating has been the subject of sporadic reform movements, but then faded into the background as accepted behavior during the past two centuries. The current effort to protect battered wives emerged in the early 1970s, when the women's movement turned its attention to the crime of rape. In the course of rape crisis intervention, the women discovered that the calls for information and help came primarily from women who were being beaten by their husbands.

Domestic violence also became a focus of advocacy by government-funded, free community legal services offices providing divorce representation to the poor. In some legal services offices, more than 80 percent of the divorce clients were women battered by their husbands.* From these two, unrelated organizations came movements in every state to expand police authority to arrest wife beaters and to create civil-legal remedies for battered women. This campaign achieved substantial successes in legislative and policy reforms, and generated public sympathy for battered wives.

---

*The writer became a legal services attorney in September 1971. She spent the next fourteen years representing poor women in Brooklyn, New York, in divorce actions. More than 80 percent of her clients were wives who had been beaten by their husbands over a period of years.

There are several technical, legal reasons for these successes in changing the laws. Ostensibly, wife beating was included in the definition of the crime of assault before the reform efforts began. Victims of domestic violence, unlike those of rape, usually have physical injuries to "corroborate" their claim of assault. "Consent" was never an issue in the crime of assault (by contrast to the crime of rape, in which lack of consent to sexual contact is the central issue); therefore, there was no requirement that the victim demonstrate "resistance" to disprove consent. Thus domestic-violence law reforms did not require revising traditional legal theories and procedures.

The legislative response to domestic violence included creation of new, civil-legal remedies for battered women. "Orders of protection" are available now in nearly every state. They may contain provisions directing abusive spouses to cease beating and threatening their spouses and children, to remove themselves from family homes, and to stay away from their spouses and children. Child custody may be awarded to victims, and visitation by offenders may be prohibited or limited to supervised settings. This relief is available on an immediate, temporary basis prior to the time set for a full hearing, and before notice is given to accused spouses. Most state statutes authorize the police to arrest spouses alleged to have violated these civil orders on the same basis that persons alleged to have committed crimes may be arrested.

Legislatures and courts also addressed wife beating as a crime of violence. They responded to pressure from the women's movement to stop domestic violence. Thus the criminal justice system became involved in protecting battered women. In spite of these successes, women's accusations are often denied the credibility accorded to mens' denials of wrongdoing. Thus the sexist attitudes so visible in the rape laws continue, in a subtler fashion, to affect the criminal justice response to violence against women. Battered women, therefore, need social workers, psychologists, nurses, physicians, and lawyers who can help them understand how to get help and can explain the nature of the problems they will encounter as they try to free themselves from violent relationships.

There is a social consensus that violence against women is no longer to be tolerated. Government action is viewed as appropriate to stop violence against women by their family members. In addition, service methods have developed in light of experiences at battered women's shelters and in community organizations.

In this volume, twenty experts examine the latest proposals and programs regarding services to abused women and accountability for abusive men. *Helping Battered Women: New Perspectives and Remedies* is a well-written, inclusive, scholarly, and practical sourcebook. It is one of the few books that succeeds in synthesizing policy and clinical concerns.

The book begins with Albert Roberts's chapter providing an overview of the family violence field and a preview of the chapters to follow. Roberts shatters the most common myths about battered women and domestic violence. He describes the latest research findings, social action, public policy, and counseling strategies.

The contributors to this outstanding book examine current issues and changes in the past ten years regarding laws and legal remedies, governmental policies, and clinical approaches, and services for battered women and their children.

Albert R. Roberts's comprehensive book provides a wealth of practical information and insights for practitioners, administrators and trainers in the field of family violence. The authors provide up-to-date information on federal and state laws, policies, and programs aimed at reducing women abuse. I highly recommend this book to all judges, court administrators, attorneys, prosecutors, court case–managers, probation officers, advocates, police officers, psychologists, social workers, nurses, physicians, and policymakers at the federal, state, and local levels.

Marjory D. Fields, Supervising Judge
Family Court of the State of New York, County of the Bronx

Contributors

Ann A. Abbott, Ph.D., President, National Association of Social Workers

Gloria Bonilla-Santiago, Ph.D., School of Social Work, Rutgers University

John C. Bricout, M.S.W., School of Social Work, State University of New York at Buffalo

Patricia Brownell, Ph.D., Graduate School of Social Services, Fordham University at Lincoln Center

Bonnie E. Carlson, Ph.D., School of Social Welfare, State University of New York at Albany

Joseph M. Caruso, Ph.D., Hudson Valley Community College

Karla M. Digirolama, New York State Office for the Prevention of Domestic Violence

Diane C. Dwyer, M.S.W., Department of Social Work, State University of New York at Brockport

Sophia F. Dziegielewski, Ph.D., School of Social Work, University of Alabama

Lisa A. Frisch, M.A., New York State Office for the Prevention of Domestic Violence

Thomas Jackson, Ph.D., Department of Psychology, University of Arkansas

Nora B. Krause, M.S.W., School of Social Work, University of Tennessee

Mindy B. Mechanic, Ph.D., Department of Psychology, University of Missouri–St. Louis

Patricia Petretic-Jackson, Ph.D., Department of Psychology, University of Arkansas

Cheryl Resnick, D.S.W., Department of Social Work, Georgian Court College

Albert R. Roberts, D.S.W., School of Social Work, Rutgers University

Susan E. Roche, Ph.D., Department of Social Work, University of Vermont

Pam J. Sadoski, M.S.W., Department of Social Work, University of Vermont

Paul R. Smokowski, M.S.W., School of Social Work, State University of New York at Buffalo

John S. Wodarski, Ph.D., School of Social Work, State University of New York at Buffalo

Theresa M. Zubretsky, New York State Office for the Prevention of Domestic Violence

Helping Battered Women

I

Social Action, Research, and Policy Reforms

1

Introduction: Myths and Realities Regarding Battered Women

Albert R. Roberts

Rachel, age thirty-four, described her abusive partner's self-destructive patterns and his death threats against her:

> He had been doing drugs, and he started getting paranoid and accused me of making signals out to someone in the hall—and there was no one out there. He asked me to go downstairs to get something and he locked himself in the room, and I knew that he was upset and I heard the click of a gun being dry fired, and I could hear him spinning the barrel and I started getting scared. Finally I convinced him to open the door. He acted like he was gonna shoot himself. I begged him not to. The kids were down the hall [sleeping]. I got angry with him and said, "Go ahead, do it"; then I said, "Give it to me—I'll do it." He gave me the gun. I put it down and went downstairs. He came after me and held the gun to my head and said, "If I can't have you, no one can!" He cocked it [the gun]. We were there for a long time. I was crying and told him I never cheated on him, and finally through talking, I convinced him not to do it. For a long time I thought I was gonna die that night.

Mindy, age twenty-two, a visiting nurse with a five-year-old son, briefly described her self-destructive coping attempts. In order to cope with the violent abuse—being hit with a lead pipe and empty beer bottles by her boyfriend—she took drugs and attempted suicide. In her words,

> I O-Ded on cocaine intravenously. Purposely! I couldn't take it anymore. I was real depressed and upset and afraid that he was going to beat our son. I went to the hospital; they pumped my stomach, then told me that I was a drug addict. Then they put me in a

ninety-day inpatient drug program which I didn't complete. The psychiatrist put me on Fisterol, an antidepressant, and then Haldane.

In Chapter 3, Albert R. Roberts describes in vivid and graphic detail typical illustrations of critical incidents during childhood and adolescence, incidents triggering the worst battering episodes, terroristic and death threats, the nature and extent of injuries, and suicide attempts among a representative sample of 210 battered women.

During the late 1970s and the 1980s, the pendulum shifted from an emphasis on providing emergency shelter and counting the high rates of spouse abuse to an emphasis in the mid-1990s on implementing legal remedies, proarrest policies, case management services, and treatment programs for battered women.

Common Myths

A number of myths and stereotypes hinder both an accurate knowledge of the nature, extent, and intensity of woman battering and effective intervention. Enormous progress has been made in the past few years in regard to major policy reforms and program developments. Recent legislation, more sensitive police and court responses, and communitywide case management approaches offer much promise to lessening the battering of women in the United States. But in order for agency policies and clinical practices to be implemented effectively, our attention needs to be directed toward the realities of domestic violence against women, rather than the myths. This book was written to debunk the traditional myths and replace them with new knowledge, research, social action, public policy, and intervention strategies.

Although considerable progress has been made in funding domestic violence programs in the past ten years, much still remains to be done. There is disproportionately less funding for victim assistance programs when compared with programs and institutions for convicted felons. For example, the Violent Crime Control and Law Enforcement Act of 1994 authorizes nearly $9.9 billion for prisons and an additional $1.7 billion for alternative detention programs, whereas the Violence Against Women Act of the 1994 crime bill authorizes a total of only $1.2 billion over five years for criminal justice programs and social services to aid battered women and victims of sexual assault.

Myth 1.   Woman battering is a problem in only the lower socioeconomic class.

Reality: Woman battering takes place in all social classes, religions, races, and ethnic groups. Although violence against women seems to be more visible in the lower class because it is more frequently reported to the police and hospital emergency rooms in inner-city poor neighborhoods, it is increasingly being recognized as a pervasive problem in middle- and upper-class homes as well. For example, the murder of Nicole Brown Simpson in 1994 received intensive media scrutiny because of reports that she had been beaten by her ex-husband, former football legend O. J. Simpson. In her new book, Georgette Mosbacher, former wife of the CEO of Fabergé, describes the battering she endured while married.

Although woman battering occurs in all socioeconomic classes, it is reported to be more prevalent in the lowest economic groups. The U.S. Department of Justice's 1994 National Crime Victimization Survey Report states that women with a family income under $9,999 were more than five times as likely to be a victim of a violent incident perpetrated by an "intimate" than were women with a family income over $30,000 (BJS, 1994).

Myth 2.   Woman battering is not a significant problem because most incidents are in the form of a slap or a punch that do not cause serious injury.

Reality: Woman battering is a very serious problem. National Crime Survey data estimate the number of visits each year for medical care resulting from domestic violence: 28,700 visits to a hospital emergency room, 39,900 visits to a physician's office, 21,000 in-patient hospitalizations, and 99,800 days of hospitalization. The total health-care costs per year is approximately $44,393,700 (McLeer & Anwar, 1989; National Crime Surveys, 1981).

For example, Delores, age forty-two, described her injuries from years of battering: "Two broken ribs, scars on my elbows and thighs, bruises on my back and neck. Broke my bridge in five places. All of my top teeth are loose. My glasses were broken." In addition, "He threatened to kill me. If he was drunk enough, I thought he would. He always said, 'If I ever catch you with another man, I'll kill you' and 'If you leave me, I'll blow your brains out'."

Myth 3.   Elder abuse (abuse of one's elderly parent) is not much of a problem.

Reality: According to the 1990 report of the House of Representatives Select Committee on Aging, *Elder Abuse: A Decade of Shame and Inaction,* more than 1.5 million older persons may be victims of abuse by their adult children. This figure is only an estimate because there is no accurate reporting system for elder-abuse incidents. See Chapter 4 for a discussion of battered elderly women, police complaint reports as a source of early case findings, the need for statutory or mandatory reporting of elder abuse and financial exploitation (as is done in child-abuse cases), and a model case-management strategy.

Myth 4.   The police do not want to arrest the batterer because they view domestic violence calls as a private matter.

Reality: I had black eyes from his hitting and punching me. I called 911 and the police came, and I said to arrest him. He told them I was nuts because I was on pills from the doctor. The house was a mess, and I had the baby. The police officer believed me, and they arrested him. One officer asked me if I had anywhere to go, so I said I was from New Jersey and my mother was there. He advised me to go back to New Jersey with the money I had. The police said otherwise it would happen again. So I called my mother; bought a ticket and left the next morning. He [the batterer] called and told me to drop the charges while I was packing to leave. I told him no.

Reality: Before 1985, the police often did not want to arrest the batterer when they were called to the scene in a domestic violence case. However, the court decision in the case of *Thurman* v. *The City of Torrington* (1985) served notice to police departments across the country to treat domestic violence reports as they would any other crime in which the perpetrator and victim do not know each other.

In this Torrington, Connecticut, case, Tracey Thurman had repeatedly begged the police for protection from her former husband, Charles "Buck" Thurman. In one instance, the police were called to Ms. Tracey Thurman's residence because her former husband was beating and stabbing her just outside her home. When the police officer finally arrived (his arrival was delayed for approximately twenty minutes while he went to the station to "relieve himself"), he asked Buck for the knife but did not handcuff or attempt to arrest him. Buck then continued to brutalize Tracey, kicking and stomping on her. Tracey suffered very serious injuries, including partial paralysis. She won her lawsuit against the Torrington police department for its negligence in not arresting Buck and for violating her constitutional rights to equal protection. Ms. Tracey Thurman was awarded $2.3 million in compensatory damages, which was later reduced to $1.9 million. Because of the large settlement in the Thurman case, this case is credited as being the catalyst for the development of mandatory arrest laws in a growing number of states.

As discussed in Chapter 6, by 1989, thirteen states had enacted mandatory arrest policies for the perpetrators of domestic violence, although in several of the states, arrest is mandatory only when the batterer violates a restraining order. In addition, Chapter 8 discusses the far-reaching changes in New York State's Family Court Act, Domestic Relations Law, and Criminal Procedural Law. New York's Family Protection and Domestic Violence Intervention Act of 1994 requires police to make arrests in cases in which there is reasonable cause to believe that a felony or misdemeanor was committed by one family or household member against another or if an order of protection was violated. As of 1991, in New Jersey, arrest is mandatory if a woman suffers an injury or complains of injury. New Jersey law states that arrest is mandatory for violating a restraining order if it involves a new act of domestic violence.

Myth 5.   All batterers are psychotic, and no treatment can change their violent habits.

Reality: The majority of men who assault women can be helped. There are two main types of intervention for men who assault women: arrest and counseling. Studies have shown that mandatory arrest has worked for some types of batterers, but not others. In their 1992 study of 1,200 cases in Milwaukee, Sherman and associates found that arrest seemed to result in an escalation of battering among unemployed minorities, whereas arrest had a deterrent effect among abusers who were employed, white, and married at the time of the study. See Chapter 6 for a detailed discussion of the recent studies of the deterrent effect of arrest on different subgroups of batterers.

The Duluth, Minnesota, Domestic Abuse Intervention Project (DAIP) conducted a twelve-month follow-up study in which battered women were asked their opinion of the intervention that the project had used in an effort to make the batterer change his violent habits. Of the women studied, 60 percent said they felt there was improvement when the batterer took part in education and group counseling, whereas 80 percent of the women stated that the improvement had resulted from a combination of involvement by the police and the courts, group counseling, and the shelter (Pence & Paymar, 1993).

Myth 6.   Although many battered women suffer severe beatings for years, only a small percentage experience symptoms of posttraumatic stress disorder (PTSD).

Reality: Tina, age twenty-five, recounted her suicide attempt and intrusive thoughts about the traumatic abusive incidents:

> I tried to kill myself because of depression over life in general. I was fed up—sick and tired of being beaten and miserable and taken advantage of. I kept having recurring nightmares about the battering and death threats. Thoughts of the beatings kept popping into my mind almost every morning. . . . My body took the drugs. I couldn't O-D [overdose]. I tried to hang myself in my backyard, but someone pulled into my driveway and rescued me. I found recently I have a lot to live for.

Three clinical studies of battered women living in shelters or women attending community-based self-help groups found PTSD rates ranging from 45 to 84 percent (Astin et al., 1990; Houskamp & Foy, 1991; Kemp, Rawlings, & Green, 1991). These studies revealed a significant association between the extent and intensity of battering experiences by abused women and the severity of their PTSD symptoms. See Chapter 12 for a detailed discussion of assessment scales, PTSD symptoms, and mental health interventions with battered women.

See Chapter 9 for a detailed discussion of the admissibility of expert testimony on battered women syndrome and PTSD to support self-defense claims made by battered women charged with homicide of their abusers. In some cases the expert testimony and the distortions of it by the press leads to a more severe sentence (e.g., fifteen to twenty years or a life sentence).

Myth 7.   Battered women who remain in a violent relationship do so because they are masochistic.

Reality: Most battered women who remain in an abusive relationship do so for the following reasons:
1. Economic need (e.g., financial dependency);
2. Intermittent reinforcement and traumatic bonding (e.g., the development of strong emotional attachments between intimate partners when the abusive partner is intermittently kind, loving, and apologetic for past violent episodes and promises that it will never happen again, interspersed with beatings and degrading insults);
3. Learned helplessness (e.g., when someone learns from repeated, unpleasant, and painful experiences that he or she is unable to control the aversive environ-

ment or escape, that person will gradually lose the motivation to change the situation);

4. The fear that the abuser will hunt down the victim and kill her if she leaves; and
5. Concern that leaving the relationship and moving to a new location will be a major disruption for the children.

See Chapter 5 for a discussion of theories and causal explanations of women battering.

Myth 8.   Children who have witnessed repeated acts of violence by their father against their mother do not need to participate in a specialized counseling program.

Reality: We had been arguing; I can't remember what about. He became violent and ripped the phone wire off because I tried to call the police. He tied me up with the wire and burned me with an iron. He ran outside and ripped some kind of plug from my car so that it wouldn't work. Both my children were there. My daughter was six, and she was screaming. My son was five, and he just stayed away and hid under his bed.

A report from the American Bar Association (1994) entitled *The Impact of Domestic Violence on Children* urges lawyers and judges to try more actively to protect children from the devastating impact (both physical and psychological) of domestic violence. The report provides the following revealing statistics about children and youth who have witnessed domestic violence: Seventy-five percent of the boys who were present when their mothers were beaten were later identified as having demonstrable behavior problems. Between 20 and 40 percent of chronically violent teens lived in homes in which their mother was beaten. Sixty-three percent of males in the eleven-to-twenty age group who are incarcerated on homicide charges had killed the man who battered their mother.

Jaffe, Wolfe, and Wilson (1990) found that although group counseling was helpful for children with mild to moderate behavior problems, more extensive individual counseling was required for children who had witnessed ongoing and severe violent episodes. Jaffe and associates reported on a four-year study of 371 children who had lived in violent homes. They found that group counseling had helped the children "improve their self-concept, understand that violence in the home was not their fault, become more aware of protection planning, and learn new ways of resolving conflict without resorting to violence" (p. 90).

See Chapter 11 for a detailed discussion of shelter-based programs and group therapy for children of battered women, as well as a review of the evaluations and outcome studies of these programs.

Myth 9.   Alcohol abuse and/or alcoholism causes men to batter their partners.

Reality: Although research indicates that among heavy drinkers there seems to be a higher rate of domestic violence than among nondrinkers, the majority of batterers are not alcoholics and the overwhelming majority of men classified as high level or binge drinkers do not abuse their partners (Straus & Gelles, 1990).

In many cases, alcohol is used as an excuse for battering, not a cause. Disinhibition theory suggests that the physiological effects of heavy drinking include a state of lowered inhibitions or control over the drinker's behavior. Marlatt and Rohsenow (1980) found that the most significant determinant of behavior right after drinking is not the physiological effect of the alcohol itself, but the expectations the individuals place on the drinking experience. Removing the alcohol does not cure the abusive personality. See Chapter 13 for a discussion of the need for two independent forms of treatment for chemically dependent batterers.

Historical Background

Women have been battered by their partners for centuries. Indeed, in most societies, brutal whippings and beatings seem to have been the most salient way of keeping spouses from leaving their husbands. In 1885, the Chicago Protective Agency for Women and Children was established, and according to feminist historian Elizabeth Pleck (1987), this organization was the most important agency effort of the nineteenth century to help women who were victims of physical abuse. This agency provided legal aid, court advocacy, and personal assistance to women victims of assault. An abused woman could receive up to four weeks of shelter at the refuge run by the Women's Club of Chicago, and in addition, battered women were able to receive an equitable amount of property in divorce settlements. The agency also helped abused women secure legal separations and divorces after proving extreme cruelty and/or drunkenness on the part of their husband.

Between 1915 and 1920, twenty-five cities followed Chicago's lead in establishing protective agencies for women.

Of these cities that followed the lead of Chicago's wealthy women advocates, only a few lasted beyond the 1940s. The new Women's Bureaus were a separate unit of the police department and were responsible for helping runaway girls, prostitutes, abused women and abused children. Although these police social workers did not provide legal aid, they did provide counseling, court advocacy, and job placement and arranged for temporary housing for abused women and transient youths. The largest number of police social workers in Women's Bureaus was in Chicago, Cleveland, Baltimore, Detroit, Pittsburgh, Los Angeles, Minneapolis, New York City, Portland, Seattle, St. Louis, St. Paul, and Washington, D.C. (Roberts, 1990). However, by the 1940s all the police Women's Bureaus had been eliminated by a new police chief, city manager, or mayor. In a few police departments the Bureaus were changed to crime prevention bureaus, and a male police administrator replaced the woman director. As a result of the downfall of the police social work movement, it was rare for any help to be offered to battered women until the women's rights movement, which began in the 1970s.

By the late 1970s, emergency shelters, twenty-four-hour hotlines, and a network of volunteer host homes were developed to aid battered women throughout the United States, Canada, and Great Britain. The first shelter, Chiswick Women's Aid, was opened in London in 1972 by Erin Pizzey. Pizzey's efforts to provide emergency shelter for abused women and their children inspired others throughout the Western world to do the same. By 1977, eighty-nine shelters for battered women had been opened throughout the United States, and during that year, the shelter's twenty-four-hour hotlines received over 110,000 calls from battered women.

The major self-reported strengths of emergency services were shelter, twenty-four-hour hotlines, peer counseling, court advocacy, legal aid, and the commitment of staff and volunteers (many of whom work fifty to sixty hours a week, evenings, and weekends). The major problems were overcrowding in the shelters, lack of stable funding, rapid turnover of full-time staff and attrition of volunteers, lack of cooperation by local police and the courts, and poor interagency relations and linkages (Roberts, 1981).

By 1990, there were more than 1,250 battered women's shelters throughout the United States and Canada (Roberts, 1990). In addition, crisis-oriented services for battered women are provided at thousands of local hospital emergency rooms, hospital-based trauma centers, emergency psychiatric services, suicide prevention centers, community mental health center crisis units, and pastoral counseling services (Roberts, 1995).

A number of states have enacted special legislation that provides funding for hotlines and shelters for victims of domestic violence. Every state and major metropolitan area in the country now has crisis-intervention services for battered women and their children. Although the primary focus of these services is to ensure the women's safety, many shelters have evolved into much more than just a place for safe lodging. Crisis intervention for battered women generally includes a twenty-four-hour telephone hotline, a safe and secure emergency shelter (the average length of stay is three to four weeks), an underground network of volunteer homes and shelters, and welfare and court advocacy by student interns and other volunteers (Roberts, 1984). Many shelters also offer peer counseling, support groups, information on women's legal rights, and referral to social service agencies.

In some communities, emergency services for battered women have expanded to include parenting education workshops, assistance in finding housing, employment counseling and job placement for the women, and group counseling for the batterers. In the all-too-often neglected area of assessment and treatment for the children of battered women, a small but growing number of shelters provide either group counseling or referral to mental health centers.

Planned social change and a sharp reduction in a major social problem usually takes place after (1) legislators, human service administrators, prosecutors, and judges become aware that the problem (e.g., women battering) affects a large number of people (more than 1 million) and is life threatening; and (2) collective action is taken by large organizations, interest groups, and statewide coalitions to remedy or lessen the problem.

In this book, the contributors document the extensive efforts, demonstration projects, research, and recent legislation on behalf of battered women. We know that the passage of legislation aimed at resolving a social problem has the most potential for encouraging a resolution of the problem if a major appropriation is attached to compliance with the legislation. For example, each state had to develop and implement a plan to deinstitutionalize all status offenders and neglected and abused youths from juvenile institutions and adult jails in order to receive federal funds from the Juvenile Justice and Delinquency Prevention Act of 1974. A number of states complied with the mandate and monitored adult jails for many years afterward to make sure that juvenile status offenders were not confined with adult offenders.

Chapter 2 documents the incremental approach to building support year after year to ultimate passage of the Violence Against Women Act of 1994. This recent legislation includes a $1.2 billion appropriation (1) to improve the criminal justice response to violent crimes against women; (2) to expand services and community support for domestic violence victims; (3) to improve safety for women in public transit and public parks and assistance to victims of sexual assault; and (4) to provide support for a variety of educational, health, and database services (e.g., educating youth about domestic violence, developing national projections of domestic violence–caused injuries and recommended health-care strategies, and improving the incorporation of data regarding stalking and domestic violence into local, state, and national crime information systems). See Chapter 2 for a more detailed discussion of national and statewide coalitions and how these advocacy groups were instrumental in encouraging legislators to pass far-reaching federal and state legislation, including the Violence Against Women Act of 1994 and stalking legislation in a growing number of states.

Starting in 1984 with the passage of the Victims of Crime Act (VOCA), millions of dollars have been allocated by the federal government through state and local agencies to support battered women's shelters and court-based victim assistance. The Violence Against Women Act (VAWA) was signed into law by President Clinton on September 13, 1994. This act provides an appropriation of $1.2 billion to improve and expand crisis services, criminal justice agency responses, housing, and community support programs for victims of domestic violence and sexual assault.

References

American Bar Association. 1994. *The Impact of Domestic Violence on Children.* Chicago: American Bar Association.

Astin, M. C., K. Lawrence, G. Pincus, and D. Foy. 1990, October. "Moderator Variables for PTSD Among Battered Women." Paper presented at the convention of the International Society for Traumatic Stress Studies, New Orleans.

Bachman, R. 1994. *Violence Against Women: A National Crime Victimization Survey Report.* Washington, D.C.: U.S. Department of Justice, Bureau of Justice Statistics.

Bureau of Justice Statistics (BJS). 1994. *Criminal Victimization in the United States, 1992.* Washington, D.C.: U.S. Department of Justice, Bureau of Justice Statistics.

Houskamp, B. M., and D. W. Foy. 1991. "The Assessment of Postraumatic Stress Disorder in Battered Women." *Journal of Interpersonal Violence* 6: 367–75.

Jaffe, P. G., D. A. Wolfe, and S. K. Wilson. 1990. *Children of Battered Women.* Newbury Park, Calif.: Sage.

Kemp, A., E. I. Rawlings, and B. L. Green. 1991. "Post-Traumatic Stress Disorder (PTSD) in Battered Women: A Shelter Sample." *Journal of Traumatic Stress* 4: 137–48.

Klingbeil, K., and V. Boyd. 1984. "Detection and Assessment of Battered Women in the Emergency Room." In *Battered Women and Their Families: Intervention Strategies and Treatment Programs,* ed. A. R. Roberts, pp. 7–32. New York: Springer.

Marlatt, G. A., and D. J. Rohsenow. 1980. "Cognitive Processes in Alcohol Use: Expectancy and the Balanced Placebo Design." In *Advances in Substance Abuse Behavioral and Biological Research.* ed. Nancy K. Mello, pp. 159–99. Greenwich, Conn.: JAI.

McLeer, S. V., and R. Anwar. 1989. "A Study of Battered Women Presenting in an Emergency Department." *American Journal of Public Health* 79: 65–66.

National Crime Surveys. 1981. "National Sample, 1973–1979." Ann Arbor, Mich.: Inter-University Consortium on Political and Social Research, University of Michigan.

Pence, E., and M. Paymar. 1993. *Education Groups for Men Who Batter: The Duluth Model.* New York: Springer.

Pleck, E. 1987. *Domestic Tyranny.* New York: Oxford University Press.

Roberts, A. R. 1981. *Sheltering Battered Women.* New York: Springer.

Roberts, A. R. 1984. *Battered Women and Their Families: Intervention Strategies and Treatment Programs.* New York: Springer.

Roberts, A. R. 1995. *Crisis Intervention and Time-Limited Cognitive Treatment.* Thousand Oaks, Calif.: Sage.

Roberts, A. R., ed. 1990. *Crisis Intervention Handbook: Assessment, Treatment and Research.* Belmont, Calif.: Wadsworth.

Sherman, L. W. 1992. *Policing Domestic Violence: Experiments and Dilemmas.* New York: Free Press.

Straus, M., and R. Gelles. 1990. *Physical Violence in American Families.* New Brunswick, N.J.: Transaction Books.

2

Social Action for Battered Women

Susan E. Roche and Pam J. Sadoski

On September 13, 1994, President Bill Clinton signed the Violence Against Women Act into law as part of the Violent Crime Control and Law Enforcement Act of 1994. The Violence Against Women Act (VAWA) is the most extensive support that the federal government has ever committed to improve, expand, and enhance services and community responses to abused women. It represents a major legislative advocacy success for the battered women's movement and its allies and took more than two decades to achieve.

For those who have a long-term commitment to ending gender violence, it is important to recognize that history "is not something that happens necessarily, but something that can be made" (Freire, 1990, p. 9). The VAWA is but one powerful example of what is "historically possible" (p. 9) in pursuing a mission of social change on behalf of battered women. Battered women's movements in the United States and globally have a twenty-year base of experience with social action and contemporary wisdom with which to inform the "critical optimism" (p. 9) in regard to sustaining their mission of social change. This chapter presents a national view of the experience and wisdom regarding social change in the U.S. battered women's movement.

The national view presented here is based on a 1991 study of social action and direct practice in U.S. battered women's shelters (Roche, 1991) and our April 1993 exploratory phase of a study of U.S. battered women's coalitions. In addition, we have drawn on our experience with shelters and coalitions, and the five-year affiliation of one of us with Rutgers University's Center for Women's Global Leadership has contributed to the global perspective.

The central focus of this chapter is the expression and maintenance of these organizations' mission of social change on behalf of abused women. One assumption about organizational missions that underlies this work is that they are made manifest through a combination of program goals and related activities. More specifically, social change missions are understood as expressed through social-action goals and activities (e.g., legislative advocacy, public awareness campaigns, and training for members of the legal system), which are intended to benefit categories of battered women such as mothers, poor women, disabled women, and elderly women. Individual change missions are carried out through direct-practice goals and activities that are intended to benefit specific battered women and children who use a shelter's services (i.e., "clients"). Examples of direct practice are crisis intervention with a caller to a hotline, expert testimony in a court case, and support groups.

The Significance of the Social-Change Mission

The social-change mission of shelters and the larger battered women's movement challenges the inevitability of abuse in women's lives by aiming to end it at all levels—cultural, institutional, and individual. It targets not only the most immediate causes of abuse, such as a partner's controlling and dangerous actions, but also the sociostructural factors underlying and reinforcing the use of abuse to influence and control.

For various groups of battered women, the social change mission can also be directed toward the multiple jeopardies that shape the particular forms of abuse, society's reactions to it, and the available resources and opportunities for escaping it. Factors of multiple jeopardy include the interaction of race, class, ethnicity, sexual orientation, and age, to name but a few.

The social-change mission is important to the work of shelters in that they are often confronted by some of the same sociostructural and cultural obstacles faced by the battered women themselves. Two general categories of such obstacles were identified by Pence and the Domestic Abuse Intervention Project (1987) as "institutional and community decisions" and "cultural values and beliefs" (p. 38). These analytic categories are useful when considering the significance of the social-change mission, as most social action is aimed at altering or eliminating obstacles in one or the other category.

Institutional and Community Decisions

When acting as obstacles, institutional and community decisions comprise all the formal and informal policies and practices compromising women's safety, human rights, and fundamental freedoms on a case-by-case basis and on a categorical basis. Case-by-case decisions can include the responses to individual women of family members, neighbors, friends, and professionals. Categorical decisions include those policies and practices that inhibit shelters' access to resources, without which women cannot exercise their basic rights and freedoms. Among these rights and freedoms are the right to "security of person" and freedom from being "subject to torture or to cruel, inhuman or degrading treatment" (United Nations, 1988, articles 3 and 5). Clearly, the abuse of women and their subsequent inability to escape such abuse, owing to their lack of resources (Davis & Hagen, 1992), violate this right and freedom.

Cultural Values and Beliefs

Practitioners from every region of the world have analyzed the relationship among culture, religion, and violence against women. The international participants in the 1991 Women's Leadership Institute agreed that regardless of the specific culture or religion, some values and beliefs create and reinforce women's vulnerability to abuse (Center for Women's Global Leadership, 1992). Although the form of abuse may vary with the culture, certain forms, such as domestic violence against women, are remarkably similar. For example, forced isolation is pervasive throughout the world, although the specific manner of individually isolating women differs among Hindu, Muslim, and Christian cultures and between heterosexual and lesbian partners.

Examples of values and beliefs in the United States that make women vulnerable to abuse are the sanctity of marriage and the heterosexual family, women's responsibility for holding families together, "either-or attitudes" that prioritize "the best interests" of children over their mothers', and the recent emergence of gender neutrality as a legal principle.

The Interaction of Culture and Institutional Decisions

As Govind Kelkar of the Asian Institute of Technology pointed out, "the institutions of family and state act together, within a cultural context" (Center for Women's Global Leadership, 1992, p. 41). Although it is analytically useful to separate values and beliefs from institutional and community decisions, they operate more simultaneously in the lives of battered women, their families, and their communities.

As an example of this dependence of community decisions on prevailing values, battered women in support groups often compare the responses they have received when seeking help. Some of the least helpful responses reveal the interaction between social institutions and culture. Women speak of being admonished by family members and clergy to try to be better wives, as if their not living up to the norms for this role were responsible for the violence against them. Others speak of "gender-neutral" child custody and visitation rulings that give their batterers direct access to them, despite the existence of restraining orders. Still others relate incidents in which their inability to protect themselves and their children has caused them such self-contempt and despair that they have seriously considered killing both their children and themselves. As they tell their stories, it becomes apparent that they are struggling with their internalized values and beliefs about the "good mother" and their realization that community institutions can offer them little in the way of protection.

For battered lesbians, the interaction between culture and institutional decisions is equally complex. They describe the fear that disclosing their abuse will lead to loss of employment, family support, and community acceptance because of the simultaneous disclosure of their sexual orientation. They also describe the internal conflict of "going public" with their abuse and contributing further to the negative stereotypes of lesbians. The actions that institutional representatives may take in response to their requests for help can seem nearly as terrifying as the abuse, especially if the lesbian is a mother who has custody of her children. In this case, the interaction of patriarchal and heterosexist cultural norms and institutions compound their abuse.

At the organizational and community level, shelter personnel often run up against ideology that idealizes family, motherhood, fathers' rights, gender neutrality, and the resulting institutional decisions. In court, judges and attorneys may make patronizing, contemptuous, and even hostile comments to advocates and the battered women they accompany (Vermont Task Force, 1991). These comments often reflect sexist attitudes toward why women are battered and, indeed, whether they are being battered at all. In public welfare offices, minority battered women's advocates talk about silently ignoring racist responses, some subtle and some not so subtle, in order keep open battered women's access to AFDC and general assistance (anonymous, personal communication, June 5, 1991). In public education presentations, the battered women's advocates face accusations of being antifamily and male hating. One of the most extreme examples is the use of lesbian baiting (i.e., calling shelter personnel lesbians), a tactic intended to intimidate and to discredit them.

A critical analysis regarding the interaction between cultural values and beliefs and institutional decisions is a necessary component of social action. Without it, strategies may be aimless, fragmented, and difficult to sustain. A powerful example of critical analysis is Celina Romany's (1992) examination of human rights law from the perspective of women.

Romany describes human rights theory as having been defined and codified by the "fathers of international laws." She asserts that this gendered conception assumes citizenship as participation in public, not private, life and establishes the indivisibility of the family and its sanctity. Women have historically been denied full citizenship, and their rights have been abrogated by the norms and beliefs locating them and their family in the domestic sphere. Thus battering is treated as a private matter rather than as a violation of the human rights to which women are guaranteed by such international treaties as the Universal Declaration of Human Rights (United Nations, 1988).

Social action on behalf of battered women requires a reconceptualization of human rights that is rooted in women's actual experiences and in their own definitions of the violations in their lives (Bunch, 1991). This is exactly what the battered women's movement's social change mission is and why social change and individual change missions are interdependent (Schechter, 1982).

The Vulnerability of the Social-Change Mission

The social-change mission is vulnerable because it rests on the issues of risk and survival, that is, the risk that social action may represent to the sociopolitical and economic survival of shelters and the resultant pressures to dilute the social-change mission.

This risk is made more pronounced by the scarcity of, and competition for, the organizations' economic resources. According to many theorists and researchers, such scarcity and competition have a major influence on their activities, development, and structure (Austin, 1981; Freeman, 1982; Hannon & Freeman, 1984; James, 1983; Potuchek, 1986; Zald & McCarthy, 1987). In order to open and to stay open, shelters require a range of human, political, concrete and collaborative resources, such as volunteers, zoning permits, in-kind donations, public and private funding, and the cooperation of social services, legal aid, and law enforcement. This places them in a somewhat dependent position, similar to that of many battered women.

Furthermore, battered women's shelters, like battered women, must depend for support and protection on institutions with gender-biased histories and contexts. One of the ironies of this contradiction is that the social changes that shelters seek target the very institutions that help support their work, particularly their direct-practice efforts. Indeed, the vulnerability of social-change missions depends largely on whether supporters or their affiliates see themselves as targets of social action, as well as how they perceive the credibility of the shelter personnel and operations. Credibility in the eyes of funders, for instance, is often measured in terms of professionalism (Potuchek, 1986), and professionalism is usually geared to providing service rather than social action.

A National View of Social Action in Battered Women's Organizations

One of the salient points regarding the relationship between funding constraints and social action is that social action does not have to be regarded as an all-or-nothing choice (James, 1983; Smith & Marcus, 1984). Shelters can and do adopt local strategies for maintaining social-change missions,[1] and they can and do join one another for state and national strategies.

Social Action in Battered Women's Shelters

The 1991 study to which we referred at the beginning of this chapter was a mail survey of all shelters listed in a 1986 national directory of battered women's organizations. A total of 622 of the 812 shelters surveyed participated in the 1991 study, represented by 1,423 individual respondents and representing every state. The average shelter participating in the survey was nine years old, had an operating budget of between $135,000 and $160,000, and had six full-time and four part-time paid staff members and twenty-five weekly volunteers. The study examined social action according to the shelters' program goals and activities.

PROGRAM GOALS

One dimension of shelters' social-change missions is their goals. A list of twelve goals commonly found in shelters, representing differing amounts of political risk,

Table 2.1.   Means and Standard Deviations of Domestic Violence Program Goals

Goals of domestic violence programs	Mean	Standard deviation
1. To increase the safe surroundings for battered women and their children.	1.03	0.181
2. To increase the access of battered women to material resources (e.g., income, housing, food).	1.14	0.377
3. To increase legal protections for battered women.	1.24	0.511
4. To reduce the battered women's isolation.	1.42	0.614
5. To change cultural beliefs and values that promote violence against women.	1.51	0.701
6. To change institutional and community decisions that support individual men's use of abusive tactics against women.	1.67	0.793
7. To end violence against women.	1.24	0.552
8. To create a model organization of shared power and leadership.	2.03	0.932
9. To build a political movement of women.	2.67	0.900
10. To increase the collective power of women.	2.28	0.936
11. To end racism.	2.20	1.011
12. To end homophobia.	2.46	1.045

Note: 1 = A lot; 2 = Some; 3 = A little; 4 = None.

was presented to the respondents, who were asked to indicate the amount of emphasis that their shelters gave to these goals. Table 2.1 shows the means and standard deviations of their answers.

Shelters emphasize those social-action goals that are most directly tied to domestic violence, as portrayed by the means presented in Table 2.1. The responses suggest that even though many shelter personnel may be aware of the connections between domestic violence and other forms of oppression, they stress those changes that best address domestic violence. However, aiding individual battered women may be so demanding that it becomes the primary mission of shelters. If so, those social-action goals that appear closely linked to the most acute issues arising in such direct practice would be strongly emphasized. If the shelters' level of change seems farther removed from the immediate issues, the social-action goals may seem less compelling, attainable, and/or justifiable to pursue.

A particular goal may be justified according to its social utility, in which the cost—risking credibility and external support—is weighed against the needs of, and likely benefits to, battered women as the primary constituents (James, 1983). This is especially true of the goals pertaining to organizational structure, political organization, and women's collective power, given the shelter funders' orientation to professionalism, referred to earlier. For example, 45 percent of the shelters in the 1991 study had changed their involvement in political activism in accordance with their funders' expectations.

In addition, the degree of a shelter's professionalization may also contribute to the justification of its goals (Ahrens, 1980; National Coalition Against Domestic Violence, 1987). If most of a shelter's employees have a professional education, the shelter may emphasize direct-practice goals. Using social work education as an example, students receive far more classroom and field instruction in direct practice than in social action (Bisno, 1984), and, in allied fields such as counseling, education, and psychology, this would be equally true, if not more so. Most of the shelters participating in the 1991 study had professional personnel. For example, 98 percent of the shelters had executive directors; 90 percent had supervisory positions; 72 percent required some or all of their employees to have a bachelor's degree; and 57 percent required some or all of their employees to have a graduate degree.

PROGRAM ACTIVITIES

Social-action and direct-practice activities are carried out fairly consistently by U.S. battered women's shelters. Most of the direct-practice activities that the survey's respondents listed are always or usually undertaken, whereas the frequency with which social-change activities are undertaken is more variable, from always to never undertaken. Table 2.2 shows the means and standard deviations for the frequency with which shelters participated in each of the program activities listed.

Items 1 through 9 refer to direct-practice activities, and items 10 through 22 refer to social-action activities. Item 23 is treated differently, as we will explain.

Similar to the social-action goals, the social-action activities most often carried

Table 2.2. Means and Standard Deviations of Program Activities

Activities	Mean	Standard deviation
1. Hotline for crisis and information.	1.04	0.299
2. One-to-one planning and problem solving.	1.17	0.415
3. Mediation and/or advocacy with systems (e.g., court, welfare).	1.47	0.651
4. Support groups for battered women.	1.24	0.597
5. A coordinated children's program.	1.75	1.025
6. Organized follow-up services.	2.35	0.923
7. Shelter for other women (e.g., homeless).	3.04	1.025
8. Direct services for other women.	2.45	1.128
9. Direct services for men who batter women.	2.99	1.203
10. Training police, judges, lawyers, and the like.	2.23	0.921
11. Training social service, health, and education personnel.	2.17	0.864
12. Assisting other domestic violence programs.	1.99	0.840
13. Testifying and/or lobbying before policymakers.	2.60	0.886
14. Conducting media campaigns about violence against women.	2.42	0.855
15. Conducting media campaigns about other women's issues.	3.21	0.787
16. Assisting battered women to organize support for themselves and other battered women.	2.20	0.964
17. Assisting battered women to advocate with resource systems for themselves and all battered women.	2.14	0.944
18. Participating in domestic violence coalitions.	1.48	0.739
19. Participating in other women's coalitions.	2.62	0.909
20. Making public education presentations about domestic violence.	1.33	0.612
21. Making public education presentations about other women's issues.	2.86	0.972
22. Assisting battered women with public education presentations.	2.83	0.842
23. Recruiting and training volunteers to staff programs.	1.33	0.648
24. Other.	1.39	0.752

Note: 1 = Always; 2 = Usually; 3 = Occasionally; 4 = Never.

out are those directly linked to domestic violence (e.g., public education presentations about domestic violence and participation in domestic violence coalitions). One exception to this pattern is that shelters only occasionally assist battered women in making public education presentations, which may reflect their protectiveness of battered women or their professionalization of public education.

Volunteer recruitment and training contain elements of both direct practice and social action. Volunteers may serve in either capacity or both. Some shelters' recruitment and training activities may have a consciousness-raising effect that extends beyond direct practice with individual women to the institutional and sociocultural aspects of the problem.

Social-Change Initiatives of Battered Women's Coalitions

A coalition may be defined as "a group of organizations working together for a common purpose" (Kahn, 1991, p. 238). Specifically, domestic violence coalitions are comprised of battered women's shelters, hotlines, safe-home projects, and, often, supportive individuals. Their common purposes are to

1. Provide services to the membership (e.g., fund-raising, training, information exchanges, print and multimedia production, and dissemination and technical assistance).
2. Organize and mobilize the membership around specific political issues (e.g., bigotry, sexual harassment, impact legislation).
3. Create public awareness regarding battering and related issues.
4. Promote sociocultural changes to benefit battered women and their families, with an emphasis on underrepresented groups.
5. Policy development and innovative legislation. (National Coalition, 1993; Pruitt, 1993; Vermont Task Force, 1991).

Every state except Delaware has at least one state coalition, for a total of fifty-three. The National Coalition Against Domestic Violence (NCAVD) is composed of state coalitions and is led by a steering committee made up of one representative from each. It has five membership categories: active member organizations, supportive organizations, supportive individuals, incarcerated women, and youth. In addition to this voluntary membership, national and state coalitions have paid staffs that vary in size.

The information presented here represents the preliminary data gathered in March and April 1993 as part of an exploratory phase of a larger study being developed on the work of battered women's coalitions. Phone interviews were conducted with staff members of the National Coalition Against Domestic Violence, and the Pennsylvania, Vermont, Texas, Connecticut, and Oregon state coalitions. All battered women's coalitions have equally valuable experiences from which we can learn, and we hope that one day we can report on the U.S. battered women's coalition experience, state by state. In the meantime, we thank those coalitions that participated in this preliminary study.

The principal questions asked of each representative were "What major initiatives has your coalition been working on during the last couple of years, and with what results?" The interviewers then followed up with more specific questions exploring the representatives' answers in more depth and covering predesignated topics. These topics were legislation, judiciary and law enforcement, media campaigns, human rights, and international networking. During the interviews, four additional topics were added to the original list: training and educating service providers, health care, housing, and community organizing.

Federal legislation initiatives that national and state coalitions have successfully promoted include amendments to the Family Violence Prevention and Services Act of 1984 (FVPSA), the Violence Against Women Act of 1994, stalking legislation, and legislation to reduce the isolation of immigrant and refugee battered women and to increase their options.

The new amendments to the FVPSA increased federal funding for battered women's shelters in 1992 and 1993 and provided funding to state coalitions in 1993. The purposes of the FVPSA are (1) to demonstrate the effectiveness of assisting states in their efforts to prevent domestic violence against women, through the provision of shelter and related assistance; and (2) to give the states technical assistance and training relating to family violence programs. This is an important piece of legislation because it reinforces the concept of coalition at the state level (B. Fowler, personal communication, March 31, 1993) and aids in organizing at that level.

For several years, advocates urged the passage of the Violence Against Women Act, as they viewed it as a vehicle to increase funding for services, implement a national standard of response for judges and law enforcement officers, provide interstate protection, and create incentives to improve the states' responses and to impose penalties for noncompliance (A. Menard, personal communication, April 2, 1993). In fact, this act was deemed so important that a loosely organized group of state coalitions as well as some national organizations, was started four years ago in order to arrange grassroots support to increase the likelihood of its passage. This group, the Domestic Violence Coalition on Public Policy (DVCOP), worked toward the passage of the bill in a number of ways. It helped arrange testimony in the House and Senate, drafted and redrafted sections of the bill, organized grassroots legislative activities, and informed state coalitions on how to move it forward.

As passed, the purposes of the Violence Against Women Act are the following:

1. To improve the response of the criminal justice to violent crimes against women.
2. To expand services and community support for victims of domestic violence.
3. To improve safety for women in public transit and public parks and to assist victims of sexual assault.
4. To support a variety of educational, health, and database services (e.g., educating youth about domestic violence, developing national projections of domestic violence–caused injuries and recommended health-care strategies, and improving the incorporation of data regarding stalking and domestic violence into local, state, and national crime information databases). (National Re-

source Center on Domestic Violence and the Battered Women's Justice Project, 1994)

The recognition of stalking as a particular form of woman abuse, its conception as a problem for policy advocacy, and the process of getting relevant public policies passed are examples of the successes of grassroots organizing by coalitions. To illustrate, in late 1992, Senator William Cohen of Maine introduced a bill requiring the development of a model statute on stalking that was later passed by Congress. The VAWA provisions regarding stalking also reflect this work.

Some coalitions have networked with other organizations to advance legislation for immigrant and refugee women who are battered. One example is their collaboration with Ayuda, a clinic that provides an array of legal services to Latina women. Ayuda helped identify the need for a means to help battered immigrant women who leave their husbands to remain in the United States if they choose to (B. Fowler, personal communication, March 31, 1993). Battered immigrant women who come to the United States on their husband's green card often fear that they will be deported if they leave their husband, a fear that he quite often manipulates in order to maintain control.

Here again, the VAWA provides various protections for this group of women and their children. For example, Subtitle G of the VAWA "permits immigrant spouses and children of U.S. citizens and legal residents who have immediate relative status to self-petition for legal resident status" (NOW Legal Defense and Education Fund, 1994, p. 5). It also "encourages [the] Attorney General to consider 'any credible evidence,' in granting battered spouse benefits" to undocumented aliens, rather than requiring the expensive professional mental health evidence previously exacted by the Immigration and Naturalization Service (p. 5).

State civil and criminal legislation has also received major attention from state coalitions. As a result of their advocacy of civil laws, many states have enacted protective-order policies addressing an array of issues, from child custody to housing. For instance, years of working with divorced mothers who are battered by their children's fathers made it clear to many coalitions that child custody and visitation decisions often create unique problems for battered women, not the least of which is their inability to remove themselves from contact with their batterers. Therefore, they promoted the consideration of domestic violence by those courts charged with determining final child custody arrangements (N. Neylon, personal communication, April 1, 1993).

Coalitions also advocated for privileged communication for personnel in battered women's shelters. The Vermont Network Against Domestic Violence and Sexual Assault is one such coalition that successfully promoted state legislation extending this professional privilege to shelter staff members.

Coalitions have directed their energy toward creating changes in criminal legislation as well. Stalking legislation has already been passed by at least twenty-eight states (Hunzinker, 1992), and some states have enacted legislation regarding the mandatory or preferred arrest of a batterer. No-drop policies, which require state attorneys to continue prosecuting a batterer once the proceedings have started, have also been implemented in some states. These policies take the responsibility off of the battered woman who might otherwise have been pressured by the batterer to drop the proceedings (N. Neylon, personal communication, April 1, 1993). Although such legislation is the subject of debate in the battered women's movement on the basis of women's right to self-determination and safety, it remains illustrative of a fairly common legislative change.

The Connecticut Coalition Against Domestic Violence (CCADV) and the Texas Council on Family Violence (TCFV) have worked on criminal legislation for the defense of battered women charged with committing criminal offenses. The CCADV has advocated the legal review of all cases in Connecticut in which battered women have been charged with killing their spouses, for alternative sanctions for these women, and for resources to retain defense attorneys.

The Texas Council advanced a bill to establish a defense for the prosecution of battered women charged with injuring their children because of omission. This is one of a number of initiatives around the country regarding coalition responses to the "failure to protect" charge. Such a claim holds battered women responsible for failing to protect their children by not physically preventing the batterer from abusing the child(ren), contacting the police or child protective services agency, and/or leaving their batterers. Many in the battered women's movement take issue with this approach because it does not take into account the complexity of domestic violence (e.g., that "women who leave their batterers are at a 75 percent greater risk of being killed by them that those who stay" National Coalition, 1993). It also places the responsibility for stopping batterers' violence on the victims rather than the perpetrators.

Judicial and law enforcement education is another initiative undertaken by state coalitions to effect social change. The Pennsylvania Coalition Against Domestic Violence (PCADV), for instance, trains law enforcement officers on the dynamics of abuse, police safety issues, and police obligations and liabilities. In addition, many other coalitions have successfully advocated the passage of legislation that requiring domestic violence training for police. Similarly, many state coalitions are directing their efforts toward passing legislation that requires judges to have such training. The Texas Council on Family violence for example, has advocated the passage of legislation that requires all judges to receive training on the problems of family violence, sexual assault, and child abuse. At the time of this research, the TCFV had extended invitations to judges for their training, and they had also trained more than 1,100 municipal court judges and 600 court personnel.

The Texas Council also created other opportunities to educate the judiciary. In one instance, it "dropped in on" a statewide meeting for judges, successfully requesting a training slot. Since 1992, the TCFV has been developing a training manual for judges, using as a guide a model created by the Family Violence Prevention Fund in California. This manual contains current statutes, relevant case law, and a protocol for responding to domestic violence cases.

Domestic violence coalitions have also undertaken the *education and training of service providers and future service providers*. For instance, the Pennsylvania Coalition has worked with drug and alcohol-service providers to help them identify battered women and develop an awareness of unique issues that they may need to take into account when working with both battered women and batterers. In addition, the PCADV created for adult educators a model manual regarding battered women and the services available to them. The PCADV wrote the manual because it believes that school can be a safe place for battered women to get information about available services (B. Fowler, personal communication, 1993).

Likewise, the Vermont Network Against Domestic Violence and Sexual Assault (VNADVSA) has established research, education, and training partnerships with the University of Vermont's Department of Social Work. Faculty members work with VNADVSA and the Governor's Commission on the Status of Women to do action research on policy and direct-practice issues to which Vermont's battered women's movement needs answers. Network staff guest lecture in undergraduate and graduate social work classes. In addition, the university's social work faculty members, in collaboration with the network, incorporates issues of gender violence, human rights, and global feminism into the undergraduate and graduate curricula, particularly in practice and policy courses. Network members volunteer their time as field instructors, research advisers, and coauthors, and faculty members volunteer their time training and giving technical assistance at the request of VNADVSA members. The intention is to prepare professional allies with values, knowledge, and skills regarding domestic violence, feminist practice, and grassroots organizing to be implemented wherever they are located in the service delivery system.

Media campaign work is another initiative undertaken by coalitions in order to create social change. During the last few years, the NCADV has been working on several media campaigns. For example, as part of this initiative, *Esquire* magazine held a contest requesting ad companies to make a poster for the NCADV. The ad chosen depicts a casket with a bouquet of flowers next to it. The caption reads: "He beat me 150 times, but only brought me flowers once." The NCADV also worked on a media campaign with the Kashi cereal company to advertise that proceeds from the use of its coupons go to the NCADV.

The Pennsylvania Coalition has also worked on a national media campaign with the Family Violence Prevention Fund (FVPF). The FVPF received a grant from the Ford Foundation to establish a plan for a multiyear national media campaign directed toward changing societal attitudes toward and perceptions of domestic violence "and moving on to having a major public policy impact and sparking grass roots activism" (Family Violence Prevention Fund, 1993, p. 2). Consultants were retained to conduct a national public opinion poll, and they convened multiracial focus groups in six U.S. cities to examine public attitudes and potential strategies to raise awareness. The FVPF's plan was accepted by the Ford Foundation, and the campaign was recently launched.

Coalitions have worked on media campaigns in their own states as well. For instance, Anne Menard of the Connecticut Coalition reported that some groups have worked with the Liz Claiborne Company to design local and state media campaigns to let battered women know that help is available (personal communication, April 2, 1993). The TCFV purchased NCADV's poster and worked with the Texas Department of Human Services to distribute the public service announcement they created from it to local television stations.

Coalitions have also become quite innovative in using one strategy to serve several purposes. For example, the Oregon Coalition Against Domestic Violence and Sexual Assault was successful in promoting public awareness of domestic violence and sexual assault and establishing a new source of funding. The coalition successfully advocated for the state to add a line to state income tax forms that reads, "Stop Domestic Violence and Sexual Assault!" Next to this slogan, taxpayers can indicate whether they want to contribute some portion of their tax returns to the coalition's work.

Health care is another important system addressed by coalitions to ensure that it meets the needs of battered women. The Pennsylvania Coalition has partnered with the Family Violence Prevention Fund on a three-year national health initiative to establish a national public policy agenda for reform. The initiative will be overseen by a national advisory committee composed of representatives from medical institutions as well as battered women's organizations.

The first step in this process has been to develop model protocols for hospital emergency departments and a training program for health-care workers. A survey of the nation's hospital emergency departments was conducted to gather information on their responses to battered women. The model protocols and training program are being tested in Pennsylvania and California. During the second year, the protocols and training program will be disseminated to hospitals throughout the country. In addition, a media campaign to raise awareness of domestic violence as a health priority will be conducted. Toward the end of the project, the focus will be on implementing a national public policy agenda to reform the health-care system's response to violence in the home (FVPF, PCADV, & Conrad N. Hilton Foundation, 1993). The NCADV has worked on national health-care initiatives as well, specifically, the passage of legislation that will provide funding for model programs and mandated training on battered women's issues for students attending professional health-care schools.

Coalitions have also worked to change the health-care systems in their own states. For instance, the Pennsylvania Coalition received funding for a three-year demonstration project to establish medical advocates in three hospitals. These advocates parallel the legal advocates in the court system in order to assist battered women throughout the hospital process.

Housing is another issue of concern for battered women. Advocacy for housing is an initiative that coalitions have undertaken on behalf of battered women. At the national level, the NCADV joined the Women and Housing Task Force, which is a broad coalition of many national groups, so that battered women's agendas can be addressed. The NCADV successfully supported getting domestic violence included as a category of homelessness in the McKinney Act, thereby creating some funding for domestic violence shelters. Most recently, the NCADV has urged that some of Section 8 housing be allotted to battered women.

Community organizing, human rights, and international networking are additional focuses of some members of U.S. battered women's coalitions that have applied a global feminist perspective to women's human rights at the local, state, and national levels. A global feminist perspective of women's human rights is a consciousness, a set of assumptions, and an appreciation.

As consciousness, global feminism is rooted in women's experiences in living and resisting patriarchal and other oppression and marginalization. As a set of assumptions it recognizes that women's inequality is universal and is maintained by the threat and reality of violence and socioeconomic and cultural ostracism; that the forms of women's inequality, abuse, ostracism, and resistance may vary according to culture, history, class, and place; and that all these forms of abuse are violations of women's human rights. As appreciation, it is a desire to truly build and work in alliances by "demonstrating knowledge of, respect for, and commitment between [women] who are in essential ways different but whose interests are in essential ways akin" (Pheterson, 1990, p. 36).

Although not all coalition members have articulated this perspective, some of the work currently being done in the U.S. battered women's movement does reflect it. Two examples illustrate the application of this perspective.

The first example reflects the local expression of a global feminist perspective. The Oregon Coalition has had a two-year women-of-color project intended to work in solidarity and alliance with women-of-color communities that have been external to the coalition. The results to date? "Now over a third of the leadership positions within the Coalition are held by women of color, and at this year's leadership conference, 12 of the 25 workshops were presented by women of color" (H. Pruitt, personal communication, April 15, 1993). Along this same line, the Oregon Coalition has a significant rural and small town presence as a result of its efforts to include a diversity of women's issues. The coalition has given added emphasis to rural women's issues by focusing its organizing efforts in twenty-five rural communities, identifying and bringing together those who share a position against bigotry in any form, including sexism, racism, and heterosexism.

The second example reflects the international expression of a global feminist perspective, the involvement of the Vermont Network and the Oregon Coalition, among others, in the world campaign for women's human rights. Both groups joined in the worldwide "Sixteen Days of Activism Against Gender Violence" initiated by the Center for Women's Global Leadership's 1991 Women's Leadership Institute. The "Sixteen Days of Activism" is now an annual international series of events organized by women's and human rights organizations between November 25 (the day that Latin American feminists dedicate to public actions against violence against women) and December 10 (International Human Rights Day).

As one of the strategies of that campaign, a petition was sent to the United Nations "to have violence against women specifically, and women's rights in general, placed on the agenda of the World Conference on Human Rights in June 1993" (International Women's Tribune Centre, 1993). More than 215,000 signatures from 117 countries appeared on the petition, which was translated into at least nineteen languages. By many accounts, this instrument and the process surrounding it served multiple functions: public education and consciousness raising, mobilization, and linking. Translating and circulating it provided an immediate, concrete role for women and men to assume in influencing international policy from a shared moral framework bridging national, cultural, religious, gender, and political differences.

At the World Conference, nongovernmental organizations from antiviolence movements around the globe continued to pressure the official conference participants. The Family Violence Fund of San Francisco, for example, contribute to the work done on behalf of battered immigrant and refugee women. Because of the success of this local–global campaign, the final declaration of the official conference states that the "human rights of women and of the girl-child are an inalienable, integral and indivisible part of universal human rights" and declares its commitment to eliminate "violence against women in public and private life." Thus, the very conception of human rights as a matter of the public domain (one from which women have historically been excluded) was significantly altered, as was the base for arguing that the abuse of women is a human rights violation.

Conclusion

One measure of the strength of the battered women's movement is the extent to which its organizations have maintained social-change missions. As the national study of shelters demonstrates, local organizations are more likely to keep their social-action frameworks specifically linked to the most obvious aspects of domestic violence. But when they join in a coalition, a different picture emerges. Perhaps because of the principle of "strength in numbers" and their particular purposes, coalitions are more broadly political, and their mission statements and actions illustrate the expanding frameworks that connect domestic violence to other issues of oppression, such as racism, classism, and heterosexism.

For social change to continue to be meaningful for all battered women, local organizations must find ways to hear and represent the emerging and different voices of battered women—battered women of color, battered immigrant women, battered lesbians, battered rural women, and battered refugee women. Adopting a global feminist perspective may enable organizations to make more inclusive social-action efforts. Building on their own experiences, coalitions can help their member organizations decide how to apply this perspective to their local work. Although the scarcity of resources must be considered when deciding how the framework should be applied locally, a broader framework may appeal more to donors who have not previously contributed to domestic violence organizations, such as those who support human rights, racial justice, or rural development projects.

Developing a global perspective and applying it to local, state, and national work can have several benefits. It can provide the sense of support and connection that comes from working in solidarity with others around the world; it can deepen the understanding of the commonalities and differences among women with essentially different social realities; and it can create better strategies and allies. "The [global feminist] task is not one of changing our issues but of expanding the frameworks from which we understand our work" (Bunch, 1987, p. 335).

Sometimes the expanded frameworks are a matter of internal priorities. The Oregon Coalition demonstrates this with its women-of-color project and rural and small-town organizing. The Vermont Network illustrates this with its international links. The Pennsylvania Coalition and the Family Violence Prevention Fund exemplify this in their collaboration with corporate funders on national media and health-care initiatives.

Sometimes the frameworks of social action are expanded by external events, as the NCADV (now located in Colorado) and the Oregon Coalition discovered when their states considered antigay legislation. Against a background of scarce resources and in the midst of media-covered controversy, both coalitions made ethical decisions to adhere to their social-change missions by taking stands against that legislation. Likewise, when former women employees of Senator Robert Packwood of Oregon accused him of sexual harassment, that state's coalition publicly stood by them. These examples illustrate the risk of jeopardizing some sources of support that is sometimes involved in social action regarding the connections among gender violence, bigotry, and formal political arrangements. They also show how balancing social-change missions against resource needs often means making difficult and usually controversial (internally and externally) ethical decisions.

Social workers can strengthen local social-action efforts on behalf of battered women in the face of scarcity of, and competition for, resources (Davis & Hagen, 1988; Pfouts & Renz, 1981), by aligning with shelter and coalition members, listening to their unique practice wisdom, and transmitting it to other members of the service system, funders, and the community at large. They can contribute professional skills and knowledge when needed. Social work educators can learn about the nature of shelter and coalition work and prepare future professional allies for it.

Sometimes social work support involves opening up channels and stepping aside to allow the voices of battered women and grassroots activists to be heard directly. At other times, it will involve joining these voices. For social workers within the battered women's movement, there may be no distinction between these voices and their own. Social action for battered women can be strengthened by such genuine grassroots–social work alliances.

Acknowledgment

The authors would like to acknowledge and thank Naomi Smith and Regina Madsen for their contributions to the conceptualization of this work.

Note

1. As James (1983) pointed out, shelters may practice "cross subsidization," in which they mix their activities, some of which net an income and some of which do not. Another way in which shelters can pursue social change is by relabeling activities to be more socially acceptable, such as calling efforts to influence law enforcement practices "police training."

References

Ahrens, L. 1980, Summer. "Battered Women's Refuges: Feminist Institutions vs. Social Service Institutions." *Aegis*, 41–46.
Austin, D. 1981. "Redistributive Service and Merit Good." In *Organization and the Human Services: Cross-Disciplinary Reflections*, ed. H. D. Stein, pp. 37–88. New York: Harper & Row.
Bisno, H. 1984. "Conceptualization of Social Work Practice in Social Work Education." In *A Quarter*

Century of Social Work Education, ed. M. Dinerman and L. L. Geismar, pp. 47–92. Washington, D.C.: National Association of Social Workers.

Bunch, C. 1987. "Bringing the Global Home." In C. Bunch, *Passionate Politics: Feminist Theory in Action,* pp. 328–45. New York: St. Martin's Press.

Bunch, C. 1991. "Women's Rights as Human Rights: Toward a Revision of Human Rights." In *Gender Violence: A Development and Human Rights Issue,* ed. C. Bunch and R. Carrillo, pp. 3–18. New Brunswick, N.J.: Center for Women's Global Leadership.

Center for Women's Global Leadership. 1992. *Women, Violence and Human Rights: 1991 Women's Leadership Institute Report.* New Brunswick, N.J.: Center for Women's Global Leadership.

Davis, L. V., and J. L. Hagen. 1988, December. "Services for Battered Women: The Public Policy Response." *Social Service Review,* 649–67.

Davis, L. V., and J. L. Hagen. 1992. "The Problem of Wife Abuse: The Interrelationship of Social Policy and Social Work Practice." *Social Work* 37: 15–20.

Family Violence Prevention Fund (FVPF). 1993. *Current Programs and Activities.* San Francisco: Family Violence Prevention Fund.

Family Violence Prevention Fund (FVPF), Pennsylvania Coalition Against Domestic Violence (PCADV), and Conrad N. Hilton Foundation. 1993. *National Health Initiative on Domestic Violence Executive Summary.* San Francisco: FVPF, PCADV, and Conrad N. Hilton Foundation.

Freeman, J. 1982. "Organizational Life Cycles and Natural Selection Processes." *Research in Organizational Behavior* 4: 1–32.

Freire, P. 1990. "A Critical Understanding of Social Work." *Journal of Progressive Human Services* 1: 3–9.

Hannon, M. T., and J. Freeman. 1984. "Structural Inertia and Organizational Change." *American Sociological Review* 49: 149–64.

Hunzinker, D. 1992, October. "Stalking Laws." *State Legislative Report.* Denver: National Conference of State Legislators.

International Women's Tribune Centre. 1993, March. "A Call to Action: A Bulletin Reporting on the Worldwide Campaign to Get Womens Rights onto the World's Human Rights Agenda." Available from International Women's Tribune Centre, 777 UN Plaza, New York, N.Y., 10017.

James, E. 1983. "How Nonprofits Grow: A Model." *Journal of Policy Analysis and Management* 2: 350–66.

Kahn, S. 1991. *Organizing: A Guide for Grassroots Leaders.* Silver Spring, Md. National Association of Social Workers.

National Coalition Against Domestic Violence. 1987, Summer. Special issue "Professionalism in the Movement." *NCADV Voice,* 9–15.

National Coalition Against Domestic Violence. 1993. "Every 15 Seconds a Women Is Battered in This Country." Brochure available from National Coalition Against Domestic Violence, P.O. Box 34103, Washington, D.C., 20043-4103.

National Resource Center on Domestic Violence and the Battered Women's Justice Project. 1994, September. "The Violence Against Women Act of 1994." Available from National Resource Center, 6400 Flank Drive, Suite 1300, Harrisburg, Pa., 17112-2778.

"No More! Stopping Domestic Violence." 1994, September–October. *Ms,* 33–64.

NOW Legal Defense and Education Fund. 1994, September. "The Violence Against Women Act." Available from NOW Legal Defense and Education Fund, 99 Hudson Street, New York, N.Y., 10013-2815.

Pence, E., and Domestic Abuse Intervention Project. 1987. *In Our Best Interest: A Process of Personal and Social Change.* Duluth: Minnesota Program Development.

Pheterson, G. 1990. "Alliances Between Women: Overcoming Internalized Oppression and Internalized Domination." In *Bridges of Power: Women's Multicultural Alliances,* ed. L. Altrechi and R. Brewer, pp. 34–48. Philadelphia: New Society.

Pfoutz, J. H., and C. Renz. 1981, November. "The Future of Wife Abuse Programs." *Social Work,* 451–55.

Potuchek, J. L. 1986, September. "The Context of Social Service Funding: The Funding Relationship." *Social Service Review,* 421–36.

Roche, S. E. 1991. "Social Change and Direct Service: Striking the Balance in Battered Women's Shelters Across the U.S." Ph.D. diss., Rutgers University.

Romany, C. 1992, June. "A Feminist Deconstruction and Reconstruction of Human Rights Law." Paper presented at the 1992 Women's Leadership Institute, Center for Women's Global Leadership, Douglass College, Rutgers University, New Brunsick, N.J.

Schechter, S. 1982. *Women and Male Violence: The Visions and Struggles of the Battered Women's Movement*. Boston: South End Press.

Smith, C. B., and P. M. Marcus. 1984. "Structural Persistence in Proactive Organizations: The Case of Sexual Assault Treatment Agencies." *Journal of Social Service Review* 7: 21–36.

Tierney, K. J. 1982. "The Battered Women Movement and the Creation of the Wife Beating Problem." *Social Problems*, 29: 207–19.

United Nations. 1988. *Human Rights: The International Bill of Human Rights*. New York: United Nations.

Vermont Task Force on Gender Bias. 1991. *Domestic Violence: Gender Bias in the Legal System*. Montpelier: Vermont Supreme Court and the Vermont Bar Association.

Wood, G. G., and R. R. Middleman. 1989. *The Structural Approach to Direct Practice in Social Work: A Textbook for Students and Frontline Practitioners*. New York: Columbia University Press.

Zald, M. N., and J. D. McCarthy, eds. 1987. *Social Movements in an Organizational Society: Collected Essays*. New Brunswick, N.J.: Transaction Books.

3

A Comparative Analysis of Incarcerated Battered Women and a Community Sample of Battered Women

Albert R. Roberts

Recent estimates indicate that between 2 million and 4 million women are beaten in their homes each year (Biden, 1993; Roberts & Roberts, 1990; Sugg & Inui, 1992). The battering of an intimate partner is much more widespread and prevalent than usually realized. Woman battering, also known as domestic violence, is finally being recognized as one of the greater social and public health problems of our times, and this recognition is increasing year by year as the number of injuries and the death toll continue to climb. Several studies have found that 22 to 35 percent of emergency room visits were made because of symptoms or injuries related to physical abuse (Hasselt et al., 1988; Randall, 1990). The habitual nature, escalation, self-destructive precursors, and lethality of woman battering are only beginning to be assessed.

Violent crimes against women, particularly assaults by husbands, ex-husbands, or boyfriends, are often brutal, degrading, and debilitating. The subject of woman battering has received widespread attention from the print and television media, with such statements as the following, which appeared in *Time:* "Women are at more risk of being killed by their male partners than by any other kind of assault" (July 4, 1994, p. 21).

Previous Research on Battered Women Who Kill

The percentage of battered women who kill their batterer is quite small. Although national estimates indicate that between 2 million and 4 million women are battered each year by their partners, approximately 750 battered women kill their abusers each year (Trafford, 1991).

This chapter looks at whether clues or predictive variables can be found in a retrospective sample of battered women who kill and those who do not. Unfortunately, hardly any data exist that compare battered women who killed their partners with those who did not. Most earlier studies of battered women relied on data from a cross section of the general population (Straus & Gelles, 1990; Straus, Gelles, & Steinmetz, 1980), police or court records (Hirschel, et al., 1992; Pence, 1983; Roberts, 1988; Sherman, 1992; Sherman & Berk, 1984), and shelter-based studies (Cascardi & O'Leary, 1992; Gondolf & Fischer, 1988, 1991; Roberts & Roberts, 1990). These studies focused on currently battered or formerly battered women who often were separated or divorced from their mates. Finally, two studies compared battered women in general with a small sample of battered women who killed their partner (Browne, 1984; Walker, 1984).

Psychologist Angela Browne's exploratory study compared forty-two battered women who had killed their partner with forty-two battered women who had not killed or attempted to kill their mate. The comparison group was a subset of battered women drawn from Lenore Walker's (1984) earlier study. Those variables that were more likely to predict battered women who would kill were the following: Women who would kill had suffered more severe injuries; their batterer used drugs and was intoxicated more frequently; their partner had threatened or made sexual assaults; the women had threatened suicide; and the women's partner had threatened to kill her (Browne, 1984).

Table 3.1 examines the similarities and differences in the major findings from Angela Browne's study and from Lenore Walker's study. In Browne's study the battered women who had killed indicated that their batterer was often intoxicated (80 percent), frequently forced them to have sexual intercourse (75 percent), and forced them to engage in sodomy and bestiality (62 percent). Similarly, Walker's homicide group reported that the batterers were frequently intoxicated (88 percent) and had threatened to kill the battered woman or her close relatives (57 percent). The primary difference between Browne's study and Walker's study was that twice as many batterers in Browne's study had been forced to engage in sodomy, bestiality, and other degrading sex acts (Browne's homicide group, 62 percent, versus Walker's homicide group, 31 percent). Surprisingly, Browne's nonhomicidal group of battered women were very similar to Walker's homicide group in regard to suicide threats and attempts (Browne's nonhomicide group, 31 percent, versus Walker's homicide group, 34 percent). In addition, the percentage of men threatening to kill their spouse or her close relatives was very similar in Browne's nonhomicide group (59 percent) and Walker's homicide group (57 percent).

According to Walker's (1984) study of fifty battered women who killed in self-defense, all had resorted to violence as a last-ditch effort to protect themselves from further physical abuse and emotional harm. In her book, Walker reviewed 150

Table 3.1. A Comparison of Two Previous Studies on Battered Women Who Kill

	Browne's homicide group %	Browne's nonhomicide group %	Walker's homicide group %	Walker's nonhomicide group %
Batterer was frequently intoxicated	80	40	88	67
Partner forced victim to have sexual intercourse	75	59		5
Partner forced insertion of objects in victim's vagina, anal sex, oral sex, and/or sex with animals	62	37	31	41
Victim threatened to commit suicide	49	31	34	
Batterer threatened to kill spouse or her close relatives	83	59	57	
Victim was frequently intoxicated			48	20

murder trials and concluded that all the battered women for whom she testified "killed as a last resort. They killed in order to save their own lives and often the lives of their children" (1989, p. 7).

Most of the fifty women in Walker's 1984 study killed their mate with a gun that belonged to him. These battered women reported that no one took them very seriously, and so in order to survive "they alone had to protect themselves against brutal attacks, and . . . they knew by observable changes in the man's physical or mental state that this time he really would kill them" (Walker, 1984, p. 40). Almost all the fifty abusive men were fascinated with weapons, especially guns. In fact, 38 or 76 percent of the battered women who used a gun to kill the abuser "used the same weapon with which he had previously threatened her" (p. 42). Walker also listed three additional factors that indicated a high risk of homicide: the batterer's excessive jealousy, the victim's social isolation from family members and friends, and frequent alcohol intoxication and drug use.

When battered women who have killed their abusers are brought to trial, the prosecuting attorney typically files charges of murder or manslaughter, and the defense attorney presents a case of self-defense. During the trial, the prosecutor usually asks: "Why didn't the woman leave him if she was really being abused?" Such a question implies that either she was not really beaten or, if she were, she could just have walked away and put an end to the violence. Increasingly, however, women who have ended a violent relationship were stalked and threatened with murder by their former partner, or the batterer frequently threatens the woman with a slow and torturous death if she should attempt to leave.

In answering the question, "Why didn't she just leave him?" defense attorneys have increasingly presented evidence of the battered woman syndrome, which is viewed as a subcategory of posttraumatic stress disorder (PTSD) in the fourth edition of the *Diagnostic and Statistical Manual of Mental Disorders* (DSM-4) (1994). Walker was the first researcher to use the term *battered woman syndrome* and to document its incidence among more than 400 abused women in her Colorado study (1984).

People who experience severe trauma (e.g., Vietnam War veterans) or who suffer from repeated and unpredictable brutality (e.g., battered women) may develop psychological symptoms that persist long after the original trauma has subsided. Ongoing trauma, such as battering, may lead the victim to develop coping mechanisms that make her unable to predict the result of her actions, and so she acts in a way that offers her the greatest safety (Walker, 1989, 1993).

The psychologist Martin Seligman developed the theoretical concept of *learned helplessness,* which Walker applied to battered women to explain why they do not flee from a violent relationship (Walker, 1984). In Walker's (1993) view, learned helplessness

> means that a woman can learn she is unable to predict the effect her behavior will have. People suffering from learned helplessness are more likely to choose behavioral responses that will have the highest predictability of an effect within the known, or familiar situation; they avoid responses—like escape, for instance—that launch them into the unknown. (pp. 50–51)

My study builds on the earlier two studies by Browne (1984, 1987) and that by Walker (1984), by examining the extent to which forced sexual acts, threats by the batterer to kill his spouse or her close relatives, alcohol and drug abuse, and/or suicide attempts were reported by the battered women in my 1992 New Jersey study. In addition, this chapter extends the findings of earlier studies by using more than 200 variables, most of which were not used in the other studies.

This research was designed to ascertain whether there were differences between a group of battered women who were incarcerated for killing their abusive partners and a random community sample of battered women. I and my six trained interviewers conducted in-depth interviews (lasting approximately one to three hours) with currently and formerly battered women.

Methodology

The sample for my study came from three sources: The prison sample was drawn from the Edna Mahon Correctional Institution for Women in Clinton, New Jersey (105 women), and the community sample was drawn from two suburban New Jersey police departments (fifty women) and two battered women's shelters in New Jersey (fifty-five women). The women in the prison sample had been convicted of killing their partners and were serving sentences ranging from three years to life. The average time they served before being paroled was nine years for the battered women in New Jersey convicted of killing their abusive partners; the overwhelming majority had been convicted of second-degree murder or manslaughter.

I gathered my data from 105 volunteer female inmates and from a community

sample of 105 battered women. To ensure the confidentiality of the information,those women who volunteered for the study signed the consent form given to
them by the superintendent's administrative assistant or the interviewer; neither the
project director nor the trained student interviewer knew the subjects' last names.

The second part of the data collection was finding a comparison group of battered
women in the community through a convenience sample. Battered women who
were similar in age, race, and occupational background were randomly selected
from two large suburban police departments and two battered women's shelters.
The data were analyzed on demographic characteristics, battering history, educational and occupational background, stressful life events, nature and extent of
criminal violence, physical and mental health problems, illnesses requiring medical
treatment, use of psychotropic and/or illegal drugs, types and utilization of social
services and agencies, coping skills, and anticipated life goals three and five years
hence.

I carefully worded each question and pretested them with a focus group of
eighteen formerly battered women at the women's prison. As a result of the pretest,
I revised the forty-page interview schedule of questions in order to maximize the
number of answerable questions.

The limitations of this study were as follows:

1. This prison sample is not representative of all battered women who have killed
   their batterer, since it does not include those women who were acquitted; who
   pleaded guilty to a reduced charge and were given probation, a suspended
   sentence, or a short prison sentence; or who entered a plea of insanity or
   diminished capacity and were committed to a psychiatric institution.
2. Both the prison and community samples are biased, since they are representative of just the state of New Jersey. However, unlike social problems such as
   drug abuse and crime, woman battering does not seem to vary from one state
   or jurisdiction to the next.
3. Since this study relied on the memory of the battered women and the most
   common source of self-report data is filtered or faulty memory recall, I cannot
   claim 100 percent accuracy. But no interview or questionnaire study that relies
   on an individual person's ability to recall past events can claim complete
   accuracy, particularly with some hidden independent variables (e.g., what
   event precipitated the first battering incident).

Results

Prison Versus Community Samples

I began my analysis with a description of the similarities and differences between
the prison sample and the community sample of battered women. Although the two
samples did have similarities, they also showed marked differences. The data in
Table 3.2 illustrate the similarities and differences in background variables (e.g.,
educational level, income, and marital status). Table 3.3 indicates the similarities

Table 3.2. Demographics and Background Variables

Variable	Prison sample N	Prison sample %	Community sample N	Community sample %
Education				
Never graduated from high school	61	59.2	15	14.6
High school graduate	42	40.8	88	85.4
Vocational training				
None	66	62.9	66	62.9
Completed vocational training	39	37.1	39	37.1
Family income in 1990				
Under $10,000	55	54.0	20	19.2
$10,001–$25,000	24	23.4	43	41.4
$25,001–$40,000	12	11.3	23	22.2
$40,001 and above	14	13.3	19	18.2
Sources of income[a]				
Public assistance	50	47.6	21	20.2
Food stamps	36	34.3	16	15.4
Unemployment compensation	1	1.0	10	9.6
Child support	8	7.6	9	8.7
Wages or salary	62	59.0	82	78.1
Marital status				
Cohabiting	59	56.2	32	30.5
Currently or previously married	46	43.8	73	69.5

[a]A number of the battered women had two or more sources of public welfare from which they received assistance (e.g., public assistance or monthly welfare checks, and food stamps).

and differences related to whether a weapon was used, severe versus less severe injuries during the worst battering incident, and death threats. These comparisons were repeated on the women's coping methods and skills, such as seeking emergency medical treatment, reporting the violence to the police, and/or being intoxicated or using drugs.

No significant difference was found in the percentage of the two samples who had been abused by an intoxicated or drug-abusing partner (imprisoned battered women, 22 or 21.0 percent; community sample, 25 or 23.8 percent) or who had never completed a vocational training course (prison sample, 62.9 percent; community sample, 62.9 percent). Other similarities between the two groups included suffering depressive and anxiety episodes, experiencing one or more severe battering episodes (prison sample, 43.8 percent; community sample, 40.0 percent), and reporting the battering to the police (prison sample, 55.2 percent; community sample 62.8 percent).

Contrary to the earlier findings by Browne and Walker, my study found almost no differences between the two groups with regard to terrorist and death threats by the batterer against the battered woman, although the community sample had a slightly higher response to this question (prison sample, 69 or 65.7 percent; community sample, 70 or 66.7 percent). In addition, the majority of both groups were repeatedly forced to have sexual intercourse with their abusive partner (prison sample, 64.2 percent; community sample, 60.2 percent).

Table 3.3.   Family Violence Incidents and Positive and Negative Coping Methods

Variable	Prison sample		Community sample	
	N	%	N	%
First incident of family violence				
Abused by intoxicated or drug-abusing partner	22	21.0	25	23.8
Abused by nonintoxicated partner	83	79.0	80	76.2
Worst incident of family violence				
Severely battered (e.g., broken bones, concussion)	46	43.8	42	40.0
Pushing, slapping, or punching, resulting in bruises or scrapes	59	56.2	63	60.0
Weapon used				
Yes	42	40.0	16	15.2
Police response				
Reported violence to police	58	55.2	66	62.8
Police helpful	35	33.3	63	60.0
Emergency medical response				
Received treatment	58	60.4	48	47.5
Substance abuse				
Drug use	60	62.5	50	49.5
Drunkenness	63	67.7	71	68.3
Death threats				
Threatened to kill victim	69	65.7	70	66.7
Threatened to kill children	19	18.0	24	22.8
Threatened to kill relative	17	16.1	33	31.4

When comparing the two samples, several differences became apparent. The battered women who killed their partner were much more likely than the community sample was to have dropped out of high school, to have been poor and on public assistance, and to have never married their abusive partner. Although the majority of both groups were from the lower socioeconomic class, almost half the prison sample (47.6 percent), in comparison with one-fifth (20.2 percent) of the community sample, had been on public assistance at the time of their worst battering incident. Although very few of the women in both groups had a college degree (prison sample, 1 percent; community sample, 5 percent), the prison sample differed significantly in the number of high school dropouts (59.2 percent of the prison sample never graduated from high school, compared with 14.6 percent of the community sample). Most of the battered women who killed had never been married and had lived with the abusive partner for a number of years, compared with less than one-third of the community sample living with their batterer (prison sample, 59 or 56.2 percent; community sample, 32 or 30.5 percent).

Critical Incidents During Childhood and Adolescence

Two major findings of my study were related to critical incidents during the women's childhood and adolescence. First, the overwhelming majority of battered women who killed their partners reported having been sexually assaulted and physically abused two or more times during childhood and adolescence, and they were considerably more likely to have had an alcoholic mother or father who was violent toward them in the aftermath of a drunken episode. In contrast, very few of the battered women in the community sample had been sexually assaulted during childhood or adolescence. Second, most of the battered women in the community sample had experienced nonviolent stressors such as divorce, death of a loved one, or moving to a new city because of their father's changing jobs.

Critical Incidents: Selected Illustrations from the Battered Women Who Kill

Tina and Gladys both experienced a horrendous series of violent, traumatic, and degrading incidents during their childhood and early adolescence: They were beaten, raped, sodomized, and humiliated by sexual assaults by their fathers, relatives, or neighbors.

Tina is twenty-five and has one daughter. She recounted several terrible events during her childhood that she will never forget:

> I was nine. I was raped and sodomized by a teenager from the neighborhood. I knew him. He was about sixteen. I kept it in for sixteen years. I kept a lot in. I'm just learning now to talk about it. . . . My father tried to kill me when I was thirteen. He was drunk. It was about 3 A.M. He came home drunk. I was sound asleep, and I woke up to him strangling me. My mother was on top of his back trying to pull him off of me. There was no reason for it. He was drunk. . . . I was raped and sodomized by my ex-fiancé when I was age seventeen. I was tied up to a chair and raped. I was beat up. My face looked like the elephant man by the time he was done with me. It happened more than once.

Because Gladys's parents were very poor, at age seven she and her five sisters were placed in foster homes, and then at age fifteen, she and her older sister went to Philadelphia to live with their aunt. Gladys was pregnant at the time. Her father had died the year before, so her mother also moved to Philadelphia to live with them. Gladys was gang-raped at age thirteen and was raped again at age fifteen and again at age sixteen:

> I was raped, actually a few times. I went to a dance hall when I was thirteen. I was just standing there, and this boy came over and he wasn't really a stranger. I seen him around before. I knew him from high school. He asked me if I wanted something to drink. I said OK, and he brought me a glass of orange soda. Then we were talking, and I started feeling kinda weird. He asked me if I wanted a ride home and I said OK. All I remember after that is getting into the car and then being in a dark house, hearing a lot of men's voices and my body being used. . . . When I was fifteen, I was drugged up again and raped by a stranger.

Critical Incidents: Selected Illustrations from the Nonhomicidal Battered Women

Typical of the battered women who did not kill their abusive partners, Amy and Consuela recalled several critical incidents from their childhoods that were neither violent or degrading. Amy, aged nineteen, remembered two incidents regarding moving and a broken romance:

> My second move was hard for me. I had to make new friends. I was a little fat kid, and everyone picked on me. I didn't like where I moved at first, but then I adjusted. . . . I was going with Eric for seven months, and my best friend Brenda went out with him on the day I broke up with him. Me and her don't talk any more.

Consuela, aged twenty-six, is a high school graduate who grew up in Central, New Jersey. She worked for several years at Saks Fifth Avenue, putting price tags on clothes, checking inventory, and loading trucks:

> When I was nine, I had to have surgery for a tumor, or I think it was a cyst in my back. It was very painful. I was in the hospital for two weeks. . . . When I was fifteen,my parents divorced. My father moved back to Puerto Rico, and I didn't get to see him very often.

Triggering Events: Drunkenness, Drug Abuse, and Extreme Jealousy

My study revealed three major findings: First, almost two-thirds of the battered women who killed their partners had had very little education (never graduated from high school), were in cohabitating relationships, had received emergency medical treatment because of the seriousness of their injuries, and had a history of being sexually assaulted by men other than their abusive partner.

Second, the prison sample seemed to be in imminent danger from specific terrorist and death threats from their batterer, threats that included the method and time when he was going to kill them. Third, most of the battered women who killed their partners first attempted suicide by overdosing on drugs as a self-destructive method of coping. When their "cry-for-help" suicide attempts failed to end the battering, they decided that the only escape was to kill the batterer before he killed them.

Triggering Events: Selected Illustrations from the Homicidal Battered Women

When the battered women shared their recollections of the events that seemed to trigger the abuse, it became apparent that the batterer was drunk, "stoned," "smashed," or doing drugs. In addition, the batterer seemed to be extremely jealous and to fear losing his girlfriend or spouse. Both Rachel and Janet observed that their abusive partner's alcohol or drug abuse frequently precipitated the violent battering incidents and that the battering quickly intensified because of the abuser's jealousy and fears that his wife or girlfriend might leave him for another man.

Rachel is a thirty-year-old woman who is married with three children and had been a bookkeeper at an auto parts store. According to her, the incidents precipitating the abuse were as follows:

> What triggered him was drug use. He would get paranoid and accuse me of things, of having a boyfriend. We started arguing, he put a gun to my head, and said if he

couldn't have me, then no one could. Some fights I would fight back. He never hit me. I got bruises from him holding me down, but he never hit me. The mental abuse was the worst part of it.

Janet is a twenty-nine-year-old widow with two children who had worked part time as a secretary for a social work agency. According to her,

The third time I went out with him, I was slapped, but I can't remember. We were outside the Quick-Check. I was twenty-three and he was twenty-four. I always think it was never his fault. I blame myself. He had an alcohol problem, and it happened after he was drinking. He always made me think it was my fault. I did something to make it happen. I'd look at someone or the dinner burnt, or I talked to a guy. I couldn't look at a man while I was talking. It would happen over anything.

Triggering Events: Selected Illustrations from Battered Women in the Community

There seemed to be four types of events that precipitated the worst battering incidents: the batterer's drunkenness, extreme jealousy, intense need to isolate his victim socially, and dependency.

Kathy, aged thirty one, is a cashier at a local supermarket. She described the events that led to her being abused:

I was living with George for a year; I moved into his apartment; he threw me out eight months ago; he was seeing someone else; he beat me up and told me to get out; he was accusing me of cheating on him, and he was the one seeing someone else.

Lynn is twenty-one, a full-time student, and a part-time waitress. For her, the events causing the abuse were as follows:

He was always very jealous of me. The first incident of abuse was when he became jealous over something stupid and we began arguing. He slapped my face. Then every time he became jealous, he would cause an argument, and he would end up hitting and slapping me. He became jealous of all men—he was jealous if I even looked at another man. He even became jealous if I spent time at my older brother's house or at my friend's house. He stopped me from spending time with all my friends. He then started to argue about every stupid little thing. . . . Every time he provoked an argument I noticed his "special mood" he had before beating me. After every time he beat me, he became "the perfect gentlemen" and would apologize and buy me roses and presents and promise he would never hit me again.

Donna, aged twenty-one, is a cashier at a toy store. She recollected the events that precipitated the abuse from her boyfriend:

Last year the abuse got real bad. I was nine months pregnant, and we were constantly arguing. We went to my brother's house, who he hates, to pick up a pair of vice grips, and he started beating me for going there. He would beat me for going or being with any of my family or friends.

Imminent Danger: Terroristic and Death Threats

The overwhelming majority of the battered women who killed received death threats in which the batterer specified the method, time, and location of their demise.

Terroristic and Death Threats: Selected Illustrations from the Battered Women Who Kill

Mary received death threats that resulted in nightmares and flashbacks. She is twenty-three and, when she was working, alternated between painting houses and doing maintenance work. When not employed she received unemployment compensation, and when that ran out she received welfare and food stamps. Her recollections of death threats are as follows:

> December 6, 1991, he tried to kill me. I was late coming home from work, and he called me a liar, this, that, and the other thing. He was drunk and drugged out. I was living at a friend's house having dinner, and he pounded on the door. I came outside to see what he wanted, and he came after me and told me he was going to kill me, and when I saw the knife I ran. He was coming right at me, and he chased me down the street. My friends had already called the cops, and the cops came and he took off. . . . I seen him one day and took off. I tried to talk to him to ask him why he wanted to kill me. He calls me all the time and leaves messages that he's gonna do this to me or that to me. I asked him why, and all he had to say was that I better drop the charges or I was gonna end up a dead man.

When Mary answered yes to the question, "Did your partner ever threaten to kill you?" her response to the follow-up question, "Can you recall some of the words he used?" gives us some insight into the specificity of method and magnitude of the death threat:

> I remember exactly what he said: "Do you remember the guy from *Goodfellas* [the movie], the crazy one? Well, I'm worse than that." He said he was gonna shoot me in the head and hang me on the tree on Cranbury Street so all my friends can see, and he said he was going to pistol-whip my roommates. I feel bad because I live there, and their lives are in danger because of me.

Delores, aged forty-two, told us:

> He threatened to kill me. If he was drunk enough, I thought he would. Especially if I was with another man. He always said, "If I ever catch you with another man, I'll kill you" and "If you leave me, I'll blow your brains out."

She described her injuries from years of battering:

> Two broken ribs, scars on my elbows and thighs, bruises on my back and neck. Broke my bridge in five places. All of my top teeth are loose. My hearing aids and glasses were broken.

Suicide Attempts

In contrast with the community sample of battered women in my study, many of the battered women in the prison sample had a history of alcoholism and or drug abuse. Those who attempted suicide frequently did so by overdosing on drugs. Theresa, Tina, and Martha tried to escape the cycle of violence by attempting suicide.

Theresa is thirty-three, an x-ray technician. She is married by common law and has two children. She tried to commit suicide twice by cutting her wrists and also by overdosing on drugs. Her girlfriend found her both times and bandaged her up because she was afraid to go to the hospital. Theresa reported that she took Valium, heroin, cocaine, reefers, and crack.

Tina, aged twenty-five talked about her suicide attempt:

> I tried to kill myself because of depression over life in general. I was fed up—sick and tired of being beaten and miserable and taken advantage of. My body took the drugs. I couldn't O-D. I tried to hang myself in my backyard, but someone pulled into my driveway. I found recently I have a lot to live for."

Martha, aged forty-eight, is a business consultant. She recounted her suicide attempt as follows:

> In 1988, I already had five children and let all my stress be buried. I realized I was married to an alcoholic and wife beater. I took a lot of pills because no one wanted to help me. My husband found me. They pumped my stomach. I was in the hospital for about five days. After that, a multitude of promises such as no more drinking, but I realized that wouldn't be the case and said I'd never let this happen to myself again.

Conclusion

As I stated in the beginning of this chapter, the purpose of my study was to examine the similarities and differences between a group of battered women who had killed their partner and a community group of battered women who had not killed their partner. After I reviewed the findings, several key points became apparent. The majority of battered women who killed their abusive partners were much more likely than the nonhomicidal group was to have dropped out of high school, to have an erratic work history of one or two unskilled jobs (e.g., part-time painter or cleaning lady), to be cohabiting with their partner, to have a drug problem, to have attempted suicide by overdosing on drugs, to have received emergency medical treatment for battering-related injuries, and to have had access to the batterer's guns. In contrast with the homicidal group, the battered women in the community sample were much less likely to be alcoholics or drug addicts, have experienced alcohol-related blackouts and/or seizures, have received psychiatric treatment, have attempted suicide, and/or have access to a gun. In conclusion, the major findings support the idea that once a battered woman has received a death threat and has failed in her attempt to "drown her sorrows" in alcohol or drugs and to commit suicide, she is likely to try to kill her batterer.

References

American Psychiatric Association. 1994. *Diagnostic and Statistical Manual (DSM-IV)*. Washington, D.C.: American Psychiatric Association.

Biden, J. R. 1993, June. "Domestic Violence: A Crime, Not a Quarrel." *Trial*, 56–60.

Browne, A. 1984. "Assault and Homicide at Home: When Battered Women Kill." Paper presented at the Second National Conference for Family Violence Researchers, Durham, N.H.

Browne, A. 1987. *When Battered Women Kill*. New York: Free Press.

Cascardi, M., and K. D. O'Leary. 1992. "Depressive Symptomatology, Self-Esteem, and Self-Blame in Battered Women." *Journal of Family Violence* 7: 249–59.

Gondolf, E. W., and E. B. Fischer. 1988. *Battered Women As Survivors: An Alternative to Treating Learned Helplessness*. Lexington, Mass.: Lexington Books.

Gondolf, E. W., and E. B. Fischer. 1991. "Wife Beating." In *Case Studies in Family Violence*, ed. R. T. Ammerman and M. Hersen, pp. 273–92. New York: Plenum.

Hasselt, V. N., R. L. Morrison, A. S. Bellack, and M. Hersen, eds. 1988. *Handbook of Family Violence*. New York: Plenum.

Hirschel, J. D., I. W. Hutchison, C. W. Dean, and A. Mills. 1992, June. "Review Essay on the Law Enforcement Response to Spouse Abuse: Past, Present and Future." *Justice Quarterly* 9: 247–83.

Pence, E. 1983. "The Duluth Domestic Abuse Intervention Project." *Hamline Law Review* 6: 247–75.

Randall, T. 1990, August 22–29. "Domestic Violence Intervention Calls for More than Treating Injuries." *Journal of the American Medical Association*. 264: 939–940.

Roberts, A. R. 1981. *Sheltering Battered Women: A National Survey and Service Guide*. New York: Springer.

Roberts, A. R. 1988. "Substance Abuse Among Men Who Batter Their Mates: The Dangerous Mix." *Journal of Substance Abuse Treatment* 5: 83–87.

Roberts, A. R., and B. J. Roberts. 1990. "A Model for Crisis Intervention with Battered Women and Their Children." In *Crisis Intervention Handbook: Assessment, Treatment and Research*, ed. A. R. Roberts, pp. 105–23. Belmont, Calif.: Wadsworth.

Sherman, L. W. 1992. *Policing Domestic Violence: Experiments and Dilemmas*. New York: Free Press.

Sherman, L. W., and R. A. Berk. 1984. "The Specific Deterrent Effects of Arrest for Domestic Assault." *American Sociological Review* 49: 267–72.

Straus, M., and R. Gelles. 1990. *Physical Violence in American Families*. New Brunswick, N.J.: Transaction Books.

Straus, M., R. Gelles, and S. Steinmetz. 1980. *Behind Closed Doors: Violence in the American Family*. Garden City, N.Y.: Doubleday/Anchor.

Sugg, N. K., and T. Inui. 1992. "Primary Care Physicians' Response to Domestic Violence: Opening Pandora's Box." *Journal of the American Medical Association* 267: 3157–60.

Trafford, A. 1991, February 26. "Why Battered Women Kill: Self Defense, Not Revenge, Is Often the Motive." *Washington Post*, p. 11.

Walker, L. E. 1984. *The Battered Women Syndrome*. New York: Springer.

Walker, L. E. 1989. *Terrifying Love*. New York: Harper & Row.

Walker, L. E. 1993. "Battered Women as Defendants." In *Legal Responses to Wife Assault*, ed. N. Z. Hilton, pp. 233–57. Newbury Park, Calif.: Sage.

4

Social Work and Criminal Justice Responses to Elder Abuse in New York City

Patricia Brownell

A sixty-five-year-old woman was hospitalized with multiple injuries to her head and body. She told her doctor that her son, daughter, and daughter's friend had held her prisoner for the past several days and beat her repeatedly for no apparent reason, threatening to kill her if she attempted escape.

Although it is not always as horrifying or dramatic as this example from a police report, elder abuse is an social problem of increasing concern to gerontologists and others in the helping professions. The United States House of Representatives Select Committee on Aging issued a report in 1990, *Elder Abuse: A Decade of Shame and Inaction,* which included the finding that one of every twenty older Americans, or more than 1.5 million people, may be victims of elder abuse. The report also stated that elder abuse is far less likely to be reported than child abuse: Whereas one of every three child abuse cases is reported, only one of eight cases of elder abuse cases is reported.

There is cause for concern for a number of reasons. First is the pain, risk, and danger to which abused elders are exposed. In addition, demographic studies point to the increasing number of aged people in our society, a phenomenon known as the *graying of America* (Gilford, 1988). Even if the proportion of abused elders in the population (currently estimated at between 3 and 12 percent of the elderly) remained constant, the sheer numbers can be expected to increase.

Defining Elder Abuse

Elder abuse is defined here as physical, psychological, and/or financial abuse or neglect by a family member who is a son, daughter, son- or daughter-in-law, stepson or -daughter, niece or nephew, or grandchild (Wolf & Pillemer, 1984). Physical abuse may be hitting, pushing, or using a weapon where physical contact occurs:

> A sixty-five-year-old woman stated that her thirty-year-old son threw her to the ground, covered her face with a pillow, and attempted to suffocate her. He lifted the pillow, looked at her, and said: "You're still alive," then placed the pillow over her face again.

Psychological abuse can be threatening, intimidating, harassing, insulting, or other behavior that causes concern on the part of the victim but does not involve physical contact:

> A seventy-three-year-old woman complained that her son, aged thirty-nine, has been constantly harassing her but flees every time the police respond. The victim was informed by her neighbor that her son told the neighbor he was going to kill his mother, who now fears for her life. The son is an alcoholic, drug user, and was recently released from prison (on parole).

Financial abuse is defined as exploiting an older person financially, such as taking or attempting to take his or her assets, income, or property through intimidation or without consent:

> An eighty-nine-year-old woman stated that her son, aged fifty-five, entered her apartment and took stocks and bonds in the amount of $54,000 without her permission or authority. The stocks and bonds are in the name of her and her daughter.

Neglect (active and passive) includes the deliberate or unintentional withholding of medication, food, clothing, or other goods and services associated with caregiving:

> An seventy-two-year-old woman, bedridden with a stroke, is being cared for by her eighty-one-year-old husband, who is frail and suffering from dementia; due to memory loss, he frequently forgets to feed her and give her prescribed medication.

> An eighty-five-year-old man is dependent on his forty-five-year-old daughter, with whom he lives, to prepare meals and keep his living space clean. She resents his living with her and her family and often deprives him of adequate food and clean linens.

Unless the withholder is a formal or legally designated caregiver, however, such as a home attendant or a court-appointed guardian, or unless care is being withheld because funds belonging to the elder are being misappropriated by the informal caregiver (family member or significant other), such actions are not codified as criminal offenses by state penal codes that do not reflect mandatory reporting laws for elder abuse. New York State, for example, is one of eight states that do not have mandatory reporting systems for elder abuse.

Because elder abuse is considered to be severely underreported as a form of domestic violence, identifying a means of case finding becomes important. The mandatory reporting of elder abuse has been legislated in a number of states; however, research into its effectiveness as a means of detecting elder abuse has shown it to be limited (Fredrikson, 1989). Some researchers have suggested that such abuse is ageist and a violation of many older adults' right to self-determination (Crystal, 1987; Faulkner, 1982). In addition, Johnson (1986) questioned whether it should not be the decision of the victim—as opposed to the professional onlooker—as to what constitutes abuse.

Concerns such as these are reflected in the growing professional interest in the diversity of older people and the meanings they assign to events in their world. Without some means of identifying abuse and mistreatment of the elderly, however, the possibilities for intervention are limited.

Adult protective service (APS) programs operate in every state to serve mentally and physically impaired adults, including older victims of domestic violence. These programs provide an important means of detecting and intervening in situations involving the abuse of older adults by relatives and significant others. They generally confine their services to the frail and judgment impaired, however, not to the competent adult. As defined in the New York State (NYS) Social Services law, for example, even involuntary protective services may be provided to judgment-impaired adults (eighteen years of age and older) who are unable to protect themselves from abuse and exploitation by others. This may include elders suffering from dementia (such as Alzheimer's disease) whose needs are overwhelming caregivers. In these latter cases, case management and social services are usually considered the interventions of choice.

Another important but overlooked source of case finding for elder abuse is the criminal justice system, most notably, the local police department. This offers a means of addressing abuse and exploitation against older adults that reflects categories of actions defined by the penal code as constituting criminal acts.

Elder Abuse and the Criminal Justice System

Research on the role of the criminal justice system as an intervention strategy for elder abuse is needed but, to date, has been considered inadequate (NARCEA, 1991). This demonstrates the difficulty with access to information even at the local law enforcement level. Among the reasons are

1. Police departments do not generally maintain domestic violence information in a form that is accessible to researchers.
2. Confidentiality mandates keep much of the recorded information on complaint reports unavailable to researchers or to service providers such as APS, home-care vendors, and not-for-profit social service workers.
3. Special computer programs are generally required in order to identify crimes against specific age groups—like the elderly—by relationship to perpetrator and type of crime.

4. Offenses as defined by the Uniform Crime Reports are not always comparable to the literature's accepted definitions of elder abuse.

As a result, much information found in police complaint reports on elder abuse is unusable or unavailable to researchers, policymakers, and practitioners (Saltzman et al., 1990).

There have been few significant studies to date on the use of complaint reports either to assess patterns of family violence or to investigate the police's response to domestic elder abuse. Two notable exceptions are, for the former, "Magnitude and Patterns of Family and Intimate Behavior in Atlanta, Georgia, 1984" (Saltzman et al., 1990), and, for the latter, *A Time for Dignity: Police and Domestic Abuse of the Elderly* (Plotkin, 1988). The Saltzman study, however, did not examine elder abuse as a form of domestic violence, and the study by Plotkin (a collaborative effort of the Police Executive Research Forum and the American Association of Retired Persons) is currently out of print. The latter study also focused more on procedures implemented in local law enforcement agencies throughout the United States identifying and responding to elder abuse than on actual cases.

Despite the paucity of research using police data to investigate elder abuse, these data are collected by all police departments throughout the country (Plotkin, 1988). The Plotkin study, in fact, identified the New York City Police Department (NYPD) as exemplary in its efforts on behalf of victims of domestic violence, including elderly victims of mistreatment. In 1989, for example, 4,000 incidents of domestic violence were reported to the NYPD (J. Ryan, personal communication, March 21, 1990). Although staff shortages have limited the capacity of the NYPD to retrieve information on elder abuse as captured on complaint reports, it is possible to make such identifications through special computer programming.

Police Complaint Reports as a Source of Information and Case Findings

A complaint report can provide important information about the demographic and structural aspects of elder abuse. In addition, because the abuse is reported either by or on behalf of elderly victims at the time of the incident, it is likely to represent the victim's perception of having been mistreated. Finally, because the complaint report also includes a brief description of the abusive event, as reported by either the victim or the witness, it provides a better picture of the event than do statistical data or crime codes alone.

These reports also provide useful information about elder abuse from the criminal justice perspective and are useful in building a bridge between the fields of criminology and gerontology, sociology, and social work. However, having information about elder abuse victims who come into contact with the criminal justice system is not sufficient to ensure that they will be protected from their abuser (perpetrator) or that the abuser will be either punished or given needed corrective services. In order for the criminal justice system to deal with elder abuse, the victims must be willing, in most cases, to prosecute the abuser. Such prosecution can take the form of cooperating with the police and/or the district attorney or seeking an order of protection through either the criminal or the family court.

In New York City, after the police completes the crime report (after responding to a complaint by or on behalf of the victim), the victim is asked whether he or she would be willing to prosecute the perpetrator. The response is recorded on the complaint report. Although the victim may later change his or her mind as to whether to follow through with the prosecution, answering in the affirmative at the time of the initial contact normally initiates a follow-up response from a detective at the local precinct. At this time, encouragement and support for the victim to follow through with prosecution can lead to intervention by the criminal justice system, a desirable outcome in that it can prevent future abuse or open the way for social service providers.

The Victims of Domestic Violence and Their Willingness to Prosecute

The use of prosecution in domestic violence situations is controversial (Mancuso, 1989). The goal of the family court system in New York, for example, is to help family members work out problems outside the criminal justice system. Therefore, when victims' rights advocates began to challenge the use of civil court to adjudicate crimes committed by family members against spouses, the option of using the criminal court for this purpose was legislated.

The spouse abuse literature argues that a victim's decision to prosecute his or her abuser is desirable if it will protect the elderly victim against further abuse. Such a decision can signal the abuser that the victim refuses to tolerate the abusive relationship. It can also result—assuming an appropriate follow-through by the victim—in, at a minimum, an order of protection being issued, permitting the immediate arrest by police if the abuser violates its conditions. The arrest may offer alternatives to incarceration, such as requiring the abuser to enter substance-abuse or mental health treatment. An order of protection forbids the abuser to contact the victim for a defined period of time, and its violation will bring a mandatory arrest of the offender.

Police reports on elder abuse can also provide an important and often overlooked source of case finding if the victim states a willingness to prosecute and therefore receives a follow-up contact by the local precinct. In a state like New York, which, again, is one of eight states with no mandatory reporting system, police reports can provide valuable information on the incidence and prevalence of abuse in particular communities.

Stating a willingness to prosecute an abuser who is a family member, such as a child, can increase an elder abuse victim's sense of empowerment and the likelihood of his or her deciding to establish limits for an abusive child. Finally, this willingness can lead to intervention by social workers collaborating with police officers to target those elder abuse victims who come to the attention of the police for follow-up services.

Services offered through such a collaboration may include supporting a victim's decision to prosecute and/or supporting the victim through the prosecution process. For victims who are not willing to prosecute their abuser, a referral to Adult Protective Services should be considered. Other service interventions are counseling and case management, referring the victim to the appropriate service network for assistance with securing broken locks and doors and providing Meals on Wheels, friendly visiting or telephone reassurance services, as well as respite and other services, as needed. In addition, the abuser's service needs should not be overlooked, particularly if the abuser appears to be an overwhelmed caregiver (of an Alzheimer's patient, for example) or a developmentally disabled or mentally or physically impaired adult. It may be useful to draw up a profile of those victims who would most likely be willing to prosecute as well as those who would not, in order to target efforts on their behalf more effectively.

Case Management of Abused Elders and Their Families

The most common response to domestic violence is crisis intervention. Experts on elder abuse, however, including Quinn and Tomita (1986) and Breckman and Adelman (1988), point to the often long-term and chronic nature of elder abuse and the difficulties of helping abused elders acknowledge abuse by a loved one, such as an adult son or daughter.

One reason that adds to the difficulties for older adult victims of family abuse to admit abuse by loved ones is fear of the loss of support. Another is the desire to protect loved ones from the consequences of arrest and prosecution. A third is fear of possible retribution by the abuser.

Community case management services can be an effective intervention strategy for victims of elder abuse and their families. As used here, case management is the coordinated access to services for neighborhood-bound elderly (Keizer, 1987; Reed, 1980). The goal of case management services for elder abuse victims is to enhance their quality of life and safety.

The "staircase model" (Breckman & Adelman, 1988) for counseling victims to participate in the service should be considered, and service plans should be developed and implemented for case managers to use with victims who have not come to terms with their abuse situation. Gerontologists like Crystal (1987) have argued that elder abuse (although thought to be underestimated) is not sufficiently common to justify a separate service delivery system for the elderly.

Under the auspices of the area aging agencies, catchment area–based systems of services have been organized. A case management approach to service elder abuse victims can tap into these already existing systems for support services. Funding for case management services to the elderly and their families has decreased in recent years, although Comprehensive Medicaid Case Management funds are still available under the Comprehensive Omnibus Budget Reconciliation Act (COBRA) of 1985. The conditions for using these funds are the state's willingness to select case management as an optional service reimbursable under Medicaid, the identification of adult domestic violence victims as a target population to be served, and the assumption that the clients served are recipients of Medicaid.

Those services available under the auspices of the Older American Act or federal/state entitlements are Medicaid, food stamps, Emergency Assistance for Adults (OAA) for back rent and utility disconnects, home care, housing advocacy, legal aid, relocation (if necessary), respite service for caregivers, Meals on Wheels, protective services for adults (if necessary), involvement of the criminal justice system including family and criminal courts, medical care, financial management, substance-abuse services, and family and individual counseling.

Case management services for elder abuse victims must often be extended to the abuser as well. First, elder abuse victims can be very protective of their abusers if they are loved ones, such as sons or daughters, and particularly if they suffer from substance-abuse or psychiatric problems. In order to help an elder abuse victim, therefore, assistance often must be extended to the abuser, particularly if he or she is impaired or providing caregiving. Intervention strategies that include involvement with the criminal justice system can be framed as assisting the abuser as well as the victim; this can be useful in persuading the victim to file a complaint with the police and follow through with prosecution.

In New York City, the district attorney's offices with special elder abuse units offer flexible sentencing options—such as mandated substance-abuse treatment—that serve to reassure elder abuse victims that their abuser will be helped, not punished. Case managers who work with local precincts and district attorneys' offices can assure elder abuse victims that they will maintain some control over the arrest and prosecution process and play a role in the abuser's sentencing.

Elder abuse victims are difficult to interest in establishing and implementing a service plan designed to improve their quality of life and safety. The reasons for their unwillingness may include the denial common to all victims of domestic violence. They may deny the abuse for fear of their personal safety, to protect the abuser, and/or to preserve the relationship with him or her (often a loved one or close family member).

The victims' belief that they have no choice but to tolerate the abuse is often indirectly validated by the professional community's belief that services for them do not exist. A case management approach to serving elder abuse victims and their families can correct that notion by using existing services, including the criminal justice system, both to assist the elder abuse victim and to address the needs of the abuser, if this reflects the wishes of the victim to ensure the eventual well-being of the abuser.

One problem in identifying elder abuse victims is the difficulty of detecting the abuse. Unlike spouse or child abuse, elder abuse may be insidious and not always visible. For example, financial abuse has been identified as the most common form of elder abuse. Although it may lead to physical consequences, such as the inability of an older victim to buy food or pay the rent to avoid eviction, it is not as obvious as a violent physical attack. Threats to injure or kill elderly, motivated by an intent to obtain money—when they are not accompanied by actual physical harm—are also forms of elder abuse that are not easily detected.

Interagency service networks for the aging may be one source for identifying elder abuse. Another, often overlooked, source of case finding is the police department. Like spouse abuse, elders who are abused may contact the police. Once the family situation has stabilized, however, the older victim may not want to follow through with his or her complaint, thereby leaving the victim open to another attack.

The Study of Police Complaint Reports of Family Crimes Against the Elderly

In order to determine the usefulness of the local law enforcement agency in identifying elder abuse and providing a profile of elder abuse that meets the criminal justice criteria of a crime according to state penal laws, we studied those police complaint reports filed with the New York City Police Department (NYPD) that indicated abuse of an older parent by an adult son or daughter. We looked at a total of 295 complaint reports filed with the NYPD in Manhattan during 1992 that reflected criminal offenses by adult children against parents aged sixty and older. All 295 complaint reports included data on age, race/ethnicity, gender, type of offense, whether the victim or another person reported the offense, and victim's and abuser's relationship and living arrangements; of these, 238 reported the victim's stated willingness to prosecute at the time of the report as well.

Purpose of the Study

The study of elder abuse and law enforcement in New York City (Manhattan) had the following objectives:

1. Describe a profile of elderly victims of domestic mistreatment by their children. The study sample is drawn from elderly Manhattan residents who came to the attention of the New York City Police Department (NYPD) in 1992.
2. Expand the knowledge base of criminal offenses reported to the NYPD in Manhattan that indicate elder abuse as defined in the elder abuse literature.
3. Test the feasibility of developing predictor profiles of elder abuse victims who state their willingness or unwillingness to prosecute their abusive children at the time the abuse incident is first reported to the police.
4. Identify policy proposals for law enforcement, implications for social work, limitations, and needed follow-up based on the study's findings.

Findings of the Study

THE STUDY'S POPULATION

The average age of the elder abuse victims in our sample was young–old, with a mean age of sixty-nine. The oldest reported victim was ninety-three years old. On average, the oldest abuse victims were white, with the next oldest being black and the youngest being Latino, although the average ages of the black and white victims were not significantly different. This pattern also held for abusers, as could be expected for abuse by children, except that significant age differences emerged among all three ethnic groups for abusers: White abusers were, on average, the oldest; black abusers were significantly younger than white abusers; and Latino abusers were younger as a group than both white and black abusers.

For those victims stating a willingness to prosecute, younger victims usually were more willing to prosecute their abusers than older victims were. An analysis of patterns within ethnic groups, however, showed that in interaction with race/ethnicity, this association disappeared and the victims' age was not found to be a key predictor variable of willingness to prosecute. Rather, it was likely an artifact of the way that the victims were grouped into "young–old" and "old–old" categories in order to make the bivariate analyses.

The victims' gender was overwhelmingly female (mothers), 74 percent, and that of the abusers was overwhelmingly male (sons). Even though Pillemer and Finkelhor (1988) challenged the notion that the victim's gender was a key defining variable, there otherwise is general agreement in the elder abuse literature that women are the predominant victims of elder mistreatment (Carlson, 1992).

Carlson identifies this finding as primarily due to the fact that women represent the majority of elderly people today. A comparison with the ratio of older women to men in Manhattan and New York City as a whole showed that it was not statistically different from that of the study population (at the .07 level of significance). Carlson also found that daughters were the primary perpetrators of elder abuse, but our study found that the overwhelming proportion of abusers were males (sons).

The greater tendency of black elders to report even low levels of abuse than other ethnic groups do supports the findings of national studies that blacks use the criminal justice system to report domestic violence more often than other ethnic groups do. This may reflect blacks' lower average income levels, which may prompt them to seek redress from local law enforcement, not as an agent of social control, but as a provider of social services or in lieu of more expensive legal services. On the other hand, Latino elders have an even lower average income in New York City (Cantor, 1993) and do not report abuse to the police at the same rate as older blacks do. This suggests that further research is needed to determine the reasons for black elders' greater reporting relative to their proportion in the population.

Race/ethnicity differences show up on other demographic variables as well. (Note that race is used in the study as a surrogate value for culture in the anthropological sense and not as a genetic indicator.) The ages of both victims and abusers are strikingly different among the ethnic groups. Though not a major focus of the study, Latino victims and abusers were significantly younger, on average, than either blacks or whites.

Physical abuse was more common among white victims and abusers, and financial and psychological abuse were more common among black victims and abusers. Although we expected this, it was not statistically significant in our sample of 238, but it was statistically significant in the analysis of the larger set of 295 complaint reports. This could suggest some support for the hypothesis by Griffin and Williams (1992) that social isolation may make white victims more susceptible to physical abuse, and the combination of extended families and economic discrimination against younger blacks may increase the risk of financial abuse of black elders. There was no pattern for Latino elders concerning the predominant type of abuse.

In a recent study of older people in New York City in the 1990s, children of

African-American respondents were the most likely (17 percent) to be living in the same household as their older parents, followed by Latino children (13 percent), and, finally, white children (8 percent) (Cantor, 1993). There were insufficient data, however, on the study subjects through the NYPD complaint reports to identify a link between reported elder abuse and family composition.

Although males were by far the most usual perpetrators of reported abuse, the main types of abuse reported as committed by them were financial and psychological. Female abusers were more likely to be reported for committing physical abuse.

Slightly more elders in the study lived with, as opposed to apart from, their abusers; however, there was close to a 50–50 split. Elders living with their abusers were less likely to be willing to prosecute their child abuser than were those who did not live with their abuser.

The fact that most elders, regardless of whether they lived with their abusers, reported the abuse to the police themselves suggests a degree of self-reliance that challenges the popular stereotype of abused elders as helpless and dependent on their abusers. But this may reflect a limitation of our study. Impaired victims may be less likely to show up in a sample drawn from police complaint reports (as opposed to adult protective services caseloads, for example).

Criminal Offenses Indicating Elder Abuse

Unlike most studies of agency reports of elder abuse, the types of abuse we examined are almost equally divided among physical, psychological, and financial abuse (using the coding scheme of counting one type of abuse per incidence report, based on a hierarchy of abuse categories: first physical, then financial, and, finally, psychological). Financial abuse in particular is considered an important form of elder abuse (Abelman, 1992). It had been overlooked as a form of domestic violence by the NYPD, however, which has to date identified only those offenses reflecting domestic violence most likely to apply across the life span (physical and psychological).

Financial abuse is one category of abuse that is particularly characteristic of elder abuse, as opposed to child or spouse abuse. This could be an indirect effect of social policies that since the passage of the Social Security Act of 1935 have increasingly raised elders to or above the poverty level and guaranteed a monthly income (however meager) through Social Security, Supplemental Security Income (SSI), and pensions.

The elder abuse victims in our study were subjected to a wide variety of criminal offenses by their children, ranging from harassment (including stalking), menacing, assault, robbery, forgery, to even rape. The litany of criminal offenses by children reads no differently from those committed by strangers against the elderly. However, although elders can take measures to protect themselves against stranger crime by refusing to admit strangers into their homes, avoiding leaving their homes in the evenings, seeking well-protected outdoor environments, and maintaining well-secured residences, these measures often offer limited protection against child abusers.

Some of the descriptions of abuse reported by elderly victims to the police are poignant examples of criminal offenses committed against them by their children: the mother who invites her son for dinner and finds—when her back is turned—that he leaves without saying good-bye, taking her radio with him; the father who opens the door to his son, only to be hit on the head and threatened with a box cutter; the grandparent who arranges a visit between his daughter and her child for whom he is caring—with the result that she steals a gold chain off the grandchild's neck and disappears. Others were horrifying:

> A sixty-four-year-old woman reported that her son, age thirty-eight, entered her bedroom, pulled off the covers, and stated: "I'm going to fuck you." She stated that she attempted to resist, but he pulled her hair and punched her in the face. He then forcibly held her down and raped her, stating: "If you go to the police, something will happen to you."

The fact the elders reported these incidents to the police could be seen as a measure of the hurt, anger, and sense of rejection they felt, as well as the trust that can be achieved between a police officer and an elderly victim.

Despite the poignancy and, in some instances, the horror evoked by the reports of abuse described in the police complaint reports, the elderly victims making the reports emerge as a spunky group willing to take steps to protest the abuse by their children. This shows that a significant number of elder abuse victims are willing to report abuse to the police on their own or to cooperate with the police if the abuse is reported by a third party.

The elders' willingness to report abuse to the police in the study was striking. In addition, the preponderance of low-level abuse reported may mean that elders are willing to report abuse in the initial stages of the abuse cycle. (Findings of studies on spouse abuse have suggested that abuse tends to escalate over time.)

Predictive Value of Variables

To test the predictive value of variables captured on police complaint reports in relation to a victim's stated willingness to prosecute a child abuser, a classification and regression tree (CART) analysis was performed. CART is a single procedure that can be used to analyze either categorical data (classification) or continuous data (regression). According to the SYSTAT (1992) manual: "A defining feature of CART is that it presents its results in the form of decision trees. . . . CART is inherently a non-parametric methodology that communicates by pictures" (p. 11).

The CART methodology elucidated the association between a stated willingness to prosecute and the identified predictor variables. The most significant predictor of a stated willingness or unwillingness to prosecute was the intensity of abuse. Of those victims who experienced very intense abuse, sixty-three (88 percent) of seventy-two stated a willingness to prosecute. This emerged as the single predictor of stated willingness to prosecute for those victims who experienced very intense abuse, supporting the findings of the logistic regression. It also was the most important predictor, regardless of gender, living situation, and race/ethnicity.

Of those who experienced less intensive abuse, blacks showed a greater likelihood of prosecuting than did nonblacks: Seventy-seven (77 percent) of 100 blacks who experienced less intensive abuse stated a willingness to prosecute, as opposed to 36 (55 percent) of 66 nonblacks. For those blacks who experienced less intensive abuse, however, the gender of the abuser was the most significant predictor of a stated willingness to prosecute: Black elders who experienced less intensive abuse from female children were as likely to state willingness to prosecute as not: Eleven (50 percent) stated a willingness, compared with eleven (50 percent) who stated an unwillingness to prosecute. When male children committed the abuse, however, black elders were significantly more likely to state a willingness to prosecute than not: Sixty-six (85 percent) stated a willingness to prosecute, and twelve (15 percent) stated an unwillingness to prosecute.

This suggests that the intensity of abuse and the abuser's race/ethnicity and gender have important interactive effects in relation to the stated willingness to prosecute. Each of these variables has different effects on the dependent variable, based on its status with respect to the other two. For example, the severity of the abuse is predictive of the victim's willingness to prosecute, but how predictive it is depends on the race (of both the victim and the abuser in the case of a child abuser) and the gender of the abuser.

The CART analysis further demonstrates that the living arrangements between victims and abusers is also not a significant predictor variable, as suggested by the logistic regression. Once race, the gender of the abuser, and the severity of the abuse are accounted for, the predictive value of the living arrangements between victims and abusers becomes insignificant.

Of the variables examined as potential predictor variables of an elder abuse victim's stated willingness or unwillingness to prosecute, the CART analysis identified very intensive abuse as the key predictor variable. This means that by knowing that a victim experienced very intense abuse, one can predict with a strong degree of certainty—according to this model—that he or she will state a willingness to prosecute his or her child abuser, regardless of age, ethnicity, living arrangement with abuser, or whether the victim self-reported the abuse to the police.

A second key predictor of a willingness to prosecute based on the CART analysis—when the victim has experienced less intense abuse—is race/ethnicity (the victim is black). A third predictor, which has an interactive effect with race/ethnicity, is the gender of the abuser (the abuser is a black male child). The majority of abuse situations (89 percent) were self-reported by victims to the police.

Advocates of mandatory reporting for elder abuse suggest that elderly victims of domestic violence by their children will not report abuse to the police, much less state a willingness to prosecute their abuser. Although the study's findings appear to challenge this, it is not possible, given the scope of our study, to determine whether there were many more victims who did not report.

At least for the group of Manhattan elders who self-reported complaints of abuse by their children to the NYPD, the position appears to be supported that elder victims of abuse not only are capable of advocating on their own behalf but also view the police as a valuable resource and as allies in ensuring protection from abuse.

The candor with which some of the victims in our study shared intimate and perhaps embarrassing details of their abuse to the responding police officer demonstrates the elderly victim's ease in speaking to the officer. This, in turn, supports findings from the literature on older people's trust in the police (Yin, 1985) and also suggests that local law enforcement can play a valuable role in communities in identifying and responding to elder abuse.

Implications of Identifying Predictors

As we noted, the implications for service intervention follow from the clients' assessed likelihood of stating their willingness or unwillingness to prosecute their child abusers. Cooperation between precinct-based police and community-based social workers is essential to ensure appropriate intervention strategies.

Elder abuse victims who are assessed as likely to state willingness to prosecute could be encouraged to report the abusive incident to the police and also to receive follow-up counseling and support. This may involve applying to the family or criminal courts for orders or protection and instructions on their use. Or it may mean working with clients in conjunction with the district attorney's office. For those clients who are reluctant to pursue prosecution with the district attorney's office if it means incarcerating the loved one who is abusing them, district attorneys' offices in New York City are expanding the alternatives to incarceration (ATI) to include mandated counseling, substance-abuse treatment, or evaluation by mental health professionals. Helping victims view prosecution as a means of obtaining help for child abusers can ease the guilt that elder abuse victims may feel while ensuring their protection from further abuse.

For these clients determined to be unlikely to be willing to prosecute, encouraging and assisting them to file a complaint report with the local precinct anyway can still be useful. That is, it can demonstrate to the elder abuse victim that the police can be useful as a resource and still allow them to maintain control over the outcome of the complaint process, if they are not ready to move more assertively against their abuser. Additional protective services can be discussed with those victims assessed as unlikely to prosecute and can be incorporated into a service plan. For non-judgment-impaired victims, these may include occasional visits by the community police; new locks for the doors; home visits or regular telephone contacts by social service professionals, aides, or volunteers; Meals on Wheels; voluntary money management; and instructions on how to contact the police in the case of an emergency. For judgment-impaired victims or those who appear be in imminent danger, more aggressive interventions such as referrals to adult protective services may be necessary. This can also apply to mentally impaired abusers of unimpaired elder abuse victims. As noted, coordination between the police and social workers to assist elder abuse victims and their families are often the key to ensuring the victims' safety and protection.

Policy Implications

Implications for Law Enforcement

Although broader implications may be drawn, in the context of the system in which our study was carried out, its findings demonstrated that at least some elder abuse victims see the police as an important resource in their seeking protection against being victimized by their children. To date, no state has specifically legislated mandatory reporting to the local police department. Indiana mandates reporting elder abuse to county district attorney offices, although the reports are received and investigated by outstationed APS workers, according to Ronald Dolan of the Ball State University School of Social Work in Indiana (telephone conversation, October 1993). The Charleston, South Carolina, police department, however, has developed a unique program that includes a twenty-four-hour hotline for reporting elder abuse, and South Carolina has a mandatory reporting system (Charleston police department, undated brochure). Most states with mandatory or voluntary reporting systems designate local or state area aging agencies or adult protective service agencies to receive and follow up on reports of elder abuse.

For states like New York that do not have a mandatory reporting system, reports of abuse may come to the attention of the local aging agency, adult protective services agency, local voluntary agency, or police. Of the available options, the police department is rarely considered an important source of reporting and follow-up for elder abuse. In addition, the problems of obtaining information on elder abuse reports from police departments make them difficult to use for social service purposes.

Despite these limitations, however, law enforcement agencies can take steps to ensure responsiveness to reports of domestic violence. Training can be required on procedures to be used in instances of child and spouse abuse. Some not-for-profit agencies, such as Victim Services (VS) in New York City, have developed relationships with local law enforcement agencies, and collaboration between law enforcement and social service agencies can include the co-location of domestic violence specialists in local precincts to follow up on complaint reports of elder abuse.

The state or local adult protective services program can also establish a relationship with local precincts to follow up on cases identified as involving criminal mistreatment or exploitation of older people. Some community-based agencies—a notable example is the West Side One Stop for Senior Services in Manhattan—have service programs for abused and exploited elders in their catchment areas, using demonstration-grant funding.

The continuing budget shortfalls for local and state government threaten the expansion of all these initiatives to address elder abuse as a domestic violence issue of concern. To ensure the continuation of efforts to remedy elder abuse through the criminal justice system, a number of steps could be taken by law enforcement agencies:

1. Strengthening the community policing program to make it an effective precinct-based link between victims of social problems like elder abuse and the agencies that can service them.

2. Modifying police-training curricula to ensure that those police officers responding on crimes reflecting elder abuse know to identify them as such to improve front-line case detection. When reported by elders to police, financial abuse by family members should be identified as a form of domestic violence. In addition, training on the "syndrome" of domestic violence, including elder abuse, that keeps some victims from agreeing to prosecute should be provided to police to counter possible frustration in responding to complaints by elder victims who express unwillingness to prosecute their abusers.

3. Institutionalizing the use of supplementary reporting forms for police that incorporate information on the formal and informal support available and/or used by elders reporting abuse by family members, for a more effective follow-up to complaints.
4. Expanding crime prevention programs to include public education and information on the detection and prevention of elder abuse.
5. Encouraging more collaboration between community-based agencies serving the elderly and the local precincts, to address the problem of elder abuse in the community.
6. Considering the addition of civilians such as forensic social workers in the law enforcement agency's workforce.

Community-based public education initiatives—part of the community policing program mandate—should stress that elder mistreatment by family members is not only a domestic violence problem but may also reflect criminal acts that could result in the arrest and prosecution of the abuser. They should also emphasize that elder abuse is not necessarily synonymous with criminal acts and that support for overwhelmed caregivers is available in communities and should be used before family problems involving an older adult escalate out of control.

Community policing offers an excellent opportunity for collaboration with community-based service agencies (McElroy, Cosgrove, & Sadd, 1993). But collaborative relationships will have only limited success as long as confidentiality mandates by the police preclude sharing information on complaint reports of elder abuse. An aggressive pursuit of ways to circumvent these restrictions by both local law enforcement and community-based and public social service agencies could improve the quality of life and safety of elderly community residents who are victims of family violence and exploitation.

Forensic social workers based in precincts who can supervise social work student units and/or community liaisons could be a vital adjunct to police on the beat and to the community policing program in evaluating the service needs of elder abuse victims. They can also ensure appropriate referrals to adult protective services, the local aging agency network, and local crime victims agencies, such as Victim Services in New York.

The education and training of police officers is an important component of any effort at collaboration between law enforcement and social services communities. A study of elder abuse and adult protective services in New York City found that only 4 percent of referrals came from law enforcement (Abelman, 1992). Although this could reflect a need for additional training to sensitize police to the problem of elder abuse and a need for appropriate follow-up, police rarely have the expertise to make the kind of sophisticated clinical assessments sometimes needed to identify an elderly victim of family abuse who is not capable of self-determination.

Implications for Social Work

The police are trained as agents of public safety and control; they are not trained social workers. Domestic violence in general and elder abuse in particular are indicative of complex family dynamics that often require the evaluation and intervention skills of trained social work professionals.

An unwillingness to prosecute could follow from a competent older adult's assessment that the present situation does not represent sufficient danger to his or her safety or will not escalate beyond the initial incident reported to the police. Or it may demonstrate an older person's fear of retribution by the abuser, a sense of loyalty, or a need to protect the child abuser that overrides the older person's survival instincts. For an impaired elder, it could be a fear of abandonment or withdrawal of even minimal caregiving support or of the incapability of accurately assessing the extent of danger.

In addition, elder abuse victims, like domestic violence victims in general, are often reluctant to report or press charges against their abusers when they are family members. Social workers who come in contact with such victims, particularly if the abuse is long term and chronic, may choose to make both persistence and patience part of their intervention strategy. This is called a strategy of "negotiated consent," as opposed to a passive acceptance of a client's right to self-determination, if the client is judged to be in danger or at risk of further abuse (Moody, personal communication, 1990).

For older victims of domestic mistreatment, a willingness to prosecute does not guarantee following through with the prosecution or obtaining an order of protection, despite the possible dangers. Our study did not track cases through the criminal justice system but reviewed them only at the initial point of contact with the police. Nonetheless, ongoing assistance may be necessary to help those victims who are willing to prosecute their abusers negotiate the criminal justice or court process to obtain needed protection. Monitoring and/or assistance with food, money management, personal care, repairing of locks, and securing of windows may be necessary, and they all can be provided by local social service agencies for the elderly if linked to the victim at the time of the report or shortly thereafter.

One of the obstacles to intervening in elder abuse cases is often the abuse victim's attachment to his or her abuser, despite the abuse. A vivid example of this was portrayed in Spike Lee's movie *Jungle Fever,* in which the actress Ruby Dee portrays a mother victimized by a beloved son who is a crack addict. Unlike stranger crime, elder abuse by their children involves family members who may have strong emotional ties. As a result, the problems and needs of the abuser may have to be treated in order to ensure the protection and safety of the victim.

For social workers, the value of differentiating among clients who report abuse by their children or who are considered to be at risk of abuse, in relation to their assessed likelihood of willingness to prosecute their abusers, is that they can better target the interventions. For the family dispute cases, family mediation counseling as advocated by Gelles (Mancuso, 1989) may be most effective. Those victims who are predicted to be unlikely to be willing to prosecute should be evaluated for adult protective services. If an APS referral is not deemed appropriate, keeping in touch with the victim by phone or through building superintendents or bank personnel could serve as a measure of protection, particularly if the victimization continues and the victim later becomes ready to take action against it.

As noted, those victims who are predicted to be likely to be willing to prosecute may need help in cooperating with the district attorney's office and/or obtaining an order of protection. In addition, the elderly victim's environment should be investigated to ensure that it is as secure as possible. The family network could be evaluated to determine whether other family members could offer protection and/or support for the elderly victim against further abuse by the child abuser. Finally, the abuser should be evaluated to determine whether the problems that led to committing the abusive act could be resolved through social services interventions or substance-abuse or mental health services.

The three major intervention models identified by Wolf (1990) are statutory or mandatory reporting (most often associated with child abuse); the legal intervention model, a criminal justice approach; and the advocacy or social service intervention model, which can be an empowerment approach (associated with spouse abuse) or a protective services approach when the adult victim appears to be incapable of protecting himself or herself against the abuse or exploitation. Several intervention models that show promise for assisting both competent and judgment-impaired elder abuse victims have been developed by social workers (for example, Breckman, with Adelman [a physician], and Tomita, with Quinn [a nurse and court investigator]; see Breckman & Adelman, 1988; Quinn & Tomita, 1986). Case management models of intervention can be adapted to serve elder abuse victims, with Medicaid case management as a potential funding source.

Financial abuse of elderly victims in inner-city communities may reflect larger social issues such as unusually high unemployment among inner-city black males, poor or nonexistent housing, easy availability of crack cocaine, and the prevalence of violence on the streets. Social policies intended to stimulate economic development, employment programs targeted to inner-city minority communities, stricter gun controls, greater availability of substance-abuse treatment and detoxification programs, more housing and environmental improvements, community-based access to social services, and other strategies for improving living conditions in inner cities for family members of all ages can help remedy some of the abuse experienced by black (as well as Latino) elders. The social work profession has a long history of advocating on behalf of social welfare programs for the poor and disadvantaged.

More and more resources are being allocated to criminal justice as they are being withdrawn from the social services community. This suggests that social work as a profession needs to look at how it can work in the criminal justice system to address issues of domestic violence. Our study's findings show that such social services programs for the elderly located in the criminal justice system would be valuable. This, in turn, could provide an opportunity for schools of social work and local law enforcement agencies to establish a social work presence in local precincts through student units supervised by field instructors on staff or outstationed from social services agencies.

Social workers based at precincts enable a timely follow-up on complaints of elder abuse. Assessments made by precinct-based forensic social workers of elderly complainants of abuse by their children can result in successful interventions for the victim.

Forensic social work is receiving more attention from the profession (Ivanoff,

Smyth, & Finnegan, 1993). Although until now it has been seen as a component of correctional services in prison facilities, there is a movement toward community-based forensic social work: A social work student unit was established in 1993 in the Mid-Town Manhattan Community Court, a demonstration project funded by the City of New York, the New York State Office of Court Administration (OCA), local business and community groups, and philanthropic organizations (among other funding sources) and administered by the Fund for the City of New York as an experiment in community-based court administration for misdemeanor crimes.

Hiring social workers at local precincts to work with community police and support police responding to domestic violence situations, particularly those involving the elderly, could provide a valuable service to the police and victims alike. In addition, this could be the needed bridge between social work practice and the criminal justice system in responding to the needs of elder abuse victims living in the community. Social workers hired for this purpose may require special orientation and training in order to work effectively with law enforcement.

Forensic social work, as defined by the Legal Aid Society, involves working in the criminal justice system to interview clients, diagnose, evaluate and develop a service plan in conjunction with criminal justice personnel, work with the district attorney's office in developing alternative sentences, serve as an advocate at court, make referrals, and provide crisis-intervention counseling. Forensic social workers can also serve as field instructors for units of social work students (as in the Manhattan Mid-Town Community Court Model) and/or supervise teams of community liaisons who network with community-based programs and other agencies (including family and criminal courts when orders of protection are needed), make home visits, and assist in developing and following up on service plans for linking victims (and their abusers, as appropriate) with government entitlements, as well as community-based social, health, and mental health programs (Legal Aid Society, 1994).

Schools of social work should consider adding some elective courses on social work within the criminal justice system. These may include an orientation to the criminal justice system and the state penal code, issues of mutual concern to the fields of social work and law enforcement—such as domestic violence and victims' services and the treatment and transitional services for the forensic mentally ill and other impaired populations who come to the attention of the criminal justice system: substance abusers, people with AIDS and tuberculosis, the physically impaired and developmentally disabled, and—increasingly—pregnant, parenting, and postpartum women.

The special concerns of older adults who are victimized by family members should reflect an understanding of gerontology and families in later life. The course work could focus not only on clinical issues, but also on policy and planning issues, in order to develop leaders in the social work community to shape the response of the criminal justice system to domestic violence victims and their families as well as other special populations. An ecological or systems approach is a good conceptual framework for understanding the relationships among individuals, family systems, community service systems, the criminal justice system, and the social welfare system.

Conclusion

Our study of family crimes against the elderly in New York City, using police complaint reports, is the first to examine the use of the criminal justice system as an intervention strategy for elder abuse. One purpose of the study was to determine the feasibility of building a predictor profile of elder abuse victims' willingness to prosecute their child abusers, using the data in the police complaint reports. The study focused on the very beginning of the engagement between elder abuse victims and the police. A willingness to prosecute was defined as an important outcome variable, as in practical terms, it usually serves as the "gate" to ongoing engagement of the criminal justice system in the abuse situation.

Both practice and program models need to continue to be developed and evaluated to ensure effective social work responsiveness to the problem of elder mistreatment and exploitation. Especially important are models that involve collaboration between social workers and the police, both to ensure effective intervention in elder abuse situations and to facilitate an ongoing dialogue between the disciplines of social work and criminal justice. Community-based case management service models that include social workers and/or elder abuse specialists working with local precincts and law enforcement agents to implement service plans that are sensitive to older victims' need for both security and self-determination, as well as concerns about abusers who may be impaired or otherwise in need of support services themselves, are promising intervention strategies.

Appendix: Case Examples

Physical Abuse (very intense)

Assault, First Degree

> Complainant was in the hospital. She had suffered multiple injuries to her head and body. Complainant states her son, daughter, and friends had held her prisoner for several days. They stated they would kill her if she left and beat her for no reason.

The sixty-six-year-old female victim stated an unwillingness to press charges against her son and other abusers (perpetrators) with whom she stated she resided.

Assault, Second Degree

> Complainant presently at hospital and is being treated for burn wounds to her legs and arms and for a possible broken hip. The home attendant, who is also a witness, states that upon arrival for work she observed the son strike the victim about her face three times. . . . The manager of the building states they have had many complaints of noise from victim's apartment.

The eighty-eight-year-old female victim refused to speak to police at the time the complaint was filed; the home attendant served as a witness. The abuser, the sixty-year-old son, was identified as residing with the victim.

Attempted/Actual Robbery

Complainant stated that above perp (son) broke into apartment, punched complainant about the body and removed the above listed property (valuable watch set with precious stones). Perp then fled in unknown direction.

The sixty-seven-year-old female victim stated a willingness to prosecute her twenty-two-year-old son.

Menacing, Physical

Victim states that the above perp (son) said: "Let me in, I need money." Then proceeded to place hand in door. Victim opened door, and perp attacked victim by punching him and menacing him with a box cutter and scissors. Victim also states that perp said: "I'm going to kill you."

The seventy-seven-year-old male victim stated a willingness to prosecute his twenty-year-old son, with whom he did not reside.

Physical Abuse (less intense)

Harassment, Physical

Both complainant and witness state that the perp [victim's son] did yell at and push complainant, resulting in no physical injury but causing said complainant to be alarmed.

The responding officer advised the victim (a sixty-two-year-old woman) and her daughter (witness) how to obtain an order of protection against her thirty-two-year-old son and issued her a crime victim's service agency card. Victim and abuser were identified as living together.

Financial Abuse (very intense)

Grand Larceny

Forgery

Complainant reports that [the] above perp (his son) has forged his signature on above checks totaling $1,500 and did cash them without his permission or authority to do so.

The sixty-year-old male victim stated a willingness to prosecute his twenty-seven-year-old son, with whom he lived.

Robbery

Victim states perp (son) came to his door and repeatedly banged on the door. The parents had an order of protection stating that he was not to come to his parents' residence and not to harass them. The father reluctantly let him in and then perp threatened father with bodily harm to give him $80 for drugs.

The eighty-four-year-old father stated willingness to prosecute his twenty-nine-year-old son.

Attempted Grand Larceny

Perp (son) called complainant/victim and stated he wanted $50. If she didn't give him [the] money, he was going to kill her. Undersigned list [en]ed to telephone threat. Canvass of area proved to be negative.

The seventy-three-year-old female victim stated a willingness to prosecute her thirty-four-year-old son, with whom she did not reside.

Menacing, Financial

Complainant states that her children frequently ask her to [give them] her apartment to sell drugs. Complainant states her daughter is the one who purchases drugs to give to her brother to sell. Daughter is also a drug dealer. Complainant states they have weapons and threaten their mother, stating: "Any kind of accident can happen to you."

The sixty-three-year-old female victim expressed a willingness to prosecute her daughter, with whom she stated she did not live.

Financial Abuse (less intense)

Criminal Mischief, Financial

Complainant stated that the above named perp the son of complainant's common-law wife did cause damage to the telephone wires and did alarm and verbally abuse them, arguing with them in search for money. Complainant and spouse both [are] senior citizens [and] are fearful of their son. Complainant was referred to family court for order of protection.

The victim, a seventy-nine-year-old man, stated a willingness to prosecute his common-law wife's eighteen-year-old son, with whom they did not live.

Larceny

Victim states perp (daughter) came to visit and removed from apartment without permission [a] set of sterling silverware and a blanket (value to be determined). Perp is a known crack addict, according to victim.

The victim, a sixty-five-year-old woman, stated a willingness to prosecute her thirty-seven-year-old daughter, with whom she does not reside.

Petit Larceny

Victim states she invited her son in for dinner. When she turned her back, son took property [a clock radio] and fled. Victim states son has a drug problem.

The sixty-eight-year-old female victim stated a willingness to prosecute her son, with whom she did not reside.

Harassment, Financial

Victim states that his son attempted to kick down his apartment door and demanded to be let in. Perp demanded $10,000 to leave father alone. Son threatened to "go all the way" if father didn't let him in. As son departed, he stated he was "getting a gun" and would return. Son has made threats in the past and is an alleged crack abuser.

The victim, a sixty-six-year-old man, was referred to family court for an order of protection against his twenty-eight-year-old son. The father and son were identified as not living together.

Psychological Abuse (very intensive)

Menacing

Above complainant states she had a verbal dispute with perp (her son) at which time perp holding knife in hand said to complainant that he was going to cut her up into little pieces. Referred to family court for order of protection.

The victim, a seventy-two-year-old woman, stated a willingness to prosecute her thirty-two-year-old son, with whom she resided.

Psychological Abuse (less intense)

Criminal Trespassing

Complainant states above listed perp who is her adopted son did enter living room window without permission or authority and upon several requests by complainant to leave. Complainant further states perp (son) does not reside at location and had not resided there for some time. Complainant states no property was removed or damaged.

The victim, a sixty-year-old woman, stated a willingness to prosecute her thirty-eight-year-old son.

Family Dispute Case Description: Example

Family offense or family dispute cases are sometimes included as elder abuse cases when reported by the police in complaint reports. Although not analyzed as part of this study, we offer a representative example here to provide a contrast between this type of complaint and those categorized as elder abuse cases in this study. The family dispute cases were reported as altercations, sometimes of long duration and usually over a specific issue or problem. An example from the complaint reports includes

Complainant states [she had] and her daughter were having an argument about mother's going out, because [the building] super[intendent] was coming to [fix] the toilet bowl.

(This is from a complaint made by a seventy-six-year-old woman; the age of the daughter was missing from the report. The officer taking the complaint made a referral for family counseling.)

References

Abelman, I. 1992. "Report on Incidence of Adult Abuse on the Protective Services for Adults Caseload in New York City." Unpublished report, New York State Department of Social Services.

Breckman, R., and R. Adelman 1988. *Strategies for Interventions into Elder Mistreatment.* Newbury, Calif.: Sage.

Cantor, M. 1993. *Growing Older in New York City in the 1990's: A Study of Changing Lifestyles, Quality of Life and Quality of Care.* Vol. 2: *The Elderly of New York City: A Demographic and Economic Profile.* New York: New York Center for Policy on Aging of the New York Community Trust.

Carlson, B. E. 1992. "Questioning the Party Line on Family Violence." *Affilia* 7: 94–110.

Crystal, S. 1987. "Elder Abuse: The Latest Crisis." *Public Interest* 88: 56–66.

Faulkner, L. 1982. "Mandating the Reporting of Suspected Cases of Elder Abuse: An Inappropriate, Ineffective and Ageist Response to the Abuse of Older Adults." *Family Law Quarterly* 16: 69–91.

Fredrikson, K. 1989. "Adult Protective Services: Changes with the Introduction of Mandatory Reporting." *Journal of Elder Abuse and Neglect* 1: 59–70.

Gilford, D., ed. 1988. *The Aging Population in the Twenty-First Century: Statistics for Health Policy.* Washington, D.C.: National Academy Press.

Griffin, L. W., and O. J. Williams. 1992. "Abuse Among African-American Elderly." *Journal of Family Violence* 7: 19–35.

Ivanoff, A., N. Smyth, and D. Finnegan. 1993. "Social Work Behind Bars: Preparation for Field Work in Correctional Institutions." *Journal of Teaching in Social Work* 7: 137–49.

Johnson, T. 1986. "Critical Issues in the Definition of Elder Mistreatment." In *Elder Abuse: Conflict in the Family,* ed. K. Pillemer and R. Wolf, pp. 167–96. Dover, Mass.: Auburn House.

Keizer, J. 1987. "Developing a Community-Based Social Service Program for the Elderly." *Journal of Gerontological Social Work* 11: 105–18.

Legal Aid Society. 1994, January 6. "Job Description for Forensic Social Worker." *New York Times,* sect. 10, p. 24.

Mancuso, P. J., Jr. 1989. "Domestic Violence and the Police: Theory, Policy and Practice." In *Family Violence: Emerging Issues of a National Crisis,* ed. L. J. Dickstein and C. C. Nadelson, pp. 127–41. Washington, D.C.: American Psychiatric Press.

McElroy, J. E., C. A. Cosgrove, and S. Sadd. 1993. *Community Policing: The CPOP in New York.* Newbury Park, Calif.: Sage.

National Aging Resource Center for Elder Abuse (NARCEA). 1991. *Elder Abuse and Neglect: A National Research Agenda.* Washington, D.C.: National Aging Resource Center.

Pillemer, K., and D. Finkelhor. 1988. "The Prevalence of Elder Abuse: A Random Sample Survey." *The Gerontologist* 28: 51–57.

Plotkin, M. 1988. *A Time for Dignity: Police and Domestic Abuse of the Elderly.* Washington, D.C.: PERF and AARP.

Quinn, M. J., and S. Tomita. 1986. *Elder Abuse and Neglect: Causes, Diagnosis and Intervention Strategies.* Newbury, Calif.: Sage.

Reed, W. L. 1980. "Access to Services by the Elderly: A Community Research Model." *Journal of Gerontological Social Work* 3: 41–52.

Saltzman, L., J. A. Mercy, M. L. Rosenberg, W. R. Elsea, G. Napper, R. K. Sikes, and R. J. Waxweiler. 1990. "Magnitude and Patterns of Family and Intimate Assault in Atlanta, Georgia, 1984." *Violence and Victims* 5: 3–17.

SYSTAT. 1992. *CART: Tree Structured Nonparametric Data Analysis: A SYSTAT Companion Product.* Evanston, Ill.: SYSTAT.

U.S. House of Representatives, Select Committee on Aging. 1990. *Elder Abuse: Decade of Shame and Inaction.* Washington, D.C.: Government Printing Office.

Vinton, L. W. 1988. "Correlates of Elder Abuse." Ph.D. diss., University of Wisconsin.

Wolf, R. 1990. "Perpetrators of Elder Abuse." In *Treatment of Family Violence: A Sourcebook,* ed. R. Ammerman and M. Hersen, pp. 310–27. New York: Wiley.

Wolf, R., and K. Pillemer. 1984. *Working with Abused Elderly: Assessment, Advocacy and Intervention.* Wooster, Mass.: University Center on Aging, University of Massachusetts Medical Center.

Yin, P. 1985. *Victimization and the Aged.* Springfield, Ill.: Thomas.

5

Domestic Violence and Woman Battering: Theories and Practice Implications

Diane C. Dwyer, Paul R. Smokowski, John C. Bricout, and John S. Wodarski

Public attention to the problem of domestic violence has escalated over the past two decades. Academics and practitioners have assessed the problem and its potential solutions using both quantitative and qualitative research methods. More recently, public-policy makers have joined in the effort. According to the U.S. Senate Judiciary Committee,

> Data we have collected from across the Nation show, for the first time ever, the terrifying extent of violence in the home every single week of the year. Projected nationally, we have found that:
>
> - In 1991, at least 21,000 domestic crimes against women were reported to police *every week*;
> - Almost one-fifth of all aggravated assaults (20%) reported to the police are assaults in the home;
> - These figures reveal a total of at least *1.1 million* assaults, aggravated assaults, murders, and rapes against women committed in the home and reported to the police in 1991; unreported crimes may be more than three times this total. (1992, p. III)

Nonetheless, although the attention has increased, the problem persists. This chapter examines the current state of affairs of domestic violence research and comments on its application to theory and practice.

The Nature and Ramifications of Domestic Violence

We selected the term *domestic violence* from a variety of descriptions. "Domestic" identifies the setting of the act, that is, in a marital or intimate cohabiting relationship, in the home. "Violence" is used because this is not a question of minor arguments or "disputes" but, rather, intentional, hostile, and aggressive physical or psychological acts. Although incidents of domestic violence certainly vary in magnitude and frequency, they are nonetheless violent acts perpetrated on a partner in a relationship, in the presumed safety and privacy of the home.

Many researchers regard such violence as a problem of both sexes (Gelles, 1974; Straus, Gelles, & Steinmetz, 1980), and they agree that domestic violence is gender neutral in definition and reality. In this chapter, however, we use the feminine pronoun to refer to the victim, not as a matter of convenience, but to support the feminist perspective that such gender neutrality minimizes the disproportionate amount of male violence perpetrated against women, overlooks the self-defense aspect of much female violence, and discounts the structural reinforcements for such violence (Bograd, 1988).

Because there is little common agreement about what constitutes an act of domestic violence, comparisons of domestic violence studies are fraught with difficulties. Some researchers limit their examination to incidents of physical aggression, whereas others include sexual assault (Hampton & Coner-Edwards, 1993), and still others attempt to incorporate components of psychological and emotional abuse (Murphy & Cascardi, 1993; Straus & Gelles, 1986). Common to all definitions is the notion that this form of violence involves the unjust exercise of force to dominate, abuse, or coerce another. Since such acts occur in the privacy of the home, any definition largely depends on the description of this behavior by the victim, the perpetrator, and, to a lesser degree, the police, the social service worker, or the medical professional. Moreover, concepts such as the legitimate use of power are culturally determined, and so those people who determine which domestic acts are, in fact, violent must reflect their societal biases.

The conventional definitions of domestic violence often focus on the act and its effect—that is, some form of observable, physical injury. In the case of the husband who intentionally strikes his wife with a baseball bat and breaks her arm and ribs, the violence is clear. But, if he misses, is this any less violent an act? This distinction may have repercussions when attempts are made to quantify the concept. Questions arise such as What are the observable measures of psychological violence? How much terror is abusive? Is a slap assaultive? Is threatened abuse a violent act? How does one gauge coercion? Another difficulty of reliably reporting and interpreting abuse stems from the distorting influence on one's perceptions of culture and societal hierarchies.

Violence in the family is a hidden problem. Protected by the privacy of the family, the institution of marriage has been viewed as a license to abuse. But even though the private nature of domestic violence makes it difficult to document and quantify, there is general consensus on several facts. The number of incidents of "minor" violence is quite high. Feld and Straus (1989) estimated that more than 50 percent of American couples experienced one or more incidents of partner assault during a marriage. Alarmingly, there is almost universal agreement that domestic violence escalates in frequency and intensity over time (Dobash & Dobash, 1984; Gelles, 1974; Pahl, 1985). The American Medical Association estimates that each year almost 4 million women are victims of severe assaults by their boyfriends and husbands and that about one in four women is likely to be abused by a partner during her lifetime (Glazer, 1993).

The manifestations of this violence run the gamut of physical behaviors from slaps and pushes to stabbing and shooting, and they frequently include verbal, emotional, psychological, and sexual abuse. Women who have experienced domestic violence come from all walks of life. Social class, family income, level of education, occupation, and ethnic or racial background make no difference (Smith, 1989). Identified in the late 1980s by the surgeon general of the United States as the number one public health risk to adult women, domestic violence is the leading cause of injuries to women between the ages of fifteen and forty-four and is more common than muggings, auto accidents, and cancer deaths combined (U.S. Senate Judiciary Committee, 1992, p. 3). Consequently, improved assessment and intervention strategies are necessary.

Assessment

Despite twenty or more years of research, estimates of the number of women abused by their partners each year vary significantly, ranging from 2.1 million in Langan and Innes's 1986 study to Straus's 1991 estimates of 8 million (Hirschel, Hutchinsen, & Dean, 1992). The true extent of domestic violence is an elusive research topic. Since there is no federal agency to coordinate data on domestic violence, there is no single source of information that can estimate the proportion of the problem. Instead, most researchers rely on a composite drawn from a variety of statistical sources, including clinical samples and official statistics. Frequently, however, the size and the specific sampling frame of these studies limit the interpretation of such reports. Additional information can be gained from the few social surveys that yield generalizable data.

Clinical studies conducted by practitioners and field researchers are a common source of data on violence in the family. The clinical setting (e.g., women's shelter, hospital emergency room) permits relatively easy access to extensive data regarding incidents of domestic violence. The principal researchers in this field (Dobash & Dobash, 1979; Giles-Sims, 1983; Gondolf, 1988; Pagelow, 1981; Walker, 1979) use this approach and have found significant variables in the cases of the most severely abused women. Moreover, these studies, often anecdotal or ethnographic, provide data useful in analyzing intervention programs.

Official reports, most notably the Uniform Crime Reports, furnish some useful data on domestic violence, especially domestic homicide. Researchers therefore often study police records to gain insight into the variables influencing incidents of domestic violence. Their value is limited, however, by the presupposition that the event must have been reported to the police. These limitations notwithstanding, many researchers use this data source to illuminate both the incidence of and the response to domestic violence.

Social surveys comprise the third major source of data on domestic violence. The victimization data collected by the Bureau of Justice Statistics's National Crime Victimization Survey is an example of such a survey. The data are derived from a continuing survey of a large representative sample of housing units in the United States. In 1991, approximately 83,000 persons were interviewed regarding certain criminal offenses both completed and attempted. The relationship between the victim and the offender was ascertained, thereby providing information regarding domestic violence. But such surveys are biased by the sensitive nature of the topic and by the perceived authority of a governmental interviewer.

Widely cited, the National Family Violence Surveys (1975 and 1985) provide the most comprehensive, nationally representative studies of family violence in general and domestic violence in particular. By using the Conflict Tactics Scale, these surveys measured the use of rational discussion, verbal or nonverbal hostility, and physical violence, in sample families, when members had disagreements or were angry with one another (Gelles, 1987). The 1985 survey found that 16 of every 100 couples in a married or cohabiting relationship reported a violent incident during the year of the survey. Sixty-three of 1,000 couples reported serious assaults (kicking, punching, biting, or choking) yielding an incidence rate of 3.4 million such assaults. In terms of prevalence, approximately 30 percent of the couples studied experienced violence in the course of their relationship (Hampton & Coner-Edwards, 1993).

The critics of these surveys note that they limit the examination of violence to conflict situations (Dobash & Dobash, 1979; Pagelow, 1981) and that the Conflict Tactics Scale did not measure the context, consequences, or outcomes of the violent acts. As Dobash et al., (1992) observed, "Such analysis obscures all that is distinctive about violence against wives which occurs in a particular context of perceived entitlement and institutionalized power asymmetry" (p. 83). Despite its limitations, however, this instrument dominates the field of family violence survey research and has resulted in considerable data for research analysis.

Methodology problems exist in each of the major data sources cited here. First, it is not possible to generalize from most clinical samples because they are not representative and comparison (control) groups are seldom used in the study design. Official data sets are often flawed by variations in definitions, different commitments to accurate recording and record-keeping techniques, and skewed samples. Similarly, surveys have their own limitations, such as response errors, deliberate or unintentional; recall selectivity; varying interpretation of questions; and reliance on large sample size to compensate for a low base rate of reported domestic violence (Weis, 1989).

Longitudinal studies of domestic violence are rare (Gelles, 1993), and the absence of data on both victims and perpetrators over time leaves serious gaps in our knowledge base. Do women who "escape" from violent relationships only to reenter another one later have different characteristics from those women who subsequently enter nonviolent relationships? What is the long-term impact of our intervention efforts with victims and perpetrators? These researchers recommend devising tracking systems for victims of domestic violence and monitoring them over time. In addition, a systematic mechanism for collecting domestic violence data is needed. Recognizing that violence, and especially domestic violence, is a public health concern, the Centers for Disease Control are investigating ways of developing such a system. Current programs and proposals for enhancing efforts in this direction are discussed later in this chapter.

Theoretical Considerations

According to Gelles (1993), causal theories of domestic violence can be divided into three general classifications: individual models (psychological), sociological models (sociopsychological), and social-structural models (feminist).

Individual Models

Individual models attribute violence primarily to characteristics of the perpetrator and, to a lesser degree, those of the victim. These may include poor self-control and low self-esteem (Green, 1984), mental illness (Steinmetz, 1980), propensity toward criminal behavior (Hotaling, Straus, & Lincoln, 1989), ability to ascribe blame or, in the case of the victim, to internalize blame (Dobash & Dobash, 1979; Gondolf, 1988), and substance abuse (Kantor & Straus, 1987). Other studies cite assertiveness deficits (Maiuro, Cahn, & Vitalino, 1986) combined with a need for power (Dutton, 1988) and heightened vulnerability (Rosenbaum & Bennett, 1988) as contributing factors to the likelihood of violent outbursts between partners.

O'Leary (1993) argued that the value of such psychological explanations "has been both empirically and conceptually validated" (p. 27). Indeed, these analyses can help characterize the risk factors associated with violence.

From a cognitive-behavioral standpoint, Gondolf and Fisher (1988) describe the process of "learned helplessness" affecting the victim in abusive relationships. They suggest that the negative intermittent reinforcement of the punishment or abuse leads the battered victim into a state of submissive passivity. The abuse lessens the woman's sense of control, and she may internalize blame or simply stop struggling to extricate herself from the abuse. Either of these behaviors enables the situation to perpetuate.

Dutton and Painter (1993) examined the construction of strong emotional attachments developed in violent intimate relationships. They posited that traumatic bonding theory—"the development of strong emotional ties between two persons where one person intermittently harasses, beats, threatens, abuses or intimidates the other" (Dutton, 1988, p. 106)—explains much of the victim's behavior in battering couples. Such relationships are characterized by a power imbalance perceived by the victim and intermittent flare-ups of abuse, conditions deemed necessary for traumatic bonding. Further, given the victim's emotional and physical exhaustion from the abuse, she is likely to develop a corresponding need for support or affection. This heightens her vulnerability to the batterer's apologies and promises. Thus the couple may once again become loving—at least until the next violent outburst. This cycle can explain the victim's reluctance to leave or prosecute her attacker.

Similarly, Dutton (1994) suggests that traumatic bonding theory clarifies why some women repeatedly return to abusive partners. When the victim leaves the abusive situation, her fears for her safety begin to decrease and her underlying attachment to her abuser manifests itself. Her vulnerability predisposes her to want the affection present, by virtue of the intermittent nature of the abuse, in her relationship with her abuser. Therefore, she may suddenly choose to return to her abusive partner.

Sociological Models

Sociological models examine social structures, particularly the institution of the family, in an attempt to ascertain how these allow and, perhaps, encourage violence among partners. Such models use an analysis of family dynamics to explain the problem. Consideration is given to "family structure, stress, the transmission of violence from one generation to the next, and family interactional patterns" (Gelles, 1993, p. 9).

Bandura (1973) suggested that aggression may serve to keep the group functioning effectively. That is, the assaultive behavior of the batterer may actually reinforce the established roles of family members in an abusive family. Any attempt, therefore, to alter this pattern only heightens the stress level of the system. According to social learning theory (Bandura, 1977), an action (battering) successfully used to obtain a sought-after goal (control) increases the probability of its being employed again. There is a similar dynamic for children who witness the battering that helps explain the intergenerational transmission of aggression (Bandura, 1973). These constructions are broad in their exegetic value, as they focus on family systems rather than a single characteristic of the violence, thereby revealing strategic target points for intervention and offering a beneficial perspective on the complicated nature of the problem.

Sociostructural Models

Finally, variables of gender inequality, societal attitudes toward violence and family, and patriarchy are analyzed by the *sociostructural models*. Based largely on feminist theory, these models contend that "domestic violence cannot be adequately understood unless gender and power are taken into account" (Yllo, 1993, p. 47). Proponents of this view see the problem of domestic violence as deeply rooted in the historical imbalance of power between men and women. As such, male violence is regarded as a form of social control over women. Critics have suggested that this is an oversimplification of a very complex problem, one that does not explain why some men are violent toward their partners but others are not. However, as Yllo (1993) argued,

> Feminist Theory does not regard patriarchy as a discrete, measurable variable (like age, sex, or socioeconomic status). Rather, patriarchy—the system of male power in

society—is very complex and multidimensional. By focusing on patriarchy, feminism is no more a single-variable explanation than sociology, with its focus on social structure. (p. 49)

This pervasive "patriarchy" might be construed to include the institutional gender bias of the lawmakers, judges, and enforcement personnel who either implicitly or explicitly support the system that subtly sanctions domestic violence and permits it to persist.

We should note that the feminist analysis of domestic violence is a purposeful outgrowth of feminist research and scholarship, and so it is closely related to social-change efforts. Social action, which is often seen as the source of feminist insight, then links this theoretical orientation to analysis and practice. As Wodarski (1987) observed, public awareness of this problem has, to a certain degree, paralleled the growth of the women's movement. Even though it does not offer a total, integrated framework for understanding the dynamics of domestic violence, the feminist perspective cannot be overlooked. In essence, although this perspective is not by itself sufficient, it is a necessary ingredient in any theoretical explanation of domestic violence.

Ecological Models

Because of the mutual exclusivity of the models just described, Edleson and Tolman (1992) used an *ecological* approach to conceptualize the abuse of women. This framework includes

> the violent man, his particular history, in direct interactions with others in varied settings that form a multitude of microsystems. This collection of microsystems forms the man's mesosystem. Others in the man's microsystem engage in relationships within other settings where the man is not directly involved, forming ecosystems in this man's ecology. Still more indirect are the cultural, ethnic group, and class rules that form his macrosystem. And, finally, there is the chronosystem, which reflects the depth of time and its effect on all the contemporary systems at play. (p. 15)

Recognizing the complexity of domestic violence, this theory integrates explanatory variables from differing levels of analysis, thus creating an synthesized approach to both explanation and intervention. For example, an intervention might involve simultaneously offering the abusive husband anger-management skills training (psychological), parenting skills training (sociological), and counseling regarding his use of violence to preserve the imbalance of power in his relationship (socio-structural).

Although the ecological model offers a comprehensive medium for theorizing about domestic violence, the absence of a commonly accepted explanatory theory has several consequences. Supporters of the theories just outlined spend considerable time and energy defending the efficacy of their particular vision perspective, which serves to diffuse the power of their effort by justifying explanations rather than addressing solutions. More important, without a unifying theory to explain domestic violence, any strategies for remediation tend to become fragmented and therefore less effective. Given the magnitude of the problem, it is incumbent on researchers and practitioners to maximize and consolidate their efforts.

Empirical Research

Characteristics of Victims and Abusers

Despite the lack of agreement about causes, some things are known. Straus (1980) identified the following as relevant characteristics in incidents of wife beating:

- Husband employed part time or unemployed
- Husband (if employed) a manual worker
- Family income under $6,000
- Spousal concerns about economic security
- Two or more children
- Spousal disagreements over children
- Spouses from violent families of origin
- Couples married less than ten years
- Spouses under thirty years of age
- High levels of family or individual stress
- Spouses verbally aggressive
- Frequent alcohol use
- Residence in neighborhood less than two years
- Family not part of an organized religion
- Wife a full-time homemaker

This study found that if none of these characteristics was present, there was no reported spousal abuse but that those families possessing more than twelve of these factors had a greater than 60 percent chance of having reported wife abuse in the previous year.

Additional studies identified the determinants of risk. Early researchers (Gelles, 1974; O'Brien, 1971) noted status inconsistency as a correlate of marital violence. For example, the husband's educational achievements may be higher than his occupational attainment or his educational or occupation status may be lower than that of his wife. The presence of other forms of family violence, most notably child or elder abuse, is also associated with spousal violence (Finkelhor, 1983; Hillberman & Munson, 1977; Straus, Gelles, & Steinmetz, 1980).

Wodarski (1987), considering the knowledge base developed by domestic violence research, drew up profiles of victims and perpetrators. The characteristics of abusers are (1) learning this behavior in his family of origin; (2) blaming the victim; (3) displacing anger meant for authority figures; (4) viewing the victim as a possession, thereby creating jealousy and control issues; (5) having unrealistic expectations for the victim; (6) forgetting details of the assaultive situation or even the assault itself; and (7) frequently using alcohol or drugs. The victim's characteristics are (1) having been raised in an emotionally restrictive home, thereby encouraging her passivity; (2) being socially isolated, thus having limited opportunities for feedback about the situation; (3) internalizing blame for the abuse, thereby assuming responsibility for the violent situation; (4) complying with the violence, viewing it as a survival mechanism; and (5) demonstrating loyalty to the relationship, rooted in her hope that he will change.

These factors must be viewed as prescriptions for change rather than predictors of some future case of domestic violence. Social-change efforts can reduce the level of risk encountered by a woman in her home, whereas using these factors to predict future violence is fallible and subjects the family to the potential negative effects of labeling.

Consequences of Domestic Violence

The consequences of domestic violence are equally well documented. Battering is the single most common cause of emergency room treatment for women and the major antecedent of injury to women, leading to approximately 25 percent of female suicide attempts and 4,000 homicides per year (Holtz & Furniss, 1993, p. 47). Rosenbaum and O'Leary (1981) argued that spousal abuse, specifically wife battering, exceeds even alcoholism in its magnitude as a health problem. Aside from the human costs, the financial repercussions to our health and mental health care system are obvious.

Domestic violence similarly takes a toll on the workforce. On a national level, the New York Victims Services Agency (1987) estimates that domestic violence costs employers $3 billion to $5 billion annually because of worker absenteeism. Abusive husbands or partners harass 74 percent of employed battered women at work, cause 56 percent of them to be tardy at least five days a month, result in 28 percent having to leave work early at least five days per month, and induce 54 percent to miss at least three full days of work per month (N.Y. Victims Service Agency, 1987). According to Schecter and Gary (1988), 20 percent of battered women lose their jobs as an indirect result of the violence. Again, the human and financial costs are high.

Program Evaluation

Program evaluation research is beginning to find its way into the literature. The Family Violence Project of the National Council of Juvenile and Family Court Judges identified eighteen "state-of-the-art" programs addressing the problem of domestic violence. These programs were selected from more than 100 for their outstanding contributions and "effectiveness in reducing, intervening and controlling family violence" (National Council of Juvenile & Family Court Judges, 1992, p. 5). This report attributes the success of these programs to the following factors:

- They borrow and build on good ideas from one another and continue to evolve.
- They stress a coordinated response by the community agencies involved.
- They rely on skilled, dedicated, and visionary leaders, often women who have organized services for battered women in the community. (p. 5)

Among the comprehensive programs cited in this research are the House of Ruth in Baltimore, the Domestic Abuse Project in Minneapolis, Templum in Cleveland, Project Safeguard in Denver, the family courts in Honolulu and Maui, the Family Violence Prevention Fund in San Francisco, Project Assist in Kansas City, and the Domestic Abuse Intervention Project in Duluth. All are distinguishable by the fact they use a multimodel approach to the multifaceted problem of validating the ecological perspective.

Through the coordination of criminal justice, judicial, and social service agencies, community intervention programs (CIPs), like those cited, strive to provide a comprehensive and sensitive response to domestic violence incidents. Empirical evaluations of CIPs cite interesting findings. Gamache, Edleson, and Schock (1988) studied the impact of three early CIPs and found that arrests, convictions, and mandated treatment increased significantly after the inception of these programs. But this did not lower the number of incidents of abuse. Similarly, Dutton (1986) found that court-ordered referrals to treatment were effective if the offender completed the treatment regimen. In broad terms, it can be said that these studies demonstrate that coordinated criminal justice responses, including arrest policies and postarrest treatment, can be effective. However, Edleson and Tolman (1992) noted that some women may face an increased risk when seeking the aid of criminal justice professionals.

Several issues remain for CIPs. Critics embracing the feminist analysis of battering find advocating change in male-dominated legislatures and courts to be painfully slow. Likewise, heavy reliance on police is also looked down on in minority communities, where the police themselves are often seen in authoritative and even abusive roles. Many minority groups are disdainful of the overuse of jails and would prefer court-mandated treatment programs with specific guidelines for quality treatment. Finally, as CIPs become larger and more diverse, they have the potential to become controlled by the criminal justice system, which may undermine their long-term change efforts and stall the advocacy movement. These issues will require careful attention and evaluation as the community intervention movement for domestic violence grows and matures.

Practice Issues and Implications

Crisis Intervention

Battered women usually seek crisis intervention only after perceiving a precipitating event as the "last straw." This particular act of violence follows many acute battering incidents that most likely resulted in serious physical injury (Roberts, 1990), but the precipitating event is no more an end point than a beginning. Because battered women are in continuous peril as long as the batterers know their whereabouts, it is critical that battered women in crisis be helped in an orderly, structured, and humanistic fashion (Roberts, 1990).

Roberts (1990) listed the necessary components of effective crisis intervention as assessment/evaluation, treatment, planning (including referral), and implementation. There are several potential avenues for crisis intervention open to the battered woman, depending on the community in which she lives. These include crisis hot-line programs, police crisis team programs, and hospital emergency room programs. Although the services provided by individual programs of each type vary considerably, all share a similar service environment and require similar competencies.

Overall, it is important that crisis interventions provide the battered woman with specially trained crisis counselors who are familiar with referral sources and can quickly access them. Because of their training, social workers are ideal for this task (for a discussion of this subject, see Chapter 10). Whatever the interventionist's professional training is, the acute needs of battered women require immediate and sensitive assessment and treatment.

Practice Implications

As with other social problems, the alliance between research and practice in the realm of domestic violence is reciprocal. Knowledge and theory propel practice efforts, and the experiences of practitioners furnish the data and access necessary to further inquiry. Recognizing this interrelationship, the current theoretical underpinnings of the domestic violence knowledge base have some intriguing implications for practice. These assumptions relate to both the proactive and the reactive levels of intervention—that is, both macro- or micropractice.

Social workers and other helping professionals must begin by defining the problem. When using a problem-solving model, the intervention than can flow from this initial statement of the concern. When the problem is domestic violence, what is defined as violent in the confines of the "domestic" relationship becomes central to the ensuing change effort, but as we stated earlier, this is not a monolithic concept. Instead, the definition of domestic violence is replete with cultural and societal implications, all of which the practitioner must consider.

It is difficult to consider codes of conduct regulating behavior between spouses or partners without reducing the heterogeneous nature of a pluralistic population. How is it possible to respect cultural variations in the role of women, the use of physical force or coercion, the marital rights of the respective spouses, and family privacy while simultaneously protecting the victim's safety? Although there are many connotations of the term *domestic violence,* the tendency is to presume that it denotes a singular entity, but often this simplification directly or indirectly contradicts the principles of ethical practice. The mutifaceted nature of the problem makes simplistic solutions impractical, and so solutions need to be fashioned with multiple components within a holistic framework.

Theoretical explanations for the existence of domestic violence also have a categorical connection to practice. Linkages can be observed between causal theories and intervention methods. Those who subscribe to *individual models* advocate treatment approaches that may include crisis intervention, psychodynamic or cognitive therapy, and rehabilitation groups for victims or batterers. Proponents of *sociological models* espouse family system intervention or resocialization by offering safe housing and counseling in a shelter program. Finally, supporters of the *socio-*

structural models pursue legislative or policy change that will enhance the status of women in the society, thereby reducing their specific vulnerability to domestic violence. The *ecological model* offers practitioners a framework for multilevel intervention and perhaps is the most useful prescription for change. It builds on the person in the environment perspective of practice and incorporates a systems approach to change at the micro-, mezzo-, and macrolevels.

Recommendations

An Ecologically Based Social Work Intervention

Based on the diverse and comprehensive nature of the ecological model, we propose a multicomponent treatment paradigm to combat domestic violence. Using the flexibility of the ecological approach, specific attention may be paid to various levels of each causal model just outlined. In this way, psychological, sociological, and sociostructural factors all may be used in assessing and treating domestic violence. Since each case will have its own blend of causal factors, a flexible, comprehensive approach adds power and applicability to the intervention.

The ecological paradigm can serve both victims and perpetrators. In no way should this fact be seen as shifting blame for the abuse; rather, it acknowledges that both victim and abuser have unique unmet needs. Both can benefit from supportive treatment and skills training in order to eradicate the abusive situation to the fullest extent possible.

Within this paradigm, the primary worker assumes several social work roles, whose responsibilities include

1. *Performing outreach.* As mentioned earlier, three-quarters of the incidents of domestic violence are never reported or treated, which only enables the abuse to persist and worsen. The social worker has primary responsibility for outreach, which is designed to encourage ambivalent victims or perpetrators to seek treatment. At the point of intervention, referrals must be made efficiently and systematically. With aggressive and purposeful outreach, the rate of successful intervention may well increase.

2. *Assessment and linkage.* A good assessment is critical to every therapeutic intervention. Because domestic violence lacks a unified definition and explanatory theory, a comprehensive assessment is even more important. Factors within each of the causal theories should be assessed to form a systemic view of treatment needs. For example, in one case, spousal abuse may be strongly attributed to dysfunctional dynamics in the spousal relationship. In another case, cultural messages regarding patriarchy and power may precipitate the abusive situation. These causal factors are not necessarily independent of one another; rather, they present themselves in various mixtures and proportions. The assessment of these factors and their implications for the specific case should subsequently be used to make linkage and referral decisions.

3. *Interventions for victims.* Coordinating and, when appropriate, providing ser-

vices for victims are critical to the helping process. Services available from battered women's shelters, medical clinics, and legal assistance programs must be combined to meet the client's specific needs. Most shelters offer twenty-four-hour hotlines, and many offer immediate, personal crisis counseling. Access to essential medical and legal services often requires the assistance and support of a skilled advocate. The victim's strengths, abilities, and resources must be identified and nurtured. Women leaving abusive relationships often need help obtaining financial assistance, job training, housing, and budgeting assistance. Skills training in these areas is critical to the women's future welfare and should be an integral part of an intervention regimen.

Peer-counseling programs can frequently be used to provide validation and friendship for the abused woman. A community of women who have survived similar situations can offer support and encouragement. Programs offering sociopolitical education on the reasons for battering are sometimes a underutilized intervention source. Linking victims to women's advocacy and social-action community groups may be a source of empowerment for the recovering victim of domestic violence. But this should be initiated with caution if the woman is still in an abusive situation, lest it exacerbate the problem. However, the strength and satisfaction that come from becoming a peer counselor for a fellow victim or from lobbying for social change may be an important source of healing for the former victim.

4. *Intervention for batterers.* Coordinating and implementing a treatment program for the perpetrator is another appropriate responsibility of social work. Both individual and group treatments urge the batterer to move past denial and take responsibility for his behavior. They stress the necessity of ending the abuse and teaching alternatives to violence. Such techniques may include relaxation training, systematic desensitization, emotional awareness training, and assertiveness training. Group exploration may center on sex roles, antisexist education, and a redefinition of manhood. Empathy, cooperative decision making, and constructive uses of power are often discussed with peer counselors, in order to alleviate the battered woman's social isolation.

Occasionally, treatments for batterers involve family therapy. The timing and utilization of couples therapy are controversial in the intervention literature (Margolin & Burman, 1993). Its few supporters believe that treating the abuser and the victim together expedites the goal of ending violence by facilitating communication and learning common coping skills. Its critics (the majority) argue that this approach jeopardizes the victim's safety by shifting the blame to the situation, rather than placing it on the perpetrator, thereby implying that the relationship should continue.

A Model for Tracking Violence

A unique, state-of-the-art computerized tracking system for domestic violence was proposed by an interdisciplinary team of investigators at the State University of New York at Buffalo (Marcus & Wodarski, 1994). The proposed pilot project, named the Domestic Violence Applied Research Institute (DVARI), is notable for its scope and design. The DVARI computerized tracking system is intended to collect comprehensive treatment and service delivery data on each identified domestic violence client (target, victim, or witness) living in a given county.

Gathering such information at the county level is important, since many states' social service funds are appropriated and distributed at the county level. The DVARI computerized system tracks the progress of each party (target, victim, witness) over time, noting both the institutions and the interventions employed. Reliable longitudinal data hitherto unavailable will, therefore, be generated.

The Buffalo–DVARI model incorporates methodological rigor, technological sophistication, an interdisciplinary perspective, and humanistic concern for the client. It is hoped that this powerful new tool will result in informed treatment and policy decisions while simultaneously building the knowledge base on the battering phenomenon.

Conclusions

Given the unique ecological perspective of social work and its commitment to social change and social justice, social workers and researchers can lead the fight to reduce violence against women in their homes. This challenge must begin with an assessment of who can benefit from maintaining the status quo, because intervention begins with analysis. Such an examination must rely heavily on the feminist perspective. Scholars, especially those in the area of domestic violence, should link their research and assessments to social action. Strategies to reduce the feminization of poverty, by fostering employment training and child-care support, might be the outcome.

There is a glaring absence of longitudinal research. That is, little is known about what happens to a woman after she has left a violent relationship. Does she later enter another damaging relationship? What are the long-term effects of the violent experience on her and on her children? Such longitudinal studies can also add useful information to the research regarding the efficacy of existing social welfare services for victims of domestic violence. What services were instrumental in helping her escape the violence and remain in violence-free relationships? It is time to bring domestic violence out into the open and to attack this complex problem on as many different levels as possible. Social workers have a key role to play in the research and practice efforts to change the current state of affairs in the field of domestic violence.

References

Bandura, A. 1973. *Aggression: A Social Learning Analysis*. Englewood Cliffs, N.J.: Prentice-Hall.

Bandura, A. 1977. *Social Learning Theory*. Englewood Cliffs, N.J.: Prentice-Hall.

Bograd, M. 1988. "Feminist Perspectives on Wife Abuse: An Introduction." In *Feminist Perspectives on Wife Abuse*, ed. K. Yllo and M. Bograd, pp. 11–26. Newbury Park, Calif.: Sage.

Dobash, R. E., and R. P. Dobash. 1979. *Violence Against Wives: A Case Against Patriarchy*. New York: Free Press.

Dobash, R. E., and R. P. Dobash. 1984. "The Nature and Antecedents of Violent Events." *British Journal of Criminology* 24: 269–88.

Dobash, R. P., R. E. Dobash, M. Wilson, and M. Daly. 1992. "The Myth of Sexual Symmetry in Marital Violence." *Social Problems* 39: 71–91.

Dutton, D. G. 1986. "The Outcome of Court-Mandated Treatment for Wife Assault: A Quasi-Experimental Evaluation." *Violence and Victims* 1: 163–75.

Dutton, D. G. 1988. *The Domestic Assault of Women: Psychological and Criminal Justice Perspectives.* Newton, Mass.: Allyn & Bacon.

Dutton, D. G. 1994. *The Domestic Assault of Women.* Vancouver: University of British Columbia Press.

Dutton, D. G., and S. Painter. 1993. "Battered Women Syndrome: Effects of Severity and Intermittency of Abuse." *American Journal of Orthopsychiatry* 63: 614–27.

Edleson, J. L., and R. M. Tolman. 1992. *Intervention for Men Who Batter: An Ecological Approach.* Newbury Park, Calif.: Sage.

Feld, L., and M. Straus. 1989. "Escalation and Desistance of Wife Abuse in Marriage." *Criminology* 27: 141–61.

Finkelhor, D. 1983. "Common Features of Family Abuse." In *The Dark Side of Families: Current Family Violence Research,* ed. D. Finkelhor, R. Gelles, G. Hotaling, and M. Straus, pp. 17–28. Beverly Hills, Calif.: Sage.

Gamache, D. J., J. L. Edleson, and M. D. Schock. 1988. "Coordinated Police, Judicial, and Social Service Response to Woman Battering: A Multi-Baseline Evaluation Across Three Communities." In *Coping with Family Violence: Research and Policy Perspectives,* ed. G. T. Hotaling, D. Finkelhor, J. T. Kirkpatrick, and M. Straus, pp. 193–209. Newbury Park, Calif.: Sage.

Gelles, R. J. 1974. *The Violent Home: A Study of Physical Aggression Between Husbands and Wives.* Beverly Hills, Calif.: Sage.

Gelles, R. J. 1987. *Family Violence.* Newbury Park, Calif.: Sage.

Gelles, R. J. 1993. "Family Violence." In *Family Violence: Prevention and Treatment,* ed. R. Hampton, T. Gullotta, G. Adams, E. Potter III, and R. Weissberg, pp. 1–24. Newbury Park, Calif.: Sage.

Gelles, R. J., and C. Cornell. 1983. *International Perspectives on Family Violence.* Toronto: Heath.

Giles-Sims, J. 1983. *Wife Beating: A Systems Theory Approach.* New York: Guilford Press.

Glazer, S. 1993. "Violence Against Women." *CQ Researcher* 3: 171.

Gondolf, E. W. 1988. "The Effect of Batterer Counseling on Shelter Outcome." *Violence and Victims* 3: 275–89.

Gondolf, E. W., and E. R. Fisher. 1988. *Battered Women as Survivors: Alternatives to Treating Learned Helplessness.* Lexington, Mass.: Lexington Books.

Green, H. W. 1984. *Turning Fear to Hope.* Nashville: Thomas Nelson.

Hampton, R., and A. Coner-Edwards. 1993. "Physical and Sexual Violence in Marriage." In *Family Violence: Prevention and Treatment,* ed. R. Hampton, T. Gullotta, G. Adams, E. Potter III, and R. Weissberg, pp. 113–41. Newbury Park, Calif.: Sage.

Hillberman, E., and K. Munson. 1977. "Sixty Battered Women." *Victimology* 2: 460–70.

Hirschel, D., I. Hutchison, and C. Dean. 1992. "The Failure of Arrest to Deter Spouse Abuse." *Journal of Research in Crime and Delinquency* 29: 1.

Holtz, H., and K. Furniss. 1993. "The Health Care Provider's Role in Domestic Violence." *Trends in Health Care and the Law* 8: 43–49.

Hotaling, G. T., M. A. Straus, and A. Lincoln. 1989. "Intrafamily Violence and Crime and Violence Outside the Family." In *Family Violence,* ed. L. Ohlin and M. Tonry, pp. 315–76. Chicago: University of Chicago Press.

Kantor, G. K., and M. A. Straus. 1987. "The 'Drunken Bum' Theory of Wife Beating." *Social Problems* 34: 213–30.

Maiuro, R. D., T. S. Cahn, and P. P. Vitaliano. "Assertiveness Deficits and Hostility in Domestically Violent Men." *Violence and Victims* 1: 279–89.

Marcus, I., and J. Wodarski. 1994. "Development and Implementation of a Tracking System for Domestic Violence in Erie County." Grant proposal.

Margolin, G., and B. Burman. 1993. "Wife Abuse Versus Marital Violence: Different Terminologies, Explanations and Solutions." *Clinical Psychology Review* 13: 59–73.

Murphy, C., and M. Cascardi. 1993. "Psychological Aggression and Abuse in Marriage." In *Family*

Violence: Prevention and Treatment, ed. R. Hampton, T. Gullotta, G. Adams, E. Potter III, and R. Weissberg, pp. 86–112. Newbury Park, Calif.: Sage.

National Council of Juvenile and Family Court Judges. 1992. *Family Violence: State-of-the-Art Programs.* Reno, Nev.: National Council of Juvenile and Family Court Judges.

N.Y. Victims Service Agency. 1987. "Report on the Costs of Domestic Violence." New York: Victims Service Agency.

O'Brien, J. 1971. "Violence in Divorce Prone Families." *Journal of Marriage and the Family* 33: 692–98.

O'Leary, K. D. 1993. "Through a Psychological Lens: Personality Traits, Personality Disorders, and Levels of Violence." In *Current Controversies on Family Violence,* ed. R. Gelles and D. Loseke, pp. 7–30. Newbury Park, Calif.: Sage.

Pagelow, M. 1981. *Woman Battering: Victims and Their Experiences.* Beverly Hills, Calif.: Sage.

Pagelow, M. 1984. *Family Violence.* New York: Praeger.

Pahl, J. 1985. *Private Violence and Public Policy.* London: Routledge & Kegan Paul.

Roberts, A. R., ed. 1990. *Helping Crime Victims: Research Policy and Practice.* Newbury Park, Calif.: Sage.

Rosenbaum, A., and K. O'Leary. 1981. "Children: The Unintended Victims of Marital Violence." *American Journal of Orthopsychiatry* 5: 689–99.

Rosenbaum, M., and B. Bennett. 1988. "Homicide and Depression." *American Journal of Psychiatry* 143: 367–70.

Schecter, B., and K. Gary. 1988. "A Framework for Understanding and Empowering Battered Women." In *Abuse and Victimization Across the Lifespan.* ed. M. Straus, pp. 76–84. Newbury Park, Calif.: Sage.

Smith, L. 1989. *Domestic Violence: An Overview of the Literature.* London: Home Office Research and Planning Unit.

Steinmetz, S. K. 1980. "Violence Prone Families." *Annals of the New York Academy of Sciences* 347: 351–65.

Straus, M. 1980. "A Sociological Perspective on the Causes of Family Violence." In *Violence and the Family,* ed. M. R. Green, pp. 7–31. Boulder, Colo.: Westview Press.

Straus, M., and R. Gelles. 1986. "Societal Change and Change in Family Violence from 1975 to 1985 as Revealed in Two National Surveys." *Journal of Marriage and the Family* 48: 465–79.

Straus, M., R. Gelles, and S. K. Steinmetz. 1980. *Behind Closed Doors: Violence in the American Family.* Garden City, N.Y.: Doubleday/Anchor.

U.S. Senate Judiciary Committee. 1992. *Violence Against Women.* Washington, D.C.: Government Printing Office.

Walker, L. E. 1979. *The Battered Woman.* New York: Harper & Row.

Weis, J. G. 1989. "Family Violence Research Methodology and Design." In *Family Violence,* ed. L. Ohlin and M. Tonry, pp. 117–62. Chicago: University of Chicago Press.

Wodarski, J. 1987. "An Examination of Spouse Abuse: Practice Issues for the Profession." *Clinical Social Work Journal* 15: 172–87.

Yllo, K. A. 1993. "Through a Feminist Lens: Gender, Power, and Violence." In *Current Controversies on Family Violence,* ed. R. Gelles and D. Loseke, pp. 47–62. Newbury Park, Calif.: Sage.

II

Criminal Justice Responses

6

Police Responses to Battered Women: Past, Present, and Future

Albert R. Roberts

It was 1400 hours on September 6, 2010. Two police officers were dispatched by headquarters on a report of a domestic violence complaint. Upon arriving at the scene, the officers spoke to the victim, Wilma R. She stated that her boyfriend, Louis, had been drinking the night before and became involved in an argument with her that ended with his punching her in the face and choking her. The officers observed that Wilma had a cut on her upper lip and swelling in the area between her nose and mouth.

When the police officers questioned Louis, he said he never touched her. He insisted that the bruises on her face resulted from her being clumsy and falling down the steps while carrying the laundry. He said she was making up the story of being beaten because she was angry at him for staying out late with his buddies the previous night.

In order to determine whether or not Louis had choked his girlfriend, the police officer went to the car and brought in the compact portable laser unit. By aiming the laser at Wilma's neck, the officer immediately obtained laser fingerprints, which he compared with Louis's. The results showed an identical match. While the first officer was matching the fingerprints, the second officer went to the car and turned on the MDT computer to run a computerized criminal history on Louis. In less than thirty seconds, Louis's history appeared on the screen: two prior convictions for simple assault against a former girlfriend and resisting arrest. The incidents had occurred three years earlier in another state. In addition, Louis's record showed two arrests during the past three years for driving while intoxicated.

The officers' next step was to obtain a temporary restraining order (TRO) to prevent Louis from having any further contact with Wilma. They obtained the TRO by entering a summary of their findings at the scene on their portable computer and using the cellular phone to call the judge to inform her that the report was being faxed to her courtroom from their car fax.

At the courthouse, the court clerk took the report from the fax machine and brought it to Judge Catherine Sloan for her signature. The court clerk then faxed the TRO back to the police car. The entire approval process took only fifteen minutes.

Next, the police transported Louis to the county jail, where the nurse practitioner implanted a subdural electronic sensor in Louis's wrist. The police also gave a sensing receiver to Wilma to wear externally, on a chain around her neck. The computer at police headquarters will monitor these sensors, as it has done with the 300 other domestic abuse cases reported to the police department during the past twelve months. The officers told Louis that if he came within a distance of 500 meters from Wilma, the sensing device would immediately alert the police officers that he had violated the TRO, and he would be sent to prison.

The Police Response to Domestic Violence in the Mid-1990s

During the past few years, domestic violence has increasingly been defined as a serious crime (i.e., a felony rather than a misdemeanor) by a growing number of state criminal codes and family court statutes. In fact, because of the prevalence and life-threatening nature of woman battering, all fifty states have passed civil and/or criminal statutes to protect battered women. In some areas, as many as 75 percent of all police calls involve domestic conflict and/or violence. In the past, police were often reluctant to respond to family violence calls, and when they did respond, they were frequently accused of taking the side of the male batterers and subscribing to the view that "a man's home is his castle." Furthermore, the court staff tended to minimize the dangers that battered women encountered and discouraged them from filing criminal or civil complaints.

But now society at large has finally recognized that beating women (wives, cohabitants, or companions) is a crime and a major social problem. This recognition of woman abuse as a major social problem grew out of four noteworthy activities: (1) the women's movement, (2) two national prevalence studies on the extent of domestic violence in the United States (Straus & Gelles, 1991; Straus, Steinmetz, & Gelles, 1980), (3) books and news articles on battered women (Fleming, 1976; Roberts, 1984; Roy, 1982; Walker, 1979, 1984), and (4) recent litigation and legal reforms (Hart, 1992). Moreover, many police departments now have a proarrest or presumptive arrest policy. But the road toward implementing effective mandatory or proarrest policies for batterers has been bumpy and uneven, and research studies on the short-term deterrent effects of arresting batterers are inconclusive. Nevertheless, Americans have come a long way from the time when the use of violence by men to control their partners was condoned. Mandatory and warrantless arrest laws are just one part of the improved police response to victims of battering. In addition, the police in highly populated cities and counties throughout the nation now provide immediate protection to battered women.

The complex constellation of social, legal, and political issues surrounding the police response to domestic violence is among the most enduring and contentious problems in the recent history of criminal justice theory and practice. The current salience of domestic violence as an issue of national concern for criminal justice theoreticians and practitioners is well illustrated by the degree of attention that this subject has recently received in so many diverse spheres and by the body of research it has generated. Particularly in the past decade, efforts to define and institutionalize appropriate roles and responsibilities for police in responding to domestic violence have led to considerable academic research, have generated a significant body of statutory and case law, and have been the subject of an uncommon degree of public and political discourse.

Social and political pressures for change, in conjunction with the passage of civil and criminal statutes to protect battered women in all fifty states, have considerably altered the way that police officers and agencies currently respond to domestic violence. Police executives and public-policy makers, as well as individual police officers, have become more sensitive to the issues involved as they have faced the burden of making appropriate choices from among a range of competing alternative strategies. Because defining and practicing an appropriate police response to domestic violence necessarily entail consideration of a broad array of practical, legal, political, and social variables, supervisors, trainers, and street officers confront a difficult task. Despite a host of opinions, policies, agendas, and programs aimed at redressing the social problem and providing relief to victims, there currently appears to be little consensus as to precisely what comprises the most desirable and effective response to domestic violence. It may be that since no single response has proved successful, a multilevel approach should be implemented, but only after more effective policy research has been completed. (For a discussion of the changes in New York State's laws and the criminalization of woman battering, see Chapter 8.)

Historical Overview

Although the recognition of domestic violence as a pervasive social problem is fairly recent, its cultural bases are deeply embedded in Western history and culture. Even a cursory review of that history reveals the extent to which law and society have traditionally served to implicitly support and perpetuate the subordination of women to their husbands. In some parts of Latin America and Asia, especially in the upper classes, killing a wife for an indiscretion has usually been acceptable, although the same privilege is not usually extended to women as perpetrators. Various cultures and societies have permitted or tacitly encouraged some degree of family violence as a means to maintain that subordination. Demographic analyses of domestic violence offenses reported to the police confirm the observation that domestic violence is most frequently perpetrated by males against their female partners, that males comprise only a small fraction of the total number of victims in domestic violence cases reported to the police.

As Richard Gelles and Murray Straus (1988) noted, domestic violence is intrinsically linked to the maintenance of power and dominance within the family unit. Family violence and spousal assaults are facilitated when there are few effective formal and informal social control mechanisms, thereby allowing the rewards of maintaining power through violence to outweigh the costs of such violence. From this observation, we can infer that cultures that define violence within the family unit as unacceptable behavior and emphatically communicate an attitude of disapproval by applying potent social sanctions (e.g., ostracizing or publicly humiliating the perpetrator) have lower rates of domestic violence than do societies that ignore the issue or tacitly approve of intrafamily violence. Similarly, the availability of formal mechanisms for social control (i.e., the legal processes of arrest and punishment) also impacts the incidence of domestic violence. Gelles and Straus (1988) concluded that people use violence against members of their families "because they can" (pp. 17–36).

History reveals that until fairly recently, men were legally permitted to employ relatively unrestrained physical force against their wives and children in order to maintain family discipline. During the 1960s, several discrete trends evolved in policing, law, and politics that ultimately converged in the 1970s and 1980s to set the stage for our current concerns and the attention paid to domestic violence issues. The confluence of these trends and pressures created a unique and powerful synergy, forcing American police agencies and lawmakers to reexamine their policies and practices and to adopt the type of strategies that prevail today.

Specialized Police Training

Police recruit and in-service training provide an important part of teaching police their roles and responsibilities. The amount and duration of domestic violence training influence whether or not new police officers will take seriously their potential role in protecting battered women.

During the eight years from 1985 to 1993, a growing number of police departments incorporated training sessions on family violence into their police academy curricula. These specialized training sessions have been implemented much more frequently in large city or county police training academies than in small towns. In addition, many police departments now require all officers to arrest a domestic violence suspect when the victim exhibits signs of bodily injury, when a weapon is involved in the commission of a domestic violence act, or when there is probable cause to believe that the named accuser has violated the terms of a restraining order or other no contact court order.

The author conducted a national survey on domestic violence training and police responses to battered women. The survey was sent to sixty police chiefs and their staff in metropolitan areas in every region of the United States. The study's findings indicated a wide variation in the amount of time devoted to specialized domestic violence training for new recruits, ranging from a total of three hours to forty hours at the police academies located in the largest cities, such as Baltimore, Boston, Indianapolis, Kansas City, Las Vegas, Memphis, Milwaukee, San Diego, Seattle, and Tucson. Most small-town police departments provide no training on domestic violence or victim rights. In these smaller towns and municipalities, state police or troopers are called in to intervene in domestic violence cases.

State troopers are responsible for protecting residents in many rural areas that have no local police department or when the nearest law enforcement agency is the county sheriff's office. The majority of state police are trained to respond in a sensitive and compassionate way to battered women. In general, state police academies provide comprehensive training to all state troopers on such policies and procedures, changes in the state criminal code, motor vehicle violations, investigative techniques, victims' rights legislation, and domestic violence.

Beginning in fiscal year 1991, the federal Office for Victims of Crime of the U.S. Department of Justice began funding and providing technical assistance to state police training academies. The purpose of these federal grants has been to develop and implement training programs for state and county law enforcement administrators and officers on the current policies and procedures for responding to family violence incidents. Each year a different group of eight to ten states receives a two-year federal training grant to develop family violence training courses and related materials.

Research on the Deterrent Effects of Arrest

Several studies have been completed on the effect that proarrest or mandatory arrest policies have had in reducing the number of repeat calls for domestic violence. The first study, known as the Minneapolis experiment, found that arrest was more effective than no arrest or mediation in deterring subsequent battering.

The Minneapolis Domestic Violence Experiment (1981–1982) was the first research study to test the short-term deterrent effect of arrest in domestic violence cases with heterosexual married and cohabitating couples and same-sex couples. In selected police precincts, domestic violence incidents were randomly assigned to one of three police methods of responding: (1) providing advice and informal mediation, (2) separating the couple by ordering the offender to leave the premises for eight hours to cool off, and (3) arresting the alleged offender and detaining him overnight in the local jail.

Three hundred and thirty eligible cases were tracked for six months. Repeat incidents of domestic violence were measured through official police department records to determine whether there were additional domestic violence calls to the same address, as well as follow-up interviews with the victim every two weeks. The findings indicated that arrest was more effective than the other two types of police response in deterring subsequent incidents of domestic violence. The violence was repeated in only 13 percent of the arrest cases, compared with a 19 percent failure rate among the cases assigned to informal mediation and a 24 percent failure rate for the cases assigned to "cool off" for eight hours.

There were several methodological problems in the experiment, however, including a small sample size, a disproportionate number of cases to which the same few officers responded, and inadequate standardization and controls over the treatments actually delivered by the officers. But despite the methodological flaws, the Minneapolis experiment received widespread national recognition and had a significant impact on arrest policies nationwide. Between 1984 and 1987, police chiefs in thousands of police departments read the favorable reports in newspaper articles and the National Institute of Justice (NIJ) report, which praised the study and stated that arrest was the best deterrent for spouse abuse.

Between 1984 and 1986, in the aftermath of the Minneapolis study, the percentage of large city police departments with preferred or proarrest "policies increased from 10% to 46%" (Walker, 1992, p. 121). By 1989, thirteen states had enacted mandatory arrest policies for domestic violence perpetrators. In some of these thirteen states, arrest is mandatory in misdemeanor- and felony-level domestic violence charges, as well as for violation of a restraining order. However, in two states, (Delaware and North Carolina) arrest is mandatory only when the abuser violates a restraining order (Buzawa & Buzawa, 1990, p. 96).

In order to determine the validity of the Minneapolis experiment, the National Institute of Justice (NIJ) funded six replications in Atlanta, Georgia; Omaha, Nebraska; Charlotte, North Carolina; Colorado Springs, Colorado; Dade County, Florida; and Milwaukee, Wisconsin. Similar to the Minneapolis experiment, the six later studies examined whether arrest was the most effective police response in preventing batterers from committing future acts of abuse.

In contrast with the Minneapolis experiment, none of the six replications found arrest to be a more effective deterrent than the other police responses. There are three reasons that arrest did not prevent further domestic violence. First, the majority of the batterers in these studies had prior criminal records: 50 percent in Milwaukee, 65 percent in Omaha, and 69 percent in Charlotte. Therefore, arrest is neither innovative nor unexpected by the lawbreaker. Second, violence is a common and chronic problem among the study samples rather than a first-time occurrence. Therefore, it is unrealistic to expect a short arrest to have much impact on a long-term, chronically violent relationship. Third, there was wide variation among the studies in the amount of time that arrested batterers were in custody. For example, in the Milwaukee study, the average amount of time in custody for a "short arrest" was 2.8 hours, and for a full arrest it was 11.1 hours; in Charlotte, the average time in custody was 15.75 hours (Dunford, 1990; Sherman et al., 1992). In contrast, for the Minneapolis study, the time in custody ranged from approximately twenty-four hours to one week (168 hours). Finally, arrest alone without formal sanctions of incarceration and fines does not constitute a strong enough societal stigma among persons with previous arrest histories.

Lawrence Sherman and his associates recently found that arrest did not have a deterrent effect among a particular subgroup of abusers in Milwaukee. The most promising finding of the studies just cited is that even though arrest may lead to the escalation of violence among unemployed persons it may prevent subsequent violence by abusers who are employed, married, and white (Sherman, et al., 1992). Because of the large sample size, 1,200 cases eligible for randomization, the researchers were able to compare many subclassifications and matched pairs. The other replications were not able to subclassify as many variables as was done in the Milwaukee study.

Pro-arrest Policies

Since 1984, the trend has been for a growing number of police departments in cities with a population of more than 100,000 to adopt a policy of proarrest or probable-cause arrests of batterers. Efforts to redefine battering as a crime were boosted significantly by the following four activities and studies:

1. The National Coalition Against Domestic Violence as well as statewide coalitions and advocacy groups are working to protect battered women.
2. The Minneapolis domestic violence experiment on the deterrent effects of arrest (Sherman & Berk, 1984).
3. The final report of the U.S. Attorney General's Task Force on Family Violence (1984), citing the Minneapolis experiment, documenting the prevalence and intense dangers of battering episodes, and concluding that domestic violence is a major crime problem and that criminal justice agencies should handle it as such.
4. Television network and newspaper accounts of the court decisions that held police liable for failing to protect battered women from severe injuries (e.g., *Thurman* v. *City of Torrington*, 595 F. Supp. 1531 [1984]).

A highly publicized Supreme Court case in the mid-1980s led to proarrest laws and mandated police training on intervening in domestic violence incidents. In this case, Tracey Thurman of Torrington, Connecticut, who had been beaten repeatedly by her husband, sued the Torrington police department. The basis for her lawsuit was the failure of the police department to protect her, even though she had continually requested police protection over an eight-month period. And even though Ms. Thurman had obtained a court order barring her violent spouse from assaulting her again, it took the police twenty-five minutes to arrive on the scene of the most violent battering. After arriving at the Thurman home, the arresting officer delayed arresting Mr. Thurman for several minutes, giving him, who had a bloody knife in hand, plenty of time to repeatedly kick his wife in the head, face, and neck while she lay helpless on the ground. As a result, Ms. Thurman suffered life-threatening injuries, including multiple stab wounds to the chest, neck, and face; fractured cervical vertebrae and damage to her spinal cord; partial paralysis below the neck; lacerations to the cheeks and mouth; loss of blood; shock; scarring; severe pain; and mental anguish. Tracey Thurman's award was unprecedented: $2.3 million in compensatory damages against twenty-four police officers. The jury found that the Torrington, Connecticut, police had deprived Ms. Thurman of her constitutional right to equal protection under the law (Fourteenth Amendment of the Constitution). The jury further concluded that the Torrington police officers were guilty of gross negligence in failing to protect Tracey Thurman and her son Charles, Jr., from the violent acts of Charles Thurman, Sr.

In the wake of the court decision in the Thurman case, police departments throughout the country began implementing proarrest policies and increased police training on domestic violence. Therefore, during the latter half of the 1980s and the first half of the 1990s, there was a proliferation of police training courses on how best to handle domestic violence calls.

By 1988, ten states had passed laws expanding the police's arrest powers in cases of domestic assault. Specifically, these new statutes require arrest when there is a positive determination of probable cause (i.e., the existence of a visible injury and/or the passage of only a small amount of time between the commission of the assault and the arrival of the police). Police departments are also legally required to arrest batterers who have violated protective or restraining orders granted to battered women by the courts. As of 1992, protective orders were available to abused women in fifty states and the District of Columbia. In more and more jurisdictions, women in abusive relationships have obtained a protective order against their abuser from their local court in order to prevent him from coming to their residence. Police are called upon to enforce the protective order and to arrest the abuser if he violates any stipulations in the court order.

Several issues, however, limit the effectiveness of proarrest policies. First, in many jurisdictions, unmarried couples are not included in the proarrest policy for domestic violence. This certainly limits the police, since it is generally recognized that the police receive proportionately more domestic violence calls from cohabiting women than from married women. Second, several studies have indicated that 40 to 60 percent of batterers flee the residence before the police arrive on the scene. Therefore, the batterer would not be arrested unless the battered victim signed a criminal complaint. The final issue relates to the fact that experienced police officers are used to making their own decisions regarding whether or not to arrest an abusive person. As a result, police compliance with a presumptive or proarrest domestic violence policy will be a gradual process, taking several years.

Despite all the limitations inherent in instituting a proarrest policy, considerable progress has been made in the past decade. Although the arrest of all suspects in domestic violence calls is mandatory in only a small number of states, thousands of police departments nationwide are now making arrests when the officer observes signs of bodily injury on the battered woman.

The Potential of Electronic Monitoring as Part of a Coordinated Community Response

Technology is beginning to protect battered women from their abusive partners. It is also deterring some violent batterers from repeating their abusive and brutal acts. Recent developments in electronic monitors, computerized tracking of offenders and victims, and video surveillance have greatly bolstered crime investigations and crime prevention efforts. The goal is to lessen and eventually eliminate violent crime by controlling the physical environment. In most severe cases, the formerly battered woman agrees to maintain an active restraining order, agrees to testify in court and cooperate with any criminal proceedings against the alleged batterer, has a telephone in her residence, and believes that she is in extreme danger of aggravated assault or attempted murder by the defendant. In these cases, a home electronic monitor (e.g., panic alarm or pendant), also known as the abused woman's active emergency response pendant, can deter the batterer from violating his restraining order.

Private security companies recently began donating and marketing electronic security devices called panic alarms to battered women. The main purpose of these portable alarms, which have a range of about 200 feet from the victim's home, is to provide the battered women with an immediate and direct link to their local police in an emergency with just a press of a button. In some jurisdictions in Colorado and New Hampshire, the electronic pendant alarms are coupled with electronic monitoring of batterers through the Juris Monitor ankle bracelet, manufactured by B.I., Inc. If the batterer comes within close proximity of the victim's home, the ankle bracelet sounds a loud alarm in the home and immediately alerts the police. ADT Security has set up electronic pendants for battered women in thirty counties and cities throughout the United States. The women are carefully selected for each program by a screening committee comprised of community leaders, including a prosecutor or deputy prosecutor, a supervisor from the local battered women's shelter, and a police administrator. In all cases, the victim has an active restraining order against the batterer and is willing to fully cooperate with the prosecutor's office. One major drawback of these alarms is that the unit will not work if the telephone line is cut or not working.

Several companies—including T.L.P. Technologies, Inc.; Transcience; and B.I. Inc.— are currently developing electronic monitors. The alarm system developed by T.L.P. Technologies works even when the phone lines are down and when there is no electrical power. In the victim's home, police install the system, which includes a radio transmitter with a battery backup, an antenna, and a remote panic or motion-detector device. T.L.P.'s Visibility Plus Radio Data Alarm System integrates both the alarm system and computer-generated data immediately into the police radio channel instead of using a private security company as an intermediary. This system has been used with hundreds of battered women in both Nassau and Suffolk Counties, New York.

The most promising device that pinpoints the location of the victim whether she is at home, at work, or in the supermarket was developed by Geo Satellite Positioning Equipment. This advanced technology works by means of a satellite that sends a special signal from a receiver on the ground to the local police computer screen. A street map comes on the screen and sends a burst of data over the network, including the alarm number and the longitude and latitude of the victim's location within 5 to 10 feet.

Because of the growing awareness of the acute injuries sustained by battered women throughout the United States, and the millions of dollars spent on health and mental health care for victims of domestic violence, I predict that the electronic-monitoring programs will be expanded to thousands of battered women in every state by the year 2010. Unfortunately, as has been the case with other new legislation, a "high-profile" crisis situation needs to occur before Congress enacts new legislation.

Both short-term emergency support and long-term security services are critically needed by battered women and their children. It seems important that emergency services, including electronic pendants, be initiated for the thousands of battered women in imminent danger of suffering repeated assaults and being murdered by their former abusive partners. Funding for the new technology should come from both corporate sponsors and government agencies. But first, research needs to be carried out to determine which emergency electronic systems are most effective in protecting battered women. Also, under what conditions does the electronic technology fail to ensure the battered women's safety? *Before new electronic technology is purchased by battered womens shelters and law enforcement agencies, it is critical that comprehensive evaluations and outcome studies be planned and carried out.*

Community-wide Intervention Programs

Some populated cities and communities have developed citywide and community-wide task forces in order to provide a well-coordinated response to domestic family violence from the police, the courts, victim/witness assistance, and social service agencies. Many of these community task forces have followed the model of the programs developed during the 1980s in such areas as Baltimore County, Maryland; Quincy, Massachusetts; Duluth and Minneapolis, Minnesota; Boulder and Denver, Colorado; Memphis, Tennessee; Milwaukee, Wisconsin; Lincoln, Nebraska; and Seattle, Washington. For coordination to be effective among battered women's shelters, police, prosecutors, victim/witness assistance programs, and batterers' counseling programs, certain policies and practices are required. For example, shelter directors should offer to speak at police roll calls and police training sessions. These program directors have an important role in educating the police command and line personnel about the vital role of police in arresting and taking the batterers into custody and transporting battered women to the hospital emergency room and/or shelter. Police chiefs should define domestic violence as a serious crime; be willing to instill this view in their captains, lieutenants, sergeants, and patrol officers; and adopt mandatory arrest policies and implement a systematic monitoring program to check compliance with these new policies. Police commissioners and chiefs should also require all officers to complete training on the myths of domestic violence, the psychosocial characteristics of battered women and their abusers, the situations in which it is appropriate to wake a magistrate in the middle of the night to obtain a temporary restraining order for the victim, and why more arrests of batterers are needed. In addition, it is critical that police chiefs work closely with prosecutors and judges to make sure that arrest policies are supported by prosecutions and sanctions in the form of fines, jail time, and/or deferred prosecution pending the outcome of six months of court-mandated batterers counseling.

Conclusion

Mandatory arrest and eight to twelve hours in jail to cool off are certainly not a panacea to domestic violence. Although substantial progress has been made in strengthening domestic violence laws and improving police training, much remains to be done. Even if arresting them helps deter otherwise law-abiding abusive partners and even if arrest deters only a small percentage of abusers, it is still much more humane than doing nothing. That is, arresting the violent abuser conveys the important message to abusive adults, children, and society at large that family violence is a serious crime. But if the police refuse to arrest the batterer, they are conveying the message that family violence is tolerated and acceptable.

Warrentless arrest by law enforcement officers is one primary part of society's improved response to victims of battering. Responsive communities must work toward an integrated response from the police, the courts, and social service agencies. Victims of domestic violence often have multiple legal, psychological, and social service needs. Therefore, a well-coordinated community-wide approach by all mental health, social service, judicial, and law enforcement agencies should be planned and implemented throughout the United States.

References

Buzawa, E. S., and C. G. Buzawa. 1990. *Domestic Violence: The Criminal Justice Response.* Newbury Park, Calif.: Sage.

Dunford, F. W. 1990. "The Role of Arrest in Domestic Assault: The Omaha Police Experiment." *Criminology* 28: 183–206.

Fleming, J. B. 1976. *Stopping Wife Abuse.* Garden City, N.Y.: Doubleday.

Hart, B. J. 1992. "State Codes on Domestic Violence: Analysis, Commentary and Recommendations." *Juvenile and Family Court Journal* 43: 3–73.

Hirschel, J. D., I. W. Hutchison, C. W. Dean, and A. Mills. 1992, June. "Review Essay on the Law Enforcement Response to Spouse Abuse: Past, Present and Future." *Justice Quarterly* 9: 247–83.

Pence, E. 1983. "The Duluth Domestic Abuse Intervention Project." *Hamline Law Review* 6: 247–75.

Roberts, A. R. 1981. *Sheltering Battered Women: A National Study and Service Guide.* New York: Springer.

Roberts, A. R. 1984. "Police Intervention." In *Battered Women and Their Families: Intervention Strategies and Treatment Programs,* ed. A. R. Roberts, pp. 116–28. New York: Springer.

Roberts, A. R. 1990. *Helping Crime Victims.* Newbury Park, Calif.: Sage.

Roy, M. 1982. *The Abusive Partner.* New York: Van Nostrand.

Sherman, L. W. 1991. "From Initial Deterrence to Longterm Escalation: Short Custody Arrest for Poverty Ghetto Domestic Violence." *Criminology* 29: 821–50.

Sherman, L. W., and R. A. Berk. 1984. "The Specific Deterrent Effects of Arrest for Domestic Assault." *American Sociological Review* 49: 261–72.

Sherman, L. W., J. Schmidt, D. Rogan, D. S. Smith, P. Gartin, E. Cohn, D. Collins, and A. Bacich. 1992. "The Variable Effects of Arrest on Criminal Careers: The Milwaukee Domestic Violence Experiment." *Journal of Criminal Law and Criminology* 83: 137–69.

Thurman v. City of Torrington, 595 F. Supp. 1521 (D. Conn. 1985).

U.S. Attorney General's Task Force on Family Violence. 1984, September. *Final Report.* Washington, D.C.: Department of Justice.

Walker, L. E. 1979. *The Battered Woman.* New York: Harper & Row.

Walker, L. E. 1984. *The Battered Woman Syndrome.* New York: Springer.

Walker, L. E. 1992. "Battered Woman Syndrome and Self-defense." *Notre Dame Journal of Law, Ethics and Public Policy.* 6: 321–34.

7

Court Responses to Battered Women

Albert R. Roberts

We have come a long way during the past two decades as responsive prosecutors, judges and legislators have begun to recognize family violence as a serious crime. All fifty states have passed civil and/or criminal statutes to protect battered women, and prosecutors' offices are beginning to implement efficient systems of screening and prosecuting cases. Police and courts in a small yet growing number of jurisdictions have set up a round-the-clock method of issuing temporary restraining orders and providing advocacy as the cases move through court. Although court-mandated, probation-operated batterers' counseling programs have been developed on a limited basis, more are needed.

The court system is still plagued, however, with many problems in its handling of family violence cases, including

- Judges, trial court administrators, case managers, and intake officers who tend to minimize the dangers that abused women encounter and who discourage them from following through with criminal or civil complaints.
- Overloaded dockets and overworked judges in large cities that result in the court's inability to schedule a hearing and a trial date in a timely manner.
- A lack of specialized training on family violence for court personnel.
- Abused women who fail to call the police or go to court because they believe that the criminal justice system will not be able to protect them.
- A lack of counseling programs to which the court can refer both the batterer and the victim.

From time to time, the court system does all it can to issue and enforce a restraining order, but still the batterer flies into a rage as a result of the court's involvement and murders the woman who had sought the court's protection. Occasionally the court itself has been the site of violence, when an enraged batterer has brought a concealed weapon into the courthouse and shot his partner while she was seeking protection from the court.

What are the statutory provisions for the effective handling of domestic violence by prosecutors, judges, and the courts? What changes were made at the end of the 1970s and the decade of the 1980s in state laws, family law remedies, and criminal assault statutes to benefit battered women? Under what circumstances, in most states, can a woman obtain a restraining or protective court order against her abusive partner? This chapter attempts to answer these questions related to changes in the legislative and judicial responses to the crime of domestic violence.

The Response of the Courts and Judges

Family courts and criminal courts are unique American institutions. Their primary function is to provide a public forum for resolving legal disputes of a criminal or family nature. The courts' powers and organizational structures vary from state to state, but for the most part, many of the states' statutes are uniform with regard to the responsibilities of judges, prosecutors, and attorneys. The overwhelming majority of criminal and family law cases are settled without a trial. A family court judge often has courtroom administrative responsibilities; that is, he or she may also preside over bail hearings, probation revocation hearings, and child custody hearings and also may issue search warrants, restraining orders, and/or protective orders.

The availability and commitment of judges to protect the legal rights of battered women differ from state to state and within the states. For example, during the mid-1980s, Cook County (Chicago), Illinois, followed by Marion County (Indianapolis), Indiana, established a special court with a specially trained magistrate to hear all domestic violence cases.

Court Orders

Judicial intervention on behalf of battered wives is a recent phenomenon. In 1976, Pennsylvania took the lead as the first state to pass legislation recognizing wife battering as a crime. By 1980, forty-four states had enacted legislation that dealt with family violence, but it was not until 1988 that all fifty states took family violence laws seriously and passed acts that created civil and criminal remedies for victims of family violence.

Temporary restraining orders (TROs) became one of the most frequently used legal options for battered women during the 1980s. Although the protection order is known by different names across the country, it is most commonly referred to as an *order of protection, a restraining order,* or a *temporary injunction.* An order of protection can stay in effect for up to one year. The purpose of these court orders has been to prevent violence by one family member against another. The court orders usually forbid the alleged abuser from making contact with the victim, and in some cases, the order specifies the distance that the abuser must maintain from the person who requested the order. Depending on the state law, the court order may mandate that the abusive spouse move out of the house, refrain from terroristic threats of abuse or further physical abuse, pay support for the victim and minor children, and/or participate in a counseling program aimed at ending the violence or chemical dependency (both the batterer and the victim may be required to enter counseling).

In the past in most jurisdictions, a battered woman needed a lawyer to prepare documents for a civil (family or domestic relations) court order. But now, in most states, an abused woman may file a petition in the appropriate court and represent herself in the hearing. The batterer is given reasonable notice of the hearing and is asked to be present. He can hire an attorney to represent him, but legal representation is not required. The hearing for the temporary and permanent order of protection is before a judge; there is no jury.

The fearful and endangered victim must convince the judge that she was physically or sexually abused. Although some judges have been very compassionate and sensitive to the needs of battered women, others tend to blame the women for provoking the assaults. The judge usually has complete discretion over whether to grant a temporary restraining order and, seven to fourteen days later, a permanent restraining order. If the judge does not believe that the woman is in danger of further abuse, the case may be dismissed.

The most serious drawback of orders of protection is that they are extremely difficult to enforce. Because the police cannot be available twenty-four hours a day, seven days a week, the courts and police rely on the victim to call them if the batterer violates the court order. If the batterer violates any of the conditions of the protection order (e.g., tries to get into the victim's apartment), he will be in contempt of court or guilty of either a misdemeanor or criminal offense (depending on the state code).

There is wide variation, from one state code to another, in the penalties for violating a restraining order. Abusers can receive from fifteen days to six months in jail, probation and mandated counseling, or up to a $500 fine. An additional disadvantage of the court order is that instead of restraining the abuser, it may provoke him into retaliating against the victim with even more violence (Gondolf & Fisher, 1991, p. 280).

Judges need specialized training on the myths, dynamics, and effects of domestic violence, as well as on the court-mandated treatment needs of abusers. In the early 1990s, several statewide judicial conferences focused on family violence issues and policies. In addition, the National Council of Family and Juvenile Court Judges initiated two demonstration projects in 1990. The first project, funded by the Department of Justice, concentrates on improving family court practices with abused women through technical assistance. The second nationwide project, funded by the Conrad Hilton Foundation, is developing training materials for the court personnel, judges, district attorneys, and probation officers (Hart, 1992).

Probation

County and city probation departments can play an important role in optimizing the delivery of services to batterers and their victims. Unfortunately, to date, only a very few probation departments offer any assistance to abusers, battered women, or their children. Probation officers can provide early identification of serious cases and presentence reports on batterers (including a detailed psychosocial history, criminal history, and relationship problems), monitor batterers' restitution orders, and either conduct or refer batterers to six-month court-mandated group-counseling programs. These types of programs are provided by the San Francisco Probation Department and the Ocean County Probation Department in New Jersey.

Law Students Providing Legal Services to Battered Women

Many attorneys are interested in representing only clients with substantial financial resources, but many battered women cannot afford to hire an attorney. Therefore, because of the scarcity of legal services available to battered women, several law schools have established clinical practicum programs on battered women's rights. Third-year law students have the opportunity to help poor battered women who often are single parents and sometimes are homeless. Three law schools that have led the way with this program are the Yale Law School, the Catholic University School of Law, and the City University of New York's Law School at Queens College.

Prosecution of Family Violence Cases

In the past, it was very rare for batterers to be held accountable and to be punished for abusing their spouse or girlfriend. As discussed in the previous section, judges in different parts of the country are beginning to receive training on the enforcement of protection orders and the necessity of sentencing violent batterers to jail and/or court-mandated counseling. Because judges are viewed as the supreme authorities of their courtroom, they wield significant power. Thus when a batterer who violates probation or a restraining order is given a stern lecture or a short-term jail sentence, it gives the perpetrator as well as the community an important message—that domestic violence will not be tolerated by the criminal justice system.

Prosecutors also have the potential to break the cycle of violence. Most victim advocates believe that more domestic violence cases should be actively prosecuted, particularly those acts involving alleged abusers with prior criminal histories. Although other advocates believe that most abusive men are generally law-abiding citizens and, at the same time, that the first- or second-time abuser has the potential to change, the victim still needs to be protected. Therefore, deferred prosecution pending the outcome of a six-week, twelve-week, or six-month batterers' counseling program is the preferred prosecutorial alternative. The least useful approach is to encourage plea agreements (plea bargains), with the sole intent of reducing the prosecutor's caseload and clearing the court's calendar, rather than protecting the victim.

Responsive prosecutors have been instituting promising strategies and policies in regard to family violence, which have improved the different stages of the prosecution process. The first innovative stage has been the early identification of abuse cases and the filing of criminal charges by the prosecutor's office. The victim/ witness assistance unit in the prosecutor's office conducts a phone interview with each violently battered woman within a few hours after her abuser's arrest. If it determines that the alleged abuser has caused serious bodily harm to the victim or that the abuser has been convicted of any assaultive crime, than the advocate will help prepare the victim to testify and collect eyewitness testimony from neighbors or photographs and x-rays of the victim's injuries. The other model, the Domestic Abuse Intervention (DAI) Programs, was developed in Duluth and Minneapolis, in which staff interview and council victims after an arrest is made. A staff member then meets with prosecutors before the arraignment hearing to make sure that the prosecutors have all the necessary information and background evidence to prosecute the case.

In order to prevent batterers from intimidating and pressuring victims to drop charges or restraining orders, a growing number of prosecutors sign the criminal complaints themselves or file charges based on the arresting officer's signed complaint. When prosecutors take official responsibility by signing and filing charges themselves, they are sending the important message that domestic violence is a serious crime against the state, not a personal matter. Several prosecutors (e.g., Madison, Wisconsin, and South Bend, Indiana) do not allow the battered women to drop charges except in the case of extraordinary circumstances. In the majority of domestic violence arrests, however, neither the prosecutor nor the police will sign a criminal complaint. And in those cases in which the victim signs the complaint, most change their mind after their spouse apologizes and swears never to hit them again.

Sentencing options include traditional probation, pretrial diversion, probation, and intensive supervision in a biweekly counseling program, a stipulated order of continuance pending completion of a diversion program, and a presumptive sentence of thirty to sixty days in jail with the sentence suspended for one year pending compliance with an agreement that the batterer have no contact with the victim and complete a counseling program. The main problem with these innovative sentencing options is that most courts and prosecutors have limited staff resources and refuse to assign enough staff to screen applicants and monitor the abusers' attendance at and cooperation with the diversion program. Even when three to five full-time staff are assigned to these projects, they often fail because the community does not have enough alcohol rehabilitation, drug treatment, and/or group-counseling programs for the hundreds of batterers in need of treatment. Nevertheless, some jurisdictions have assigned adequate staff to operate a comprehensive domestic violence treatment program. The Minneapolis project employs thirteen full-time staff members augmented by nearly fifty trained volunteers. In both Minneapolis and Duluth, when the civil courts determine that abuse has taken place, the batterer is required to participate in educational and counseling groups. The court can also order a chemical dependency and psychological evaluation, and the abuser is required to sign a contract stipulating his responsibility to participate in the court-ordered treatment program. The staff regularly monitors his compliance with all aspects of the court order, including limited or no contact between the defendant and the victim. Then, in the few cases in which the abuser violates the court order, the prosecutor has the documentation to obtain a conviction.

Conclusion

Navigating the court system is generally a time-consuming and overwhelming ordeal for victims of violent crime. But for a woman who has been a victim of repeated physical abuse, degradation, and terroristic threats by a spouse or boyfriend, "the thought of going to court may be so intimidating that no effort is made to get legal protection" (Roberts, 1981, p. 97).

Protection or restraining orders are now available in every state as well as the District of Columbia. Thirty-two states have passed child custody statutes, which mandate courts to consider domestic violence when making custody awards and granting visitation rights. As of January 1993, fourteen states and the District of Columbia had enacted statutes mandating arrest for perpetrators of domestic violence. Thirty-three states also now have preferred or proarrest policies at the discretion of the police officer.

In order to ensure that the legal rights of battered women are fully protected, however, more needs to be done. Every court clerk, case manager, legal advocate, and judge in state and county courts throughout the United States needs specialized training in handling battered women and their abusive partners. All courts need systematic guidelines, simplified mandatory forms, and step-by-step instructions for processing court orders. Police officers and court clerks should have a brochure available to disseminate to all victims of domestic violence. This brochure should provide information on the battered woman's legal rights and options, instructions on how to obtain a court order or restraining order, and a list of local community resources.

References

Buzawa, E. S., and C. G. Buzawa. 1990. *Domestic Violence: The Criminal Justice Response.* Newbury Park, Calif.: Sage.

Finn, P., and S. Colson. 1990. *Civil Protection Orders: Legislation, Current Court Practice, and Enforcement.* Washington, D.C.: Department of Justice.

Gondolf, E. W., and E. Fisher. 1991. "Wife Battering." In *Case Studies in Family Violence*, ed. R. T. Ammerman and M. Hersen, pp. 273–92. New York: Plenum.

Hart, B. J. 1992. "State Codes on Domestic Violence." *Juvenile and Family Court Journal* 43: 3–44.

Hirschel, J. D., I. W. Hutchison, C. W. Dean, and A. Mills. 1992, June. "Review Essay on the Law Enforcement Response to Spouse Abuse: Past, Present and Future." *Justice Quarterly* 9: 247–83.

Pence, E. 1983. "The Duluth Domestic Abuse Intervention Project." *Hamline Law Review* 6: 247–75.

Roberts, A. R. 1981. *Sheltering Battered Women: A National Study and Service Guide.* New York: Springer.

Roberts, A. R. 1990. *Helping Crime Victims.* Newbury Park, Calif.: Sage.

Schmidt, J., and E. H. Steary. 1989. "Prosecutorial Discretion in Filing Charges in Domestic Violence Cases." *Criminology* 27: 487–510.

8

The Criminalization of Woman Battering: Planned Change Experiences in New York State

Lisa A. Frisch and Joseph M. Caruso

Each year, a staggering number of women, children, and the elderly are abused by intimates, family members, caretakers, and cohabitants. Although such violence impacts a wide range of victims, the abuse of adult women in intimate relationships is a problem that has long been inadequately addressed and continues to be a troublesome policy issue for criminal justice officials. This chapter focuses on woman battering, its legal and social history, and the various attempts to change the social, legal, and political responses to the problem.

The terms *domestic violence, woman battering, partner abuse, wife beating,* and *spouse abuse* are often used interchangeably and are generally defined as physical abuse between those engaged in an intimate relationship (Rush, 1991, p. 106). The nature of the relationship however, is not the only distinction between domestic violence and stranger assault. Domestic violence is unique in that it embodies a continuum of coercive behaviors that includes physical, sexual, psychological, emotional, and/or economic abuses that tend to escalate in frequency and severity over time (Carter, Heisler, & Lemon, 1991; Hart et al., 1990). A range of tactics such as threats, physical beatings, isolation, and the manipulation of fear and other emotions are used to establish a pattern of behavior that maintains power and control over one or more persons (Pence et al., 1985, p. 28; Walker, 1989, p. 35). This imbalance of power is fixed and rigidly maintained, and the abuse often remains unidentified, owing to the private confines of the close, interpersonal relationship in which it occurs. The term *battering* therefore goes beyond physical beatings to include the pattern of controlling behaviors that effectively maintain the fixed imbalance of power over the victim. Women are by far the most common victims of battering in intimate relationships. According to the U.S. Justice Department, 91 percent of the reported cases of domestic violence are of women victimized by their male partners (BJS). The director of the Bureau of Justice Statistics (BJS) stated that "the violence women suffer is more frequently caused by people with whom the victims have had a prior relationship" (Department of Justice Press Release, January 13, 1991). Results from the National Crime Survey indicate that women are six times more likely than men are to be victimized by a spouse or other intimate partner (BJS, 1991, p. 1).

Only recently have the public and its governmental institutions begun to identify domestic violence against women as a social problem. Battering is now recognized as the single major cause of injury to women, more frequent than auto accidents, muggings, and rapes combined (Stark & Flitcraft, 1988). Many of these assaults cause serious injury or even death to the victims. The National Crime Survey reports that injuries inflicted in domestic violence cases are at least as serious as the injuries inflicted in 90 percent of all violent felonies (BJS, 1986) and that one-third of women murdered are killed by husbands or intimate partners (BJS, 1991). According to the National Crime Survey, over two-thirds of violent victimizations against women were committed by someone known to them. In contrast, victimizations by intimates and other relatives account for only 5 percent of all violent victimizations against men (Bachman, 1994, p. 1). Accordingly, the former U.S. surgeon general, C. Everett Koop, announced that domestic violence is a public health menace and that "the home is actually a more dangerous place for American women than the city streets" (*New York Times,* October 17, 1991).

The recent realization that intimate violence against women is a social problem is one that evolved slowly and is largely the result of efforts made by women themselves. Lack of understanding of the dynamics of woman battering and a strong social tolerance for the behavior have been obstacles to recognition of the problem, which is rooted in long-standing historical traditions.

Historical and Cultural Perspectives

Women have been battered for thousands of years. Frederick Engels postulated that the phenomenon began with the emergence of the first monogamous pairing relationship and the patriarchal social and economic system (U.S. Commission on Civil Rights, 1978, p. 207). In many cultures, women and children were considered to be the "chattel," or property, of their husbands and fathers. Social customs and written laws gave men the right and responsibility to control their wives and to use force when necessary to preserve "order" in their families. Husbands' right to discipline their wives was codified in law as early as ancient Rome. Until the late nineteenth century, common law and written statutes regulated, but did not prohibit, the physical abuse of wives. Men were allowed to discipline their women as they saw fit, backed by strong community tolerance and hampered by little or no interference from the outside world. Blackstone (1765), in reference to a husband's power to discipline his wife, stated: Because "[t]he husband . . . is to answer for her misbehaviour, the law thought it reasonable to intrust him with his power of restraining her, by domestic chastisement, in the same moderation that a man is allowed to correct his apprentices or children" (Dobash & Dobash, 1979, p. 61).

Throughout the nineteenth century, American legal decisions reflected societal tolerance of and ambivalence toward the battering of women (Reynolds, 1987, p. 7). In 1824, the Mississippi Supreme Court upheld a man's right to assault his wife in response to her "misbehavior," without having to face prosecution, because a trial would result in public shame "that is unwarranted." Similar decisions, mirroring Blackstone's principles, followed in other states. In 1864, the North Carolina Supreme Court upheld the notion of domestic privacy, stating that the law "will not invade the domestic forum or go behind the curtain" but, rather, will "leave the parties to themselves" unless "some permanent injury be inflicted or there be an excess of violence" (Dobash & Dobash, 1979, p. 62).

Laws that promoted or regulated domestic violence were for the most part repealed in the early twentieth century, but the patriarchal control of women by men continued to be culturally tolerated and socially acceptable. The traditional view that a man's home was his private domain prevailed as America entered the twentieth century. The activities in a man's home were seen as "private matters" and thus exempt from public scrutiny and concern. The development of the family court (1899) further reinforced the notion of family affairs being private, since this legal system was devised within civil law (private torts) rather than criminal law (public wrongs) (N.Y.S. Governor's Commission 1988, pp. 7–9).

From 1900 through the 1960s, woman battering did not come to public attention because it was considered a "private matter" and not the business of public officials and often was redefined as a "family problem," "personal squabble," "dispute," or "disturbance" that did not require an active response by the criminal justice system. Police, prosecutors, and the courts maintained a hands-off attitude in these cases, which were considered an annoyance and tended to be minimized or avoided whenever possible (Pleck, 1987, pp. 182–83).

During the last twenty-five years, many police were trained to diffuse "domestic disturbances" by applying arbitration, mediation, and negotiation techniques. This widespread training stemmed from an experimental program developed in 1967 that involved forming a family crisis unit within the New York City Police Department (U.S. Commission on Civil Rights, 1982, pp. 53–55). This program, funded by the Law Enforcement Assistance Agency (LEAA), was an early attempt to upgrade and professionalize the police by linking the fields of law and psychology. The eighteen officers selected to participate in the project were trained intensively in crisis intervention, interpersonal conflict–management techniques, and the use of referrals to social service agencies. At the end of the two-year experiment, the relationship between the social sciences and law enforcement was claimed to be a major success, and the family crisis unit received national publicity. The results of the experiment were unclear, however, in regard to whether this response by the police actually resulted in a reduction of calls or injury to officers (Loving, 1980, p. 35). Nevertheless, police agencies across the country, eager to find a tool to deal with the vexing problem of domestic calls, embraced the use of crisis intervention and mediation in these cases.

According to the Police Executive Research Forum (Loving, 1980, pp. 33–35), the original purpose of the experiment was to teach skills to police for handling verbal disputes only, and these intervention techniques were not intended to replace arrest in cases involving violence. Regardless of the intent, crisis-intervention techniques soon became the preferred method to reconcile all "domestics." Even in cases of serious injury, arrest continued to be used as a last resort, because of cultural values that were deeply rooted in legal tradition and the belief that battering was an individual pathology rather than a crime deserving punishment (Buzawa & Buzawa, 1990, p. 78). According to the police, in the 1970s when they did attempt to arrest violent husbands or boyfriends, their supervisor would reprimand them for doing a poor job in dealing with the situation.[1] Domestic calls were thus viewed as "nuisance calls," and most police administrations considered arrest in these cases to be a failure.

The policy of arrest-avoidance by police led to successful litigation by battered women making constitutional and procedural claims, which accordingly began to change the way in which police were expected to handle domestic violence calls (N.Y.S. Governor's Commission, 1988, p. 10). The first major lawsuit, *Bruno* v. *Codd* (396 N.Y.S.2d 974 [1978]), was a class-action suit filed against the New York City Police Department by twelve married battered women who claimed that the police were not arresting their abusers because they were married to them and thus they were not being given "equal protection under the law" as other assault victims were. This case resulted in a consent decree that created the first police policy on domestic violence and mandated training for the entire department (*Bruno* consent decree, 1978, pp. 1–4). This consent decree marked the beginning of the formal criminalization of domestic violence in New York State and the nation.

Criminalization

The term *criminalization* describes the process(es) by which substantive and procedural criminal laws are written, amended, and applied to specific behaviors that were previously socially tolerated, for the purposes of general and specific deterrence, punishment, and social control (Beirne & Messerschmidt, 1991, pp. 24–25). Thus to criminalize a set of behaviors is to assign them a criminal status in written law based on perceived social harms and to enforce such laws when violations become known. Written laws describe behaviors that are considered harmful and authorize an official response. The enforcement or nonenforcement of these laws plays a critical role in shaping public attitudes toward the seriousness of particular actions. Predictable law enforcement conveys the message of wrongfulness and social rejection and educates victims, offenders, children, neighbors, and the public at large that such behavior will not be tolerated. Criminalization focuses the legal authority and coercive power of the criminal justice system on a set of behaviors now perceived as socially dangerous and currently not manageable using informal means of social control. Criminalization is thus more than the manipulation of law. The process includes the planned change of individual perceptions, organizational policies and procedures, and, ultimately, the status quo of community life.

Understanding criminalization as planned change provides an analytical framework for examining the various attempts to promote change in the response to woman battering in New York State. All planned changes either accommodate external pressures or reflect an internal awareness that current practices need to be modified. Thus change is reactive, proactive, or a combination of both. Reactive change can be a direct response to external pressure or an indirect accommodation of some external change. Proactive change is promoted by the willingness to improve a practice, policy, or procedure in order to increase its effectiveness. Most proactive changes are, in fact, a response, at least in part, to some external force; therefore, pure proactive change is rare (Toch & Grant, 1982, p. 135). The following analysis uses this planned-change perspective to examine the criminalization of domestic violence in New York State.

The Reactive Criminalization Process

Reactive change is generated primarily in an adversarial context in which public officials are pressured by "a diverse set of special interests and other constituency groups from *outside* arenas" to change official policies and procedures (Nakamura & Smallwood, 1980, p. 32, italics added). The insider–outsider dynamic that pervades the reactive-change process results in reform strategies that rely chiefly on external means, including adversarial victim-advocacy, grassroots activism, public demonstrations, public hearings, public relations campaigns, lobbying and consensus building, and civil litigation. Such efforts, led by *external forces*, target changes in laws, policies, and procedures and often result in penalties for agency or individual noncompliance. Such changes, therefore, are made as a last resort, tend to be resented, are often more symbolic than substantive, and inspire defensive posturing and resistance (Nakamura & Smallwood, 1980, pp. 59–60).

Understanding the linkage that often exists between proactive-change efforts and their external origins suggests that reactive change can be a primary tool to promote proactivity. Thus reactive criminalization efforts must be examined as a prerequisite to analyzing criminalization as a planned-change process. Reactive criminalization includes (1) initial recognition of the problem, (2) efforts to change public opinions about the problem, (3) efforts to change the law, and ultimately, (4) efforts to improve law enforcement.

Initial Recognition of the Problem

Before the feminist movement of the 1970s, victims of wife battering had only three avenues for assistance: "their own individual strategies of resistance; the help of relatives, friends, and neighbors; and the intervention of child-welfare agencies." None of these could adequately protect the victim. The superior power of the husband and the sanctity of the institution of marriage easily outweighed the first two options, and child welfare advocates did not satisfactorily represent the interests of the women (Gordon, 1988, p. 271). There were attempts, however, to recognize and assist victims of domestic violence through efforts by the suffrage and temperance movements at the turn of the century (Pleck, 1987, pp. 3–10). But because at that time, public discussion of wife beating was not acceptable, the women's rights movement during the late nineteenth century addressed the problem indirectly, through temperance, child-welfare, and social purity campaigns. Battered women were depicted as the victims of drunken, brutal husbands rather than as the victims of a patriarchal system supporting male supremacy (Gordon, 1988, pp. 254–55).

The stage for modern feminism was set in the 1950s and 1960s during the civil rights, antiwar, and black liberation movements. Women who were working against racial oppression began to question their own social position and also gained political experience that helped them prepare for the feminist movement (Schechter, 1982, p. 30). The efforts to identify violence against women through the early women's liberation movement began with the creation of rape crisis centers. Schechter (1982) states that the "anti-rape movement articulated that violence is a particular form of domination based on social relationships of unequal power. Through the efforts of the anti-rape movement, it became clear that violence is one mechanism for female social control" (p. 34). This became clearer as great numbers of women who were being battered and sexually assaulted by their husbands or boyfriends called the rape crisis hotlines for assistance (Fields, 1991, p. 1).

Battered women turned to the rape crisis hotlines for assistance in the early 1970s because, for them, there was simply nowhere else to go. Not only did police and the courts typically ignore the problem (U.S. Commission on Civil Rights, 1978), but married battered women who attempted to leave their abusers were also denied welfare and were left with virtually no housing options. Battered women who fled their homes were forced to find temporary housing in the same shelters as fire victims or alcoholics, were offered no specialized assistance, and were often turned away for lack of space. Before the battered women's movement, there were only a few isolated attempts to house homeless battered women. As early as 1964, for example, Al-Anon opened a shelter for victims of what was then labeled "alcohol-related" violence (Schechter, 1982, p. 55).

The battered women's movement of the 1970s arose from the work of feminists, community activists, and the battered women themselves. Shelters specifically for battered women and their children evolved from women's centers and individual women who opened up their homes to those in need (Schechter, 1982, pp. 56–57). This movement encouraged women to discuss and share their victimization experiences, to help victims recognize that they were not to blame for the violence and were not alone in having had such experiences. The movement not only supported victims, but it also began to articulate the nature of the problem of woman battering and the failures of society to respond adequately to it. In a number of states in the late 1970s, women working to end this violence formed grass-roots coalitions, including New York State's Coalition Against Domestic Violence and the National Coalition Against Domestic Violence. In 1979 in New York State, Governor Hugh Carey created the New York State Task Force on Domestic Violence[2] to study and articulate the problem, increase public awareness, and make policy recommendations to the state's leadership.

Efforts to Change Public Opinion

With more knowledge of the problem came awareness of the inadequacies of public information and traditional governmental responses to domestic violence. The New York State Coalition Against Domestic Violence ran public education campaigns and promoted the formation of community coalitions to pressure local officials to recognize the problem. In 1979, the Governor's Task Force, drawing from the experience and knowledge of its diverse members, issued a list of recommendations for change. Of the original twenty-one recommendations, four were strategies to educate the public, and six focused on changing official attitudes toward the problem (N.Y.S. Governor's Commission, 1988, pp. 13–14). These recommendations included developing a statewide public information campaign, updating and disseminating written information on services for victims, and establishing a twenty-four-hour toll-free hotline to provide information and assistance to victims and the public.

Recommendations regarding strategies to change official attitudes included the development of domestic violence training programs for all human service and criminal justice personnel; the development of curricula on domestic violence for all institutions of professional education licensed by the state, including medical schools and law schools; the implementation of treatment protocols for hospital emergency room staff; the improvement of official data collection; and the coordination of additional services such as alcoholism treatment, medical care, legal representation, and emergency public assistance (N.Y.S. Governor's Commission, 1988, pp. 13–14).

In 1983, Governor Mario Cuomo established the New York State Governor's Commission on Domestic Violence, which was mandated "to assist the state in its efforts to identify and alleviate the legal, medical and social problems posed by domestic violence and its aftermath." The commission's goals were (1) the development and promotion of prevention programs; (2) the development and implementation of training for professionals; (3) the provision of effective public information and community outreach; and (4) the evaluation, coordination, and promotion of legal protections and services (N.Y.S. Governor's Commission, 1988, p. 5).

One example of an effective attempt to change official attitudes in New York State occurred in September 1985 when the Governor's Commission, with the state Department of Correctional Services (DOCS) and the Division for Women, cosponsored a public hearing at the Bedford Hills Correctional Facility for Women (N.Y.S. Governor's Commission, 1988, p. 1). This hearing was motivated by a 1982 study conducted by DOCS that found that nearly one-third of the women committed to New York State prisons reported having been abused by their husbands or live-in partners. At this hearing, twelve inmates (ten of whom had killed their abusers) spoke movingly about the circumstances of the crime for which they were incarcerated and of their experiences with physical, sexual, and psychological abuse. The women testified before a panel that included several state legislators and directors from many state agencies. Few members of the panel had heard before, first hand, about the horrors that battered women experienced or of the dearth of services available to them. Many of these women had made numerous contacts with the justice or social service systems, and yet their victimization was never effectively dealt with or even adequately documented. For example, the majority of presentence investigation reports prepared by county probation departments failed even to discuss the issue of battering in these women's lives—even when the women were convicted of killing their abusers. The hearing promoted the understanding that the current methods for dealing with woman battering were ineffective and that change in the official response was imperative. This in turn allowed greater access to systems such as criminal justice, health care, and social services to improve public policy and professional training.

Efforts to Change the Law

Much of the effort to change the justice system's response to battered women during the late 1970s and 1980s concentrated on changing the law. Before this movement to legislate change, the law reflected the ambiguity of our social attitudes toward violence in the home. In 1962, legislation was passed in New York State that gave the family court, a civil court, sole authority over wife abuse cases. A statement by the then administrative judge of the family court summed up the reason for the legislation: "The Family Court is not geared with punishment as a primary objective. We're trying to stabilize the family," (Martin, 1981, pp. 103–4). A battered wife seeking legal relief was thus faced with a system whose primary objective was not her protection but her family's stability. In addition, she was not permitted access to the criminal court even if she wanted to have her abuser prosecuted.

Unmarried women received no better legal protection at that time. Police did not have the authority to make arrests in misdemeanor cases unless they had personally witnessed the offense—an unlikely occurrence. Since misdemeanors represented a significant percentage of domestic violence, many women who were ineligible to go before the family court, because they did not fit the definition of a "family member," were left unprotected and without legal redress, either civilly or criminally. Then, in 1970, police were given the authority in New York State to make warrantless arrests in both misdemeanor and felony offenses when they had a reasonable belief that a crime had been committed (Chapter 996, Laws of 1970; amended by Chapter 997, Laws of 1971). This change, at a minimum, gave police the discretion to arrest those who had committed misdemeanor assaults against intimates. But married women continued to be denied the right to have their abusers prosecuted until seven years later, when victims of family offenses were allowed to have their cases heard in either family or criminal court (Chapter 449, Laws of 1977).

The New York Task Force/Governor's Commission on Domestic Violence facilitated several other landmark legislative changes, mainly those between 1979 and 1986. These legislative changes helped clarify the ambiguity of existing law and helped promote more effective legal protection for victims of battering. In 1980, first-degree assaults were removed from the list of family offenses, giving the criminal court exclusive jurisdiction over these serious crimes (N.Y. Fam. Ct. Act

§812(1), 1980). When Governor Hugh Carey introduced this bill, he stated that "such serious acts of violence cannot in any way be tolerated because they occur in the family or the home. Such violence is a breach of public order and safety. It is as offensive to public policy as violence in the streets" (press release, June 3, 1980).

The following year, the original purpose of family court proceedings—keeping the family unit "intact"—was amended to reflect the goals of stopping the violence, ending the disruption to the family, and assisting victims in obtaining protection (Fam. Ct. Act §812 [2] [b] and Civ. Prac. L. §530.11 [2] [b]). Victims of family violence began to achieve equitable status with other crime victims through an amendment to the Executive Law in 1983, which made abuse victims eligible for compensation to the same extent as other crime victims (Chapter 805, Laws of 1983). The Family Court Act was then amended in 1984 to allow unmarried parents and former spouses to request orders of protection in either family court or criminal court[3] (Chapter 984, Laws of 1984).

Changes in case law had an impact as well. Also in 1984, the New York State Court of Appeals, in *People* v. *Liberta* (64 N.Y.2d 152), held that New York's marital rape exemption was unconstitutional. As a result, a husband may now be prosecuted for raping his wife, even if they are living together when the crime is committed.[4] The rights of victims of family offenses became the focus of legislation in 1986, when the police were required to give these victims notice of community services and available rights and remedies (Chapter 620, Laws of 1986). This was significant, as the police are often the first and only contact a victim of domestic violence may have, and the information she receives at that juncture can be critical.[5]

Perhaps the most significant change in the law in New York State in a decade was the passage of the Family Protection and Domestic Violence Intervention Act of 1994, which was signed into law in June 1994 (Chapters 222 and 224). This law is far reaching, as it amends numerous sections of the Family Court Act, the Domestic Relations Law, and the Criminal Procedural Law. Perhaps most relevant to the criminal justice response is the new language clarifying the law enforcement role in domestic violence cases. The law now requires police to make arrests in cases in which there is reasonable cause to believe that a felony or misdemeanor was committed by one family or household member against another, or if an order of protection was violated. The sole exception to the arrest requirement is in misdemeanor cases in which the victim, without prompting by the officer, requests that an arrest not be made. In such cases, the officer has the authority to make the arrest but is not required to do so. In addition, the police must complete full, written reports of the incident, whether or not an arrest is made. The information on these reports will be collected statewide and used as a database to analyze both the numbers of domestic violence offenses that are reported to police and the response by law enforcement. Although this new law reflects the formal policies of the majority of law enforcement agencies in New York State, it does not necessarily reflect the actual practice of all officers. Training and policy development assistance for police are included in the law, in recognition of the fact that simply passing a law will likely have limited impact on police response.

Although legislation alone cannot change the system's response and certainly cannot mandate a change in attitude, the efforts made in passing and enforcing new laws can have an impact. The lobbying efforts of the grassroots service providers, the New York State Coalition Against Domestic Violence, and the educational and outreach work of the New York State Office for the Prevention of Domestic Violence helped enlighten both the public and the lawmakers. The efforts to solicit support for the newly passed Family Protection and Domestic Violence Intervention Act is an excellent example of this. The bill's original sponsor, State Senator Stephen Saland, held a series of legislative hearings across the state during the year before its passage, asking for recommendations from a vast array of domestic violence advocates, police, district attorneys, judges, and many others in order to create a bill that incorporated the concerns of a diverse constituency.

Once a bill becomes law, at least some adherence to the change becomes necessary; thus there often is a public appearance of attitude change, if not a true one. Over time, however, this public perception can ultimately affect private attitudes. Legislation is necessary for achieving social change, as it sets the groundwork for the change. As Del Martin (1976) stated nearly twenty years ago,

> [W]hatever progress we can claim in "legislating attitudes" has resulted from enforcement of new laws, not the laws themselves . . . when a law is enforced, it eventually becomes a part of the social fabric, a given in the daily lives of citizens. Only then does the collective change in attitudes have a lasting effect. (1976, pp. 175–76)

It is the next phase—enforcing the law—that presents the greatest challenge to the planned-change process.

Efforts to Improve Law Enforcement

By the mid-1970s, it became apparent that formal legal modifications were not enough to guarantee actual change in the official response to woman battering. In light of the role of police as "gatekeepers of the criminal justice system" (Goolkasian, 1986, p. 29) and the reality of selective rather than full enforcement of the criminal laws, police discretion was targeted for change. Police discretion has been defined as "the choosing of some laws to enforce vigorously and others to enforce reluctantly, if at all, and the selection from among the probably guilty of those to take into custody and those to release" (Newman & Anderson, 1989, p. 148). The principal methods used by external agents to change the decision by police to investigate and make arrests in woman battering cases included (1) *civil litigation* to force changes in both officer and command discretion and to establish organizational and municipal policies on domestic violence, (2) *research* on the effectiveness of various police techniques for handling domestic violence calls, and (3) *formal policy recommendations* by special-interest groups and influential government task forces and commissions that were directed to study the problem and make suggestions for effective change.

CIVIL LITIGATION

Arrest avoidance by police led to successful state and federal litigation by battered women, based on claims that their constitutional rights to equal protection and due process were violated when the police failed to enforce the law in domestic violence cases (Buel, 1988, p. 218). In equal protection cases such as *Bruno* v. *Codd* (1978) and *Thurman* v. *City of Torrington* (1984), both state and federal courts mandated that victims of domestic assault may not be treated differently from other victims of assault simply because of their relationship with the offender. In *Bruno,* the New York City police, the probation department, and the family court were accused of denying battered women the legal protection to which they were entitled under state law. The trial court ruled that the police owe a special duty of protection to battered wives and required them to "exercise their discretion to arrest in a reasonable, non-arbitrary manner and not to automatically decline to make an arrest solely because the assaulter is married to the victim" (Gundle, 1986, p. 261). The judge further observed that "only the written law had changed; in reality, wife beating is still condoned, if not approved, by some of those charged with protecting its victims" (90 Misc. 2d 1047; 396 N.Y.S.2d 974; Sup. Ct. 1977). Before the appellate review, the police made an out-of-court agreement with the plaintiffs to develop a proarrest policy on woman battering and to require training for all members of the NYPD (which at the time employed 28,000 officers) on the appropriate police response (*Bruno* consent decree, 1978, pp. 1–6).

In 1984, a federal court in Connecticut awarded Tracey Thurman, a battered woman, $1.9 million in her lawsuit against the city of Torrington and twenty-four city police officers as the result of the department's policy and practice of nonintervention and nonarrest in domestic violence cases (Buel, 1988, pp. 218–19). *Thurman* was the first civil rights case in which a battered woman was permitted to sue a police department for its failure to protect her from her batterer. The judge ruled that official behavior that reflects an ongoing pattern of deliberate indifference to victims of domestic assault violates the equal protection clause of the Fourteenth Amendment (595 F. Supp. 1531). Equal protection claims target the "custom or policy" of discriminating against victims of domestic violence, and case law has created a set of objective criteria to assess overall police response in light of such claims. In *Watson* v. *Kansas City* (Kan. Ct. App. 10, No. 86-2501 [1988]), the victim presented statistics that revealed a 31 percent arrest rate by local police in nondomestic assault cases and a 16 percent arrest rate in response to domestic assaults. The victim also presented evidence that the police received training that encouraged them to diffuse domestics and to use arrest as a last resort. The U.S. Court of Appeals ruled that such statistical comparisons and supportive evidence are acceptable proof of an equal protection claim (National Woman Abuse Prevention Project, 1988, 1989, p. 11).

Due process litigation by battered women targets specific police officers, supervisors, and administrators whose official actions or inactions constitute gross negligence or who fail to protect them, even though they have a "special right" to such protection (Fields, 1987, pp. 1–3). Carrington (1987, p. 2) identified six types of failure to protect claims that have been successful in domestic violence cases: (1) the failure to respond to requests for assistance, (2) the failure to arrest or restrain an obviously dangerous person, (3) the failure to protect when a special duty to protect has been voluntarily assumed by authorities, (4) the failure to protect persons whom authorities have brought into contact with assailants, (5) the failure to protect persons who have assisted authorities, and (6) the failure to investigate a report of crime.

In *DeLong* v. *County of Erie* (1983), the New York Appellate Court determined when police must respond to requests for assistance. When police failed to respond to a 911 call from a woman and she was subsequently murdered, the court ruled that when police receive notice of a specific danger and there is reliance on police protection, a special duty to protect exists. The court argued that "when police do not respond in such cases, their actions increase the danger the victims is in. This constitutes gross negligence and violates due process of law" (469 N.Y.S.2d 611). In *Jones* v. *County of Herkimer* (1966), a young woman was threatened by a man over a period of years but received no protection from local police. When the offender, the son of a local judge, chased the victim into the village hall and shot her to death, nothing was done to protect her or to restrain an "obviously dangerous person." The court found that a special relationship had been created (272 N.Y.S.2d 925).

In *Sorichetti* v. *City of New York* (1979), an estranged husband had repeatedly threatened his wife and daughter, and a family court order of protection had been issued. But the police failed to investigate when the daughter did not return home from a visitation with her father, despite evidence that the child was in serious danger. Indeed, the father had attacked the child with a knife and nearly amputated one of her legs. The court of appeals upheld a $2 million award to the daughter and noted that police are required to arrest violators of judicial orders of protection when violations are known (408 N.Y.S.2d 219). Issuance of a judicial order to protect indicated that a special duty to protect had been assumed by the authorities (Alexander, 1985, p. 17; Carrington, 1987, p. 3).

In *Baker* v. *City of New York* (1966), a battered woman was shot by her estranged husband, a police officer, in the waiting room of the domestic relations court. The police had disregarded a court order of protection, telling the victim that it was "only a piece of paper." A probation officer, knowing the husband was dangerous, did nothing to restrain him and even ordered the victim to share the waiting room with her husband, where he shot her to death. The court found a special duty to protect was owed, based on the order of protection and further held that there had been a failure to restrain an obviously dangerous person (269 N.Y.2d 515). The factors to be considered when determining a special relationship as articulated by the court in *Jenson* v. *Conrad* (1986) are "whether the victim or perpetrator was in legal custody, whether the state had expressly stated its desire to provide affirmative protection to a specific individual and whether the state knew of the victim's plight" (747 F.2d 194–95). By using this special relationship criteria, due process claims by battered women effectively challenged police discretion not to respond seriously to domestics, not to enforce orders of protection, and not to arrest obviously dangerous persons.

RESEARCH

Changes in law enforcement were further prompted by research on the effectiveness of various techniques for handling domestic violence calls. Nearly a decade after crisis intervention was adopted as the primary police response, there had been virtually no empirical validation of its effectiveness (Loving, 1980, p. 35). In February 1973, the Police Foundation funded research to explore the relationship between domestic disturbances and the crimes of homicide and aggravated assault in Kansas City, Missouri (Police Foundation, 1977, p. 22). After analyzing domestic homicides, it was determined that in 85 percent of the cases, the police had previously responded at least once to domestic disturbances at the address and that in half the homicides, the police had responded on more than five earlier occasions (Buel, 1988, pp. 215–16). These data raised the question of whether the police could have intervened more effectively in these cases, before the murder was committed.

The Minneapolis domestic violence experiment was perhaps the pivotal study affecting criminalization, specifically in regard to arrest. The experiment, funded by the National Institute of Justice, was conducted from 1981 to 1982 by the Police Foundation in cooperation with the Minneapolis Police Department. The researchers sought to determine which technique—mediation, separation, or arrest—was most effective at reducing subsequent violence against the victim. When the police arrived at the scene of a misdemeanor domestic assault where both parties were present and there was probable cause that a crime had been committed, one of the three police responses was applied, based on a lottery selection.

Incidents of repeat violence were measured over a six-month follow-up period using official police reports and biweekly interviews with victims. Using both official and unofficial measures of repeat violence, the study found that arrest was the most effective response, as there were nearly twice as many incidents of repeat violence by offenders who were not arrested, as compared with those who were arrested (Community Council of Greater New York, 1988, pp. 3–4). A summary of the results was published in 1985 by the Police Foundation and was made widely available to police agencies across the country. Also in that year, an analysis of 783 reported woman-battering incidents in Santa Barbara, California, between 1981 and 1983, found that arrest reduced recidivism in domestic violence cases (Berk & Newton, 1985, p. 256).

Other studies during this period addressed arrest in relation to homicide and police callbacks to the scene. As in the Kansas City study, police in Newport News, Virginia, found that 50 percent of the homicides in the city were between family members and that in half those cases police had responded to an earlier domestic disturbance call. After the police adopted a mandatory arrest policy, domestic homicides fell from 50 percent of all homicides to less than 30 percent (Evans, 1987, pp. 1–4). Arrest policies also appeared to contribute to a reduction in domestic violence calls to police. The Duluth (Minnesota) Police Department reported a 47 percent decrease in repeat calls after instituting a mandatory arrest policy. And after Connecticut adopted a statewide mandatory arrest law, domestic violence incidents reported to the Hartford Police Department decreased 28 percent (Buel, 1988, p. 216).

The deterrent effect of arrest was called into question by some, however, following the publication of the results of the "replication" studies, funded by the National Institute of Justice, of the original Minneapolis police experiment. These studies were conducted from 1985 to 1990, and the results were published for five of the six locations: Omaha, Milwaukee, Colorado Springs, Metro-Dade, and Charlotte. Although much attention has been called to the results of the Milwaukee experiment, which offered data indicating that arrest may actually escalate the violence of unemployed batterers (Sherman et al., 1992, p. 137), each of the studies found a positive deterrent effect in the short term—no small achievement for battered women seeking a measure of safety. This short-term deterrent effect should have been considered supportive of the original Minneapolis experiment, given the understanding of domestic violence as a pattern of behavior that generally escalates in frequency and severity over time, and so even a short-term break in the violence could be a window of opportunity for the victim to find a safe haven (Frisch, 1992, pp. 213–14).

Richard Berk, one of the original Minneapolis experiment researchers, wrote in his analysis of the replication studies that no other intervention proved to be better than arrest at any of the six sites. He concluded "[I]f on legal or ethical grounds arrest is the preferred response, one is not depriving the community of a superior criminal justice intervention. Put another way, one can do no better than arresting the offender" (1994, p. 2).

The researchers' finding that unemployed, socially marginal batterers are not deterred by arrest (Sherman et al., 1991, pp. 158–59, 167–69) is no less surprising than the fact that our entire criminal justice system fails to deter the majority of socially marginal criminals from committing *any* crime. Our society continues to use arrest as the preferred option for burglars, armed robbers, drug dealers, and sex offenders, even though it rarely deters them in the long term (Frisch, 1992, p. 213). The Milwaukee researchers, however, concluded that arrest may actually escalate the violence of these socially marginal batterers and postulated that perhaps "punishment should be made less severe in order to reduce an escalation effect (Sherman et al. 1991, p. 168). When these batterers assaulted their victims after having been arrested, the researchers presumed that the assault was the direct result of the arrest, rather than the choice and responsibility of the offender. Should we then assume that other criminals, such as burglars or car thieves, who return to crime after being arrested are doing so *in response to* the arrest? When researchers analyzed the replication studies in search of a specific deterrent effect of arrest, they seem to have forgotten that long-term deterrence is only one of many goals of the criminal justice system and is largely an unattainable ideal. If crime could be prevented permanently, arrest would be only one component of the process and long-term deterrence would require a "basic modification of cultural values, revision of opportunity structures, reorganization of social class systems and elimination of economic imbalance" (Newman & Anderson, 1989, p. 45). Few people, particularly those familiar with law enforcement, would presume that arrest alone could produce such a sweeping, societal change.

Accordingly, an additional fundamental flaw in the studies' research design was the researchers' failure to consider the impact of the decisions of the prosecutors and the courts after the arrest. The effect of arrest was considered in isolation from the remainder of the criminal justice system. When the research did include data on the prosecution of these cases, very low rates of prosecution and even lower rates of conviction were found, which would clearly seem to dilute the impact of arrest. In Milwaukee, only 5 percent of the offenders were actually charged, and only 1 percent were convicted. In Charlotte, less than 1 percent of offenders were charged and convicted (Zorza & Woods, 1994, pp. 2–3). Studying the effect of arrest without considering the role of the remaining actors in what should be a systemic response means little when determining the impact of criminal justice intervention on domestic violence or, for that matter, on any other crime. But it is the crime of battering that has historically been treated less seriously than other crimes, therefore making the response of the entire system beyond arrest even more critical. Sadly, the emphasis on deterrence that emanated from these highly funded replication studies also blinded many to the most significant reasons for using the imperfect tools of our criminal justice system—public protection (in this case, equal protection) and justice.[6]

FORMAL POLICY RECOMMENDATIONS

Early police involvement in making formal policy recommendations suggests that this phase of the change process is both reactive (recommendations come from "outside" the organization) and proactive (some making suggestions for change are actually from within the profession).

In the ten-year period that followed the NYPD's historic agreement to develop the first proarrest policy on woman battering (*Bruno* v. *Codd* [1978]), a number of influential groups made formal policy recommendations after studying the problem. As early as 1976, the International Association of Chiefs of Police (IACP) issued Training Key 245, *Wife Beating*, which stated, "Increased awareness of the extent and significance of family violence in our society is needed to stimulate action to control the problem. Wife beating, in particular, has not received adequate attention from society at large or any of its institutions" (IACP, 1976, p. 35). Training Key 246, *Investigation of Wife Beating*, directed police to treat wives who had been physically assaulted as crime victims and not to shield violent husbands from prosecution. Step-by-step procedures for handling the calls as a crime scene were discussed in some detail (Loving, 1980, p. 182).

In 1980, the Police Executive Research Forum (PERF), a national organization of chief executives from municipal, county, and state law enforcement agencies, issued the report *Responding to Spouse Abuse and Wife Beating: A Guide for Police* after an intensive, year-long examination of the problem. PERF staff interviewed numerous police practitioners, lawyers, victim advocates, and service providers and scrutinized hundreds of documented cases from local police files and family court and district attorney records. The report concluded that a policy of arrest in all felony cases and misdemeanor cases involving serious injury or the threat of injury was appropriate and that such administrative action did not devalue the officer's discretion but, rather, professionalized and preserved it, by calling for individualized assessments in each case. The report offered guidance for developing policies and procedures for responding more effectively to woman battering and provided an outline for training seasoned officers and new recruits (Loving, 1980, pp. iv–v).

Between 1978 and 1982, the U.S. Commission on Civil Rights issued three formal reports on woman battering, each containing policy-relevant information for police. The Civil Rights Commission's authority to study and report on the problem of woman battering stemmed from its statutory mandate to investigate official patterns of denying equal protection of the laws based on age, race, or gender. The first report contained formal testimony, research, and position papers of recognized experts on the problem which were presented at a conference entitled "Battered Women: Issues of Public Policy," held in Washington, D.C., on January 30 and 31, 1978. Although no formal policy recommendations were made, the report contained persuasive evidence that the traditional police practices of nonintervention and arrest avoidance clearly denied equal protection of the laws to battered women, and it called for future study and research (U.S. Commission on Civil Rights, 1978, pp. 519–20).

The second report was directed specifically to police and contained findings of direct policy relevance, including the practice of arrest avoidance, inappropriate use of mediation and separation in lieu of arrest, and the tendency to rely on the victim to perform civilian arrests or pursue civil remedies.

The third report summarized the appropriate governmental response to domestic violence. In regard to the police response, the report concluded that "police discretion should be limited, with clear-cut guidelines for making arrests," that "arrests be made on the basis of the crime committed, regardless of the relationship of the abuser to the abused," and that "the police should be no less willing to arrest in domestic cases than in incidents with equivalent levels of violence between two strangers" (U.S. Commission on Civil Rights, 1982b, pp. 25–26).

In September 1984, U.S. Attorney General William French Smith released a report on family violence prepared by a specialized task force, appointed by President Ronald Reagan, and charged with identifying the scope of the problem in the United States and making suitable policy recommendations. This task force was created on the recommendation of the 1982 President's Task Force on Victims of Crime, which recognized violence in the family as a major social and criminal justice problem that must be addressed (President's Task Force on Victims of Crime, 1984, pp. 49–50). In its report, the task force recommended that this violence be recognized and treated as criminal activity by the justice system as a whole and that law enforcement officials, prosecutors, and judges develop a coordinated response to all forms of family violence, including wife battering, physical and sexual child abuse, and elder abuse (Attorney General's Task Force on Family Violence, 1984, p. 10). The task force specifically recommended that all law enforcement agencies publish operational procedures requiring that family violence be treated as a crime and establishing arrest as the preferred response.

In the preface of the report, Assistant U.S. Attorney General Lois Haight Harrington stated,

> Anyone who lives in a violent home experiences an essential loss. The one place on earth where they should feel safe and secure has instead become a place of danger. . . . These victims are uniquely isolated. . . . Reporting violence to authorities carries its own risks. All too often police, prosecutors or judges minimize or ignore the problem and the victim is left alone to face an attacker who may respond with anger at being reported. We as a nation can no longer allow these victims to suffer alone. (Attorney General's Task Force, 1984, pp. iii–iv)

After the task force report was released, the Bureau of Justice Statistics of the U.S. Department of Justice issued the first of a series of brief reports on the problem. The purpose of the reports was to provide relevant research and other state-of-the-art information to criminal justice practitioners for their use in structuring policy, training, and planning efforts. The first report, *Family Violence,* was compiled to support the work of the task force by bringing together available criminal justice data, specifically results from the National Crime Survey (NCS) (Klaus & Rand, 1984). Two years later, the report *Preventing Domestic Violence Against Women* was released, updating information from the NCS and summarizing the research experiments conducted in Kansas City and Minneapolis. The director of the National Institute of Justice, Steven R. Schlesinger, wrote,

> The main source of our fear is violent crime by strangers. But for a great many Americans, the source of their most intense fear is not crime by unknown attackers but crime by non-strangers, in particular, family members and close friends. . . . In many cases, they feel they have nowhere to go to feel safe and secure; all too often, they find a criminal justice system unresponsive to their pleas for help. (BJS, August 1986, p. 1)

Also in 1986, the Research in Brief *Confronting Domestic Violence: The Role of Criminal Court Judges* was published (The report was a summary of Goolkasian [1986a].) The report provided an overview of the criminal justice response to the problem, along with recommendations for improved practice for each area of the system: law enforcement, prosecution, and the judiciary. The author, Gail Goolkasian, wrote: "More and more justice officials are realizing that a domestic violence incident constitutes a crime and, as with other crimes, the responsibility for taking legal action against an offender should rest with the justice system rather than with the victim" (Goolkasian, November 1986b, p. 3).

In November 1986, the NIJ released the Research in Brief *Danger to Police in Domestic Disturbances—A New Look* which reported that although domestic violence incidents do pose a risk to officers, the actual danger to police in these cases was overstated and that in fact other police assignments were far more dangerous. The director, James K. Stewart, stated in the report that the information provided could contribute to informed policymaking by helping police chiefs revise and improve training for officers in how to deal with one of the most common calls they receive. He described the implications of this and other research on police responses:

> Many police departments are currently rethinking their approach to handling domestic violence cases. . . . By giving us new information on the limited threat to officers from domestic disturbances, the research reported here frees police managers to explore alternative ways to deal with those assignments that better meet the needs of the victims of such violence. (BJS, 1986, p. 1)

In 1990, the formal recommendation phase of the change process involving law enforcement culminated with the IACP's publication of a model police policy and concept paper on domestic violence (IACP, 1990, pp. 1–7). The background statement that prefaces the policy not only summarizes the reactive forces that led to its creation, but it also indicates how precise the recommendations to criminalize the problem had become:

> Greater public understanding and factors such as community concern, legislative initiatives, law enforcement research, and police liability have focused on the need for law enforcement agencies to intervene effectively in domestic violence incidents. Progressive police departments can no longer look on domestic violence as a "spat" or "quarrel" but, rather, as a criminal incident requiring arrest if probable cause and legal authority exist. A message must be sent to the offender that his violence will not be tolerated and that the police, not the victim, will initiate criminal action. (IACP, 1987, p. 1)

In retrospect, reactive criminalization efforts increased public awareness and stimulated changes in the law but did little to effect substantial changes in everyday law enforcement practices. A study by the Crime Control Institute found that in 1984, only 10 percent of the 146 large urban police departments surveyed had a proarrest policy for domestic assaults (Cohn & Sherman, 1987, p. 1). Although by 1987 the number of such policies had risen to 46 percent, the FBI reported that in this country a woman was beaten every fifteen seconds and that despite reform efforts, the incidence of woman battering seemed to be increasing, not decreasing (Law, 1991, p. 14). The most important impact of the reactive criminalization process was on the opportunities and tools created that could be used to foster proactive, planned change.

Proactive Criminalization as Planned Change

Criminalization is never the result of a pure "proactive" change process because it is generally motivated by diverse external pressures. When change involves a complex problem such as woman battering, the challenge of transforming these outside pressures into an internal, or proactive, desire for change is especially great. Effective planned change can best be achieved through the active participation of those who will be most affected by the change. All change, particularly sweeping changes in police response, are naturally resisted. In general, future behavior is best predicted by past behavior, and most members of an organization have a vested interest in the status quo. Change inherently triggers uncertainty and suspicion, particularly when it is associated with "outsiders." In regard to woman battering, the outsiders attempting to motivate change were necessarily critical of the status quo, and consequently, resistance became the norm for those targeted to change their behavior. For example, in those states where mandatory arrest laws for battering were enacted, the police found ways to sabotage the mandatory arrest policy by arresting both the perpetrator and the victim. Other departments adopted "paper policies" that were never enforced, and other actors in the criminal justice system also resisted the change by diverting cases to civil court, dismissing the charges, or refusing to issue orders of protection.

Although criminalization requires changes throughout the criminal justice system, for a variety of reasons, the police are often the focus of these changes. The role of police in the criminal justice system is unique. They are, in fact, the "gatekeepers" of the system, using their front-line discretionary power to define which behaviors require an official response. Thus, the police's interpretation of the law greatly determines the public perception of crime. The police act as both an arm of the public conscience and an educator of the community as to what is considered "actionable" criminal behavior. Their educational role in both the criminal justice system and the larger community cannot be underestimated. The police are also the most vulnerable to external pressures for criminalization—changes in the law, research, and, most important, civil liability.

To change law enforcement, the organizational varieties of police behavior must be taken into account. James Q. Wilson's (1978) study of the extent that variations in community structure influenced police practices led him to identify three primary varieties of police behavior. Which "style" of policing a particular department adopted was contingent on the nature of the local community. In large cities like Syracuse, New York, where a reformist government had recently emerged, Wilson found a "legalistic style" of policing that stressed law enforcement as the appropriate response to most disturbance situations. In smaller cities like Albany, where local governments were dominated by one-party, machine politics, he found a "watchman style" of policing that stressed handling most discretionary matters informally and avoiding arrest whenever possible. In small, homogeneous middle-class communities like Brighton, New York, a suburb of Rochester, Wilson found a "service style" of policing that stressed making referrals, performing public services unrelated to law enforcement, and responding to disturbances with counseling rather arrest. Compared with legalistic departments, service departments did not arrest as often, but compared with watchman departments, arrests were made relatively frequently.

In considering the police response to domestic violence, Wilson's study provides an interesting mechanism for applying an organizational context to the process of criminalization as planned change. In light of Lewin's work with force-field analysis, we could hypothesize that police agencies, regardless of their organizational style, would generally resist changing their response to woman battering. Furthermore, we could postulate that the organizational style and sociopolitical nature of the local community would influence the agency's receptivity to the planned-change process. Recognizing variations in police organizational styles would help in the critical identification of specific driving forces (allies of change) and resisting forces (obstacles to change) that exist in each organization and community (Toch & Grant, 1982, p. 138). This understanding is essential to the development of effective strategies for implementing change in individual police agencies. Moreover, these strategies must be developed with a recognition of the dynamics of the "interorganizational field," or the interactions among the many agencies in the community (Warren, 1978, pp. 269–73). In attempting to shift from a noninterventionist response to a proarrest policy, a "watchman-style" police agency, for example, would likely face numerous obstacles in its particular criminal justice community. These resisting forces must be identified for each department, not only to assist in the planned-change process, but also to promote the interorganizational changes necessary for effective criminalization.

In devising planned-change strategies for individual police departments, it must also be recognized that these agencies rarely have the same operational goals or the same standards for evaluating their activities. Departments differ because "different police chiefs rarely find a common forum within which to share information, develop productivity standards or define police roles" (Duffee, 1980, p. 107). To make the desired change in New York State, it was determined that such a "common forum" had to be found in order to maximize participation, to develop a consistent view of the problem, to determine appropriate policy responses, and to identify methods to evaluate the police's effectiveness.

The Political Interaction Model

Nakamura and Smallwood's (1980) "political interaction model" provided the method for structuring the planned-change experiences with police departments in New York State. This model rejects the classical administrative assumption that organizational change is most effectively imposed from the top down, with little or no participation by those most affected by the change. Traditional hierarchical views assume that the written policy is the ultimate goal for change and thus ignore the need to transform policy statements into predictable police practice. In contrast, Nakamura and Smallwood describe effective policymaking as cyclical, with three distinct yet interrelated processes: policy formulation, policy implementation, and policy evaluation, which are best viewed as overlapping circles (p. 27). Each "circle" represents a unique environment with distinct actors and activities. The "overlap" is the linkages or connections among these environments, reflecting communication and interaction among the key actors that tie the policy system together into an "interactional arena." This arena encompasses social rather than physical space, which "concerns itself with the systemic ways in which people and organizations interact within and across sectors of local concern" (Warren, 1978, p. 418). In regard to maximizing participation, the larger the interactional arena is, the more effective the policymaking process will be. This does not mean that all actors in the cyclical system must have equal power in order to dominate the process. But it does imply that the actors in any particular policy environment can significantly influence other actors in the planned-change process. Consequently, "the political and communications linkages that exist within and between the different environments and outside the system take on crucial importance" (Nakamura & Smallwood, 1980, pp. 27–28).

Environment I: Policy Formulation

The policy formulation environment is the most formally structured of the three, owing to its' focus on traditional policymaking. Its principal actors are legitimate policymakers such as police chiefs, who are authorized to assign priorities and commit resources within their organizations, and various special-interest groups from outside arenas, which use external pressure to influence the policymaking process. Special-interest groups that can influence police policy on woman battering include service providers, prosecutors, the U.S. Justice Department, police unions, and municipal insurance companies. The goal of the activities in this environment is to draft or revise departmental policy based on (1) a clear understanding of the problem of woman battering, (2) a recognition of the need to change organizational practices in relation to the problem, and (3) an awareness of the full scope of related interests that constitute the interactional field, both inside and outside the organization.

The New York State Police Policy and Training Project

In 1986, we, as staff and consultants to the Governor's Commission/Office, devised a three-part seminar for police executives, to help them draw up formal policies on woman battering. This seminar, cosponsored by the New York State Division of Criminal Justice Services and the state Sheriffs Association, provided a common forum in which a diverse set of participants[7] with similar policy concerns came together to consider objectively all the information relevant to making informed policy decisions. In the first phase of the seminar, the participants received information on the nature and dynamics of the problem, the reactive criminalization process, changes in the law, research findings on police responses, successful civil liability rulings involving the police, special interests that could affect police policies on woman battering, and different strategies for effecting intraorganizational and interorganizational change. The information exchange took place in an academic environment[8] that encouraged critical debate and discussion, thereby facilitating a greater understanding of and group investment in the policymaking process. Because of this experience, the participants moved from being passive reactors (change targets) to active leaders in the criminalization process (change agents). A change agent is "any individual or group from within or outside the organization whose role involves the stimulation, guidance or stabilization of change" (Swanson, Territo, & Taylor, 1988, p. 534). This transformation from target to agent is critical, since effective organizational change requires the identification of an internal change agent. This person should be in a respected position in the department, be familiar with both the formal and informal organization, and be aware of the potential sources of support and resistance to the change effort.

A unique aspect of New York's planned-change experience is the development of an ongoing partnership between the identified internal change agent and project staff (the external change agents).[9] This partnership responds to the concerns of depending solely on one person in the department who may not be accepted by peers as an "expert" on the problem and who is automatically in a position of continually balancing agency goals with the often negative complications brought on by the change. This partnership was promoted in a variety of ways, including having the project staff accompany the police on domestic calls and having the police attend local task force meetings held by service providers and victims' advocates. Such experiences helped narrow the gap that originally existed between the project staff and the police participants.

Another unique aspect of the New York experience was the three- to four-week interval between the first and second part of the policy formulation seminar. During this time, the participants returned to their local departments to draft their agency policy. The drafting process required obtaining input on the policy internally, from representatives of all levels of the organization, and externally, from domestic violence advocates in their community. The seminar participants thus enlarged their role as change agents by encouraging an active role by those that would be most affected by the proposed change. This information sharing also helped tailor the policy to meet the needs of the organization and the community. The participants met again for the second part of the seminar to share their experiences in the drafting process and to present their policies to the group. As a group, the members reviewed and critiqued each policy, arriving at an agreement on policy standards and goals and ultimately reaching a consensus on their responsibility in the criminalization process. Of the approximately 300 police departments that have participated in these policy formulation seminars to date, nearly all now have formal, written proarrest policies on woman battering. But translating that policy into practice is the next step that not all departments choose to take, although it is the critical phase of the policymaking process.

Environment II: Policy Implementation

Although a written policy on responding affirmatively to woman battering is a major objective of the New York State Project, the ultimate goal is the actual change in daily police practice. Policies must be implemented at all levels of the department as well as in the interorganizational field of action—specifically the criminal justice community. The policy must be understood and accepted by line officers and supervisors, as it is well recognized that in police agencies, discretion increases as one descends the hierarchical ladder. Even the most complete policy becomes impotent when not carried out by those charged with enforcing it. Beyond the policy formulation, therefore, is the need to bring as many people as possible, both inside and outside the organization, into the implementation circle.

The project experimented with a variety of strategies for expanding this circle. As expected, the "style" of the participating departments and their surrounding political cultures determined the policymaking process (Wilson, 1978, p. 233). Recognizing these styles helped both the external and internal change agents decide on the most potentially helpful mechanisms for change and identify the likely obstacles and supports for the policy.

All departments were expected to be resistant, but the overall style of the organization offered differing environments in which to promote change. In a "watchman" style department, for example, the style of policing is order maintenance for virtually all offenses, including domestic violence. Arrests are used as a last resort, and discretion is extremely broad. In order to criminalize domestic violence in these departments, the focus must be on obtaining strong support from the administration of the department and the local criminal justice community. Strategies for change in these departments can include meeting with the local district attorney and/or judges to gain their political support. In one department, the police chief called a televised press conference to announce the policy, along with the district attorney and judge—all publicly declaring that in that community. "If you hit a woman, you're going to jail."

It would appear that "legalistic" departments, which theoretically "enforce a single standard of community conduct" would be the most receptive to this change (Wilson, 1978, p. 172). Not necessarily. These departments operated under the same belief that domestic violence was not a crime but, rather, a private disturbance that was best dealt with informally so not to take too much time from responding to "real crime." The primary challenge here is to educate the police to the criminality of battering and the negative role it plays in relation to other offenses such as homicide, child abuse, and juvenile delinquency. The focus must be on equal protection of the law and the ability of the police to help prevent crime by arresting batterers. Ongoing departmental training at all levels is necessary to achieve this perceptual change. Participation by the local prosecutor in formulating and implementing policy in legal departments is extremely important, not only in a political sense (as in watchman communities), but also in the more concrete role of supporting the policy through the prosecution phase of the system.

"Service" style departments often serve homogeneous middle-class communities which may not be receptive to admitting to the problem of women battering. Even today, with all of the recent media attention to the problem of domestic violence resulting from the O.J. Simpson case and the greater intellectual understanding that domestic violence can occur in essentially any family, social class, or ethnic group, there remains the denial that someone like the bank president or our children's high school principal could be a batterer. These departments, therefore, tend to deal with domestic violence through the criminal justice system only when necessary to maintain order. In some cases, these departments became receptive to change only after the need for change was first recognized and supported by the local government. One strategy is to work through the municipality's insurance company or to obtain the support of the county executive, mayor, or district attorney. In the experience of this project, service-style departments are often one of the last in their communities to make formal changes, but once the policy is adopted, its implementation is taken relatively seriously.

Departmental style notwithstanding, a variety of implementation strategies have been put into action across the state. In one phase of the project, instructor development, or "train the trainer," courses are offered to certified police instructors. In New York State, as in many jurisdictions, police are solely responsible for training their colleagues. These trainers are expected to provide instruction in a multitude of topic areas, whether or not they are expert in them. Domestic violence is one such area in which many police trainers felt ill equipped. Particularly now that liability has become an issue for the police, possessing the most current information is a necessity. The project therefore includes a multiday class for police instructors for training on domestic violence. The credibility of the instructor development course is strengthened by its cosponsorship by the U.S. Department of Justice, which funded the project from 1990 to 1993; the New York State Bureau for Municipal Police, and the New York State Sheriffs Association. Participants are given a curriculum, a binder of materials, and two training videos. The information provided in the course is generally consistent with that offered in the policy development seminar, but the focus is on training design rather than policy formulation. When they return to their department to conduct in-service or basic recruit training, the participants are strongly encouraged to train as a team with a domestic violence advocate. This helps strengthen the link between the police and advocates and is most effective in bringing the most relevant information to the police.

In-service training for supervisors has also been found to be an important link between policy formulation and implementation. If the supervisors of a department do not support the policy change, there will be no change. These training courses have been conducted in a number of ways, with the staff of a single department, with supervisors from several departments in the same community, and with representatives from other agencies, such as victim services, district attorney, or probation, in attendance. These training programs are designed under the guidance of the internal change agent, who has the most insight into the workings of the formal and informal organization. Whenever possible, in-service training should be conducted off-site, so as to minimize interruption and maximize a sense of open-mindedness and professionalism on the part of participants. Supervisors as well as trainers and line personnel should be invited to question and critique the policy, and their suggestions should be welcomed by the administration. In our experience, the input from the supervisors, though not extensive, contributed significantly to the overall effectiveness of the change and to their feeling of "ownership" of the policy.

A variety of implementation strategies have been used in police agencies with all three organizational styles, including in-service training, meetings with prosecutors and judges, dispatcher training, press conferences and print-media press releases, and linkages between service providers and police. These strategies cannot be temporary, or the change will be temporary as well. Rather, the training must be updated each year, with written memoranda regularly issued. Communication must be ongoing with the other key members of the interorganization field, such as the district attorney, judges, other area police agencies, and, most important, local domestic violence advocates. Some of the more proactive police officials in the state have gone further and assumed leadership roles in the local domestic violence task force or coalition. Policies must be enforced internally as well. Officers who do not comply with the policy must consistently be held accountable, or the department's inaction will implicitly undermine even the best written policy. In sum, the status quo of the organization's core must change, which requires a continuing partnership between the external and the internal change agent, with the local battered women's advocate filling the role of the external motivator. As G. Patrick Gallagher, director of the Institute for Liability Management, noted, both personal and organizational change is the result of "gentle pressure, relentlessly applied."[10]

Environment III: Policy Evaluation and Assessment

In the nine years since the first policy formulation seminar, more than one-half the police departments in New York State have sent participants to the subsequent policy forums. But of the departments that attempted to implement their new policy through in-service training and other strategies, a significant number were unsuccessful. In addition, of those that did implement their policy, even a smaller percentage evaluated the outcome of the policy. When a policy was evaluated, it tended to be methodologically unsound, "success loaded," "failure-loaded," or incomplete, in part because there was little agreement on the definition of successful criminalization. But even if exceptionally proactive police departments consistently carried out the intent of their policies, would that be significant if battered women were still being discouraged by the prosecutor from going to criminal court or were unable to obtain orders of protection form the local family court? What if the victims were actually "less safe" than they had been when the police did not have a proarrest policy? Clearly, it is necessary to distinguish successful proactivity (making the changes for the long term) from merely initiating temporary changes or "paper changes" that barely make a ripple in the status quo. To make this distinction, the reasons that the policy failed (in formulation and implementation) must be considered and methods devised to assess the effectiveness of police and community responses to the crime of woman battering.

The three-environment "political interaction model" is a useful method for describing both policy failures and policy successes. Reactive policy failures generally occurred in the formulation environment. Some police officials were never convinced that they needed a proactive policy, and thus none was written, or "paper policies" were written but never implemented. Proactive failures generally occurred in the implementation environment. In 1980, Feeley and Sarat identified seven reasons that policy changes involving the police failed in the 1970s: (1) lack of coordination with other policies, (2) commitment of policy initiators to other incompatible policies, (3) the department's simultaneous commitment to "more important" programs, (4) lack of commitment by those entrusted to implement the change, (5) differences of opinion over how to administer particulars of the policy and accountability, (6) legal and procedural differences between new policies and ongoing programs, and (7) disagreement over policy goals. We found this typology to be still accurate in describing challenges to policy implementation from 1986 to the present. For example, a strong prior commitment by one police department to the use of crisis-intervention teams and mediation in family offense cases seriously limited the department's ability to implement a proactive arrest policy. In another department, a newly appointed chief, who had bypassed many of the older supervisors in the department for the position, knew that unless he could persuade these midlevel managers to support "his" policy change, the proposal was doomed to fail. In another department, an internal assessment of the policy revealed that one of the eight shift sergeants was not requiring his officers to complete the necessary crime reports. When the division lieutenant confronted the supervisor with the evidence and informed him that the other supervisors were indeed enforcing the new policy, he ultimately complied. According to the "political interaction paradigm," most of the implementation failures occurred because the internal change agent did not actively participate in both the formulation and implementation environments or was ineffective in expanding the involvement of relevant others in all three policymaking arenas.

The policies usually succeeded when there was maximum participation in their formulation, implementation, and evaluation stages, and when those who would be affected by the planned change were involved at some level in the change process. Swanson, Territo, and Taylor (1988, pp. 545–46) argued that successful organizational change generally includes a commitment by leadership to make the change, a thorough reexamination of past practices by all levels of the department, input from all levels into new practices and procedures, and consistent efforts to "spread" the change until it is permanently absorbed into the organization's way of life.

As more and more departments participated in the project, it became apparent that the definition of "success" was inconsistent and badly defined. Those police departments that had a written policy and attempted any of the implementation strategies often automatically assumed "success," even when battered women's advocates confronted them on their continued poor response to victims. Since the notion of success has been so unclear in this area, appropriately evaluating this change requires the development of assessment criteria to judge the effectiveness of policy outcomes as well as the overall community response.

Assessment strategies tend to be either quantitative or qualitative and generally try to measure changes in knowledge, attitudes, or performance. Quantitative assessments of domestic violence policies may include the number of reports to police, the percentage of arrests made in domestic cases, the number of referrals made by police for victim services, and the increase in number of training hours devoted to the problem. Evaluation plans that are purely quantitative are often narrow in focus and are conducted in isolation from the interorganization field, for example, the effects on battered women. In contrast, qualitative assessments take a more holistic approach, assessing the policy change in relation to a variety of factors, such as attitude change and increased knowledge through training and supervision. In addition, this approach examines the impact of the policy on the other actors in the criminal justice system and other related agencies, as well as the victims' perception of increased safety and system access. The most effective evaluation strategy contains both quantitative and qualitative measures that focus on the assessment of the internal policy implementation program and on the external, community-based, implementation process. Just as the other two policy environments require internal and external change agents, the ongoing evaluation phase must include objective assessments by victim advocates and battered women in addition to others in the community, such as the prosecutor or judge. Assessment must be built into the program from its inception by including those affected by the change in defining "success," again creating active agents from passive targets. This participation helps reduce the alienation often felt by those who fear that evaluation can detect only the negative (Toch, Grant, & Galvin, 1975, p. 3). An effective evaluation design must look at the positive factors as well as the problems, and all members of the organization should be made aware of these varied goals.

Although the police have been the major focus on this project, the overall goal is to promote a consistent, coordinated community response to victims of woman battering. Duffee (1980) suggested that when the community's response is the context for planned change involving criminal justice agencies, then measures of those community functions affected by the change, such as social control (crime prevention) and mutual support (services provided to victims), must become part of the assessment plan. This means examining the procedures of the interorganizational field such as prosecutor and probation policies, court-mandated programs for batterers, judicial sentencing trends, and family court intake proceedings. Furthermore, the community's response to domestic violence goes beyond the criminal justice system to include health care, social services, substance abuse, mental health, clergy, and other areas of the human service system—which battered women call on whether or not they seek help from the police. Most important, the impact of the police policy and the community's response must be evaluated in light of the ultimate goal—safety for victims of battering (Jones, 1994).

Although it is inaccurate to assume that having a proarrest policy will ensure the victims' safety, it is hoped that such a policy will not *increase* their danger. Although there is some disagreement as to whether arrest leads to more violence for unemployed batterers (Sherman et al., 1991), the concern for battered women's safety in light of these new policies is real. Since 1984, when such policies began proliferating, an increased number of victims began to feel that they now had more options to help them. More women began to make official reports of these crimes to the police—a 100 percent increase in New York State since 1983.

Despite these new policies, battered women continue to die: an average of four women each week in New York State alone. It is troubling that publicizing these policy "changes" will increase the battered woman's expectation of assistance when the actual level of change in the community is more modest. For example, victims may assume that the police will surely arrest their batterer when they call for help, though even in pro-arrest departments, the arrest rate for batterers is generally less than 30 percent of all domestic calls. And victims may assume that they can readily obtain an order of protection from the court, even though the process is extremely lengthy and arduous and many women are, understandably, discouraged from following through. And they may assume that their batterer will be held accountable for his violence, even though only a tiny percentage are actually convicted and an even smaller number are punished.

The question remains, then: Does the development of police policy reflect the achievement of criminalization? We think not. It seems clear from this project and the experiences in other states that the focus for further study must be on the interorganizational field and that it must assess changes in the community beyond law enforcement. Proactive police policies are an integral part of this change, but moving toward positive changes in response to domestic violence requires the coordination of the community, both inside and outside the criminal justice system, with agreement on all levels that the changes must take place. Success as it must be reframed, cannot be achieved until there is agreement that such violence will not be tolerated, that violent persons will be held accountable, and that the goal of safety for victims is paramount. Otherwise, as Edelman (1977) so aptly put it, we will be left only with "words that succeed and policies that fail."

Notes

1. Many police officers who were employed during the 1970s told us that they had had this experience.

2. Thirty-four members of the advisory board were appointed to the task force, from all geographic areas of the state, representing virtually all agencies or systems that were affected by the problem of domestic violence, including education, health care, alcoholism and other substance abuse, social services, labor, criminal justice, and the state legislature.

3. In New York State, "family offenses" are acts that would constitute disorderly conduct (not in a public place), harassment, aggravated harassment second degree, menacing, reckless endangerment, second- or third-degree assault, or attempted assault between spouses or former spouses, members of the same family, or persons who have a child in common, regardless of whether such persons have been married or lived together at any time (Fam. Ct. Act, Article 8, §812, 1990, 1994, 1995).

4. Many police in New York continue to be unaware of this change, however, as the penal law has not yet been modified to conform to case law.

5. Although information on this requirement had been communicated in writing to police chiefs in the state by the director of the State Division of Criminal Justice Services, in our experience, the police often failed to comply unless they were operating under a written policy on domestic violence.

6. For further discussion regarding a critique of the Minneapolis replication studies, see E. Stark, "Mandatory Arrest of Batterers," *American Behavioral Scientists,* May–June 1993, p. 651; and J. Zorza, "The Influence of Criminology on Criminal Law: Evaluating Arrests for Misdemeanor Domestic Violence." *Journal of Criminal Law and Criminology* 83 (Spring 1992): 46.

7. Participants in the original seminar included police executives from seventeen different departments, representing urban, suburban, and rural agencies from various geographic areas of New York State.

8. This seminar was offered on a local college campus in the capital district of New York State.

9. The project staff consisted of a male–female team of a college professor of criminal justice and a representative from the office. It was helpful to use a male–female team whenever possible and to balance the training among domestic violence, law enforcement, and policy development issues. Regional representatives from domestic violence victim services programs were also invited to attend and participate in the program, as should be the case in any local law enforcement training sessions.

10. Gallagher presented this insight during a workshop on liability management, sponsored by the U.S. Department of Justice, Office for Victims of Crime, September 5, 1991, in Washington, D.C.

References

Attorney General's Task Force on Family Violence. 1984. *Final Report.* Washington, D.C.: Department of Justice.

Alexander, F. 1985, July 17. "Municipal Negligence: Failure to Provide Police Protection." *New York Law Journal,* p. 17.

Bachman, R. 1994. *Violence Against Women: A National Crime Victimization Report.* Washington, D.C.: Bureau of Justice Statistics.

Beck, L. 1987. "Protecting Battered Women: A Proposal for Comprehensive Domestic Violence Legislation in New York." *Fordham Urban Law Journal* 15: 999–1048.

Beirne, P., and J. Messerschmidt. 1991. *Criminology.* San Diego: Harcourt Brace Jovanovich.

Berk, R., and P. Newton. 1985. "Does Arrest Really Deter Wife Battery? An Effort to Replicate the Findings of the Minneapolis Spouse Abuse Experiment." *American Sociological View* 50: 253–62.

Berk, R. 1994, Summer. "What the Scientific Evidence Shows: On Average, We Can Do No Better Than Arrest." *Domestic Violence Project Research Update.* pp. 1–4.

Buel, S. M. 1988, Spring. "Mandatory Arrest for Domestic Violence." *Harvard Women's Law Journal* 2: 213–26.

Bureau of Justice Statistics (BJS). 1986. *National Crime Survey.* Washington, D.C.: Department of Justice.

Bureau of Justice Statistics. 1988. *National Crime Survey.* Washington, D.C.: Department of Justice.

Bureau of Justice Statistics. 1991. *Violent Crime in the United States.* Washington, D.C.: Department of Justice.

Buzawa, E. S., and C. Buzawa. 1990. *Domestic Violence: The Criminal Justice Response.* Beverly Hills, Calif.: Sage.

Carrington, F. 1987, July "'Failure to Protect' Is Emerging Area of Liability." *Criminal Justice Digest* 1–5.

Carter, J., C. Heisler, and N. Lemon. 1991. *Domestic Violence: The Crucial Role of the Judge in Criminal Court Cases. A National Model for Judicial Education.* San Francisco: Family Violence Prevention Fund.

Cohn, E., and L. Sherman. 1987. "Police Policy on Domestic Violence, 1986: A National Survey." In *Crime Control Reports.* Washington, D.C.: Crime Control Research Corporation.

Community Council of Greater New York. 1988, August "Arrest and Domestic Violence: Trends in State Laws and Findings from Research." *Research Utilization Update,* pp. 1–9.

Dobash, R. E., and R. P. Dobash. 1979. *Violence Against Wives: A Case Against the Patriarchy.* New York: Free Press.

Duffee, D. 1980. *Explaining Criminal Justice.* Cambridge, Mass.: Oelgeschlager, Gunn & Hain.

Edelman, M. 1977. *Political Language: Words That Succeed and Policies That Fail.* New York: Academic Press.

Evans, M. 1987. "Domestic Violence: A Proactive Approach." *Virginia Police Journal.* Reprinted in *The Law Enforcement Response to Family Violence,* pp. 1–4. New York: Victims Services Agency.

Feeley, R., and L. Sarat. 1980. *The Policy Dilemma.* Minneapolis: University of Minnesota Press.

Fields, M. D. 1987, September. *Municipal Liability for Police Failure to Arrest in Domestic Violence Cases.* Albany: New York State Governor's Commission on Domestic Violence.

Fields, M. D. 1991, October. "Rape and Domestic Violence Legislation: Following or Leading Public Opinion?" Unpublished paper.

Frisch, L. 1992, Spring. "Research That Succeeds, Policies That Fail." *Journal of Criminal Law and Criminology* 83: 209–16.

Garner, J., and E. Clemmer. 1986. *Danger to Police in Domestic Disturbances—A New Look.* Washington, D.C.: National Institute of Justice.

Goolkasian, G. 1986a. *Confronting Domestic Violence: A Guide for Criminal Justice Agencies.* Washington, D.C.: National Institute of Justice.

Goolkasian, G. 1986b. *Confronting Domestic Violence: The Role of Criminal Court Judges.* Washington, D.C.: National Institute of Justice.

Gordon, L. 1988. *Heroes of Their Own Lives.* New York: Penguin Books.

Gundle, R. 1986, Fall. "Civil Liability for Police Failure to Arrest: Nearing v. Weaver." *Women's Rights Law Reporter* 9: 259–65.

Harlow, C. W. 1991, January. *Female Victims of Violent Crime.* Washington, D.C.: Department of Justice, NCJ-126826.

Hart, B., Stuehling, J. Stuehling, M. Reese, E. Stubbing. 1990. *Confronting Domestic Violence: Effective Police Response.* Reading: Pennsylvania Coalition Against Domestic Violence.

International Association of Chiefs of Police (IACP). 1976a. "Investigation of Wife-Beating." *Training Key 246.* Gaithersburg, Md.: IACP.

International Association of Chiefs of Police (IACP). 1976b. "Wife-Beating." *Training Key 245,* Gaithersburg, Md.: IACP.

Jones, A. 1994. *Next Time She'll Be Dead: Battering and How to Stop It.* Boston: Beacon Press.

Klaus, P., and M. Rand. 1984. *Family Violence.* Washington, D.C.: Bureau of Justice Statistics.

Langan, P., and C. Innes. 1986. *Preventing Domestic Violence Against Women.* Washington, D.C.: Bureau of Justice Statistics.

Law, S. 1991, Winter. "Every 18 Seconds a Woman Is Beaten: What Judges Can Do in the Face of This Carnage." *Judges' Journal,* pp. 12–15, 40–41.

Loving, N. 1980. *Responding to Spouse Abuse and Wife Beating: A Guide for Police.* Washington, D.C.: Police Executive Research Forum.

Martin, D. 1981. *Battered Wives.* New York: Simon and Schuster.

Nakamura, R., and F. Smallwood. 1980. *The Politics of Policy Implementation.* New York: St. Martin's Press.

National Woman Abuse Project. 1988, 1989, Fall–Winter. "Downplaying Domestic Violence May Result in Police Liability." *The Exchange,* p. 11.

Newman, D. J., and P. R. Anderson. 1989. *Introduction to Criminal Justice.* New York: Random House.

N.Y.S. Governor's Commission on Domestic Violence. 1988. *Domestic Violence: A Curriculum for Probation and Parole.* Albany: New York State Governor's Commission.

Pence, E., 1989. *The Justice System's Response to Domestic Violence.* Duluth: Minnesota Program Development.

Pennsylvania Attorney General's Task Force on Family Violence. 1989. *Domestic Violence: A Model Protocol for Police Response.* Harrisburg, Pa.: Office of the Attorney General.

Pleck, E. 1987. *Domestic Tyranny: The Making of American Social Policy Against Family Violence from Colonial Times to the Present.* New York: Oxford University Press.

Police Foundation. 1977. "Domestic Violence and the Police: Kansas City." In *Domestic Violence and the Police: Studies in Detroit and Kansas City,* pp. 22–33. Washington, D.C.: Police Foundation.

President's Task Force on Victims of Crime. 1984. *Final Report.* Washington, D.C.: Department of Justice.

Reynolds, G. 1987, April. "Men Who Abuse Women: When the Law Allowed Abuse." *Northeast Woman,* pp. 7–9, 35.

Rush, G. E. 1991. *The Dictionary of Criminal Justice,* 3rd ed. Guilford, Conn.: Dushkin.

Schechter, S. 1982. *Women and Male Violence: The Visions and Struggles of the Battered Women's Movement.* Boston: South End Press.

Sherman, L., J. Schmidt, D. Rogan, P. Gaiten, E. Cohn, D. Collins, and A. Bacich. 1991. "From Initial Deterrence to Long-Term Escalation: Short-Term Custody Arrest for Poverty Ghetto Domestic Violence." *Criminology* 29: 821–49.

Sherman, L., J. Schmidt, D. Rogan, D. Smith, P. Gartin, E. Cohn, D. Collins and A. Bacich. 1992. "The Variable Effects of Arrest on Criminal Careers: The Milwaukee Domestic Violence Experiment." *Journal of Criminal Law and Criminology* 83: 137–69.

Stark, E., and A. Flitcraft. 1988. "Violence Against Intimates: An Epidemological Review." In *Handbook of Family Violence,* ed. V. D. Van Hasselt, A. Bellack, and M. Hersen, pp. 159–99. New York: Plenum.

Steinman, M., ed. 1991. *Women Battering: Policy Responses.* Cincinnati: Anderson.

Swanson, C. R., L. Territo, and R. W. Taylor. 1988. *Police Administration Structures, Processes and Behavior,* 2nd ed. New York: Macmillan.

Toch, H., and J. Grant. 1982. *Reforming Human Services.* Beverly Hills, Calif.: Sage.

Toch, H., J. Grant, and R. Galvin. 1975. *Agents of Change: A Study in Police Reform.* Cambridge, Mass.: Schenkman.

U.S. Commission on Civil Rights. 1978. *Battered Women: Issues of Public Policy.* Washington, D.C.: U.S. Commission on Civil Rights.

U.S. Commission on Civil Rights. 1982a. *The Federal Response to Domestic Violence.* Washington, D.C.: U.S. Commission on Civil Rights.

U.S. Commission on Civil Rights. 1982b. *Under the Rule of Thumb: Battered Women and the Administration.* Washington, D.C.: U.S. Commission on Civil Rights.

Victim Services Agency. 1989. *The Law Enforcement Response to Family Violence: The Training Challenge.* New York: Victim Services Agency.

Walker, L. E. 1989. *Terrifying Love: Why Battered Women Kill and How Society Responds.* New York: Harper & Row.

Warren, R. L. 1978. *The Community in America,* 3rd ed. Chicago: Rand McNally.

Wilson, J. Q. 1978. *Varieties of Police Behavior.* Cambridge, Mass.: Harvard University Press.

Zorza, J., and L. Woods. 1994. *Mandatory Arrest: Problems and Possibilities.* New York: National Center on Women and Family Law.

9

Battered Women, Homicide, and the Legal System

Mindy B. Mechanic

In recent years, expert testimony on the battered woman syndrome, or BWS, (Walker, 1979, 1984b) has been offered to support self-defense claims made by battered women charged with the homicide of their abusers (Blackman, 1986; Ewing, 1987; Kinports, 1988; Walker, 1984b; Schneider, 1986).[1] The aim of expert testimony in battered women's homicide cases is to provide the jury with information about the nature of violent relationships and the psychological consequences resulting from repeated abuse. Specifically, expert testimony on battered woman syndrome is used to explain to the judge or jury how the experience of repeated abuse shaped a battered woman's perceptions and judgments, leading to her belief that she was at risk of imminent death or bodily injury (one of the requirements for self-defense), even though she might have committed the homicide at a time other than in the midst of a battering incident. The general purpose of expert testimony is to give jurors a cognitive schema or social framework (Walker & Monahan, 1987) within which complex and unfamiliar information can be organized, thereby placing the defendant's case within a larger theoretical framework (Blackman & Brickman, 1984).

Expert testimony on BWS was admitted for the first time in a battered woman's homicide case in 1977. According to the appeals court in this case, expert testimony on battered woman syndrome was admissible because it "supplied an interpretation of the facts which differed from ordinary lay perception advocated by the prosecution that the battered woman could have gotten out of the relationship" (*Ibn-Tamas* v. *United States* [1979]). Because potential jurors have been found to lack accurate knowledge about the dynamics of battering (Greene, Raitz, & Linbald, 1989); subscribe to myths and stereotypes of battered women (Ewing & Aubrey, 1987:

Gentemann, 1984; Saunders et al., 1987); sanction the use of violence against women (Greenblat, 1983, 1985); and blame the victim (Frieze, 1987; Kalmuss, 1979; Taylor, 1983), it has been argued that viable self-defense claims on behalf of battered women are compromised.

Galvanized by concerns that laypersons and legal professionals harbor myths about domestic violence and by allegations of gender bias throughout the legal system, a number of jurisdictions have begun to study gender bias in the courts. By 1989, twenty-seven states established task forces to study gender bias in the courts (Pagelow, 1992). The following passage from the Maryland Special Joint Committee on Gender Bias in the Courts (1989) illustrates the challenge facing battering women seeking legal justice:

> The reason I don't believe it is because I don't believe that anything like this could happen to me. If I was you and someone had threatened me with a gun, there is no way that I would continue to stay with them. . . . Therefore, since I would not let that happen to me, I can't believe that it happened to you.

Amid the backdrop of alleged sex bias and lack of understanding, expert testimony on behalf of battered women who killed their abusers has been introduced in an attempt to combat the self-referential, victim-blaming reasoning implicit in the passage just quoted. Questions remain however, about whether and in what ways expert testimony meets this formidable challenge. This chapter describes some of the work that has been done on the use of expert testimony on battered woman syndrome in battered women's homicide cases. First, background information on rates of spousal violence will be presented, followed by discussion of the following topics: gender patterns in homicide, spousal homicide research, and data on battered women who have killed their abusive mates. Next, the myriad legal issues involved in battered women's homicide cases will be tackled, including legal dispositions in battered women's homicide cases, the admissibility of expert testimony, the content and impact of BWS expert testimony, the relationship between battered woman syndrome and posttraumatic stress disorder, juror understanding of battering, and experimental research on the impact of expert testimony on battered woman syndrome. The final section will conclude with a description of recent legislative changes limiting judicial discretion over whether expert testimony is permitted in battered women's criminal cases. With a focus on future, the chapter will close with thoughts and suggestions about battered women facing the legal system.

Rates of Spousal Violence

Research documenting spousal violence[2] has been limited by methodological problems, including the use of restricted samples such as hospital emergency rooms (e.g., Stark, Flitcraft, & Frazier, 1979), community mental health centers (e.g., Rounsaville, 1978), and police reports (e.g., Levens & Dutton, 1980, cited in Dutton, 1988). Epidemiological surveys of large national samples provide more accurate estimates of intimate violence in the general population. However, due to the sensitive nature of questions on this topic and social desirability, bias, it is likely that results of large-scale surveys also underestimate the true extent of the problem.

Recent estimates of spousal violence in a current relationship (obtained using the Conflict Tactics Scale [CTS]: Straus, Gelles, & Steinmetz, 1980) ranged from 21 percent in a Kentucky survey (Schulman, 1979) to 27.8 percent in a large national survey (Straus et al., 1980) and 27.4 percent in a midwestern community survey (Clarke, unpublished data). Sixteen percent of the respondents in the Straus study reported violence during the year before the study. Moreover, severe violence (those actions with the greatest potential for physical injury) was estimated to occur at rates of 8.7 percent (Schulman, 1979), 10.2 percent (Clarke, unpublished data), and 12.9 percent (Straus et al., 1980). Several limitations of these studies are important to note. First, because the Straus et al. national study used only intact married couples as respondents and other researchers had documented extremely high rates of violence in separated and divorced couples (Browne, 1987; BJS, 1991a; Schulman, 1979), the rates obtained by Straus et al. are lower than would be expected if nonintact couples had also been included. Second, the method used to assess violence failed to account for the motives and consequences of the battering incidents, resulting in prevalence estimates that do not reflect the context in which battering incidents might be understood (e.g., self-defense). Although, there are other methodological problems associated with the CTS, a detailed discussion of them is beyond the scope of this chapter. In spite of methodological shortcomings, it is evident that spousal violence is a problem of substantial proportions.

Gender Issues in Female Homicide

The role of gender in homicide patterns was explored in a recent study comparing theoretical models of female criminality (Jurik & Winn, 1990). Using official court reports (presentence investigations), Jurik and Winn compared a sample of males ($n = 108$) with the total population of females ($n = 50$) initially charged with a nonnegligent manslaughter or murder and convicted of that or a lesser charge, from 1979 to 1984 in Maricopa County, Arizona. Convicted male and female offenders were compared on five dimensions thought to be relevant to gender patterns in homicide: (1) the demographics of the offender, especially race; (2) the location of the offense; (3) the relationship between the victim and the offender; (4) the situational dynamics, including the motivation for the homicide; and (5) the method and style of inflicting injury. In a logistic regression analysis using these five predictors, all the hypothesized variables except the method of inflicting injury significantly predicted the sex of the offender. Females were more likely than males to kill in an interpersonal context in which the victim initiated the violent encounter leading to the homicide. The victims of female homicide offenders tended to be male romantic partners on whom the women depended for economic survival. In contrast, the homicides committed by males resulted from violence initiated by the male perpetrators themselves. Previous conflicts with the victim in male-perpetrated homicides had been relatively infrequent and generally did not involve physical aggression. Males were also more likely to kill strangers or acquaintances instead of intimates. Guns were the weapon of choice for more than half the offenders of both sexes. These data are consistent with other data (described later) that highlight the self-defensive nature of female perpetrated homicides.

Spousal Homicide

Although most incidents of spousal assault do not culminate in homicide, data for the year 1991 indicate that almost 2,000 deaths resulted from homicide between intimate partners (U.S. Department of Justice, 1991). Of those, slightly more than two-thirds were women killed by male partners, and the remaining 30 percent were males killed by female partners. As already pointed out, the general pattern observed in homicide research suggests that victims of female-perpetrated homicides tend to be male romantic partners, whereas victims of male-perpetrated homicides are usually strangers or acquaintances (Browne & Williams, 1989; Jurik & Winn, 1990).

The self-defensive nature of homicides committed by women against the men who abused them is particularly important to understand in light of recent legal cases arguing that battered women's lethal actions against their abusers are often instances of legally justifiable homicide (Bochnak, 1981; Gillespie, 1989; Kinports, 1988; Schneider, 1986). Self-defense arguments on behalf of battered women are often advanced despite fact patterns that do not parallel the requisite elements of traditional self-defense law (Blackman, 1986; Ewing, 1987; Gillespie, 1989; Walker, Thyfault, & Browne, 1982). For example, a woman strikes her sleeping husband (issue of imminence), or she attacks an unarmed spouse with a lethal weapon (issue of equal force). The legal requirements of traditional self-defense doctrine are discussed later in this chapter.

Self-Defensive Actions by Women Versus Those by Men

In a classic paper, Wolfgang (1967) advanced the notion of "victim-precipitated homicide" to explain the phenomenon in which homicide victims contributed to their own deaths by being the first one in the lethal encounter to use violence or threats of violence. In his study, 60 percent of husbands who were killed by their wives brought about their own deaths by striking out first. This contrasts with the 9 percent of wives killed after striking out first against their husbands. Further support for the notion that women are less likely than men are to initiate an unprovoked homicide comes from data reviewed by Browne (1987), who stated: "Women don't usually kill other people; they perpetrate less than 15 percent of the homicides in the United States. When women do kill, it is often in their own defense. . . . [H]omicides committed by women were seven times as likely to be in self-defense as homicides committed by men" (p. 10). Moreover, data collected from women incarcerated in state and federal prisons indicate that among those inmates reporting a history of abuse, 32 percent were serving sentences for killing a relative or intimate partner (BJS, 1991b). Clearly, there is a link between prior abuse and homicide by battered women in at least some cases.

In a study designed to clarify the motives (defending self, initiating, and fighting back) of battered women who used severe and nonsevere violence against their abusers, the findings showed that women perceived their actions to be motivated by either self-defense or fighting back (Saunders, 1986). Interestingly, many of the women in this study perceived self-defense and fighting back to be essentially equivalent. Social desirability (as measured by the Crowne–Marlowe Social Desirability Scale) was not related to five of the six categories of motive for violence, and in the sixth case (fighting back with severe violence) the relationship was in the unexpected direction; that is, social desirability was related to reports of fighting back with severe violence. The self-report nature of the data and the use of subjects recruited from battered women's shelters and a counseling agency limit the study's generalizability.

These findings, in conjunction with other research (Chimbos, 1978; Daniel & Harris, 1982; Saunders, 1986; Totman, 1978; Wilbanks, 1983a, 1983b; Wolfgang, 1958, 1967), have been used to argue that female-perpetrated homicides tend to be self-defensive acts committed in an interpersonal context, rather than instrumental acts of violence. Despite the variety of methodological approaches used to study gender issues in homicide, several trends seem to emerge. First, in contrast to homicides committed by males and property crimes committed by females, the rate of violent crime committed by women has remained relatively stable over time (Simon & Landis, 1991). Second, it appears that female-perpetrated homicides differ from those committed by men, not only in number, but also in context. Most notable is the interpersonal context and the precipitation by the victim frequently observed in homicides committed by females.

Battered Women Who Strike Back

Several researchers have suggested that when battered women do strike back against their abusers, lethal incidents are the "final chapter in a history of physical abuse" (Thyfault, Bennett, & Hirschorn, 1987, p. 72; see generally Browne, 1987). In these cases, multiple attempts to receive assistance were made from various sources, including family, mental health professionals, and the police, before the final lethal incident (Browne, 1987; Browne & Williams, 1989; Lindsey, 1978; Thyfault et al., 1987). Contrary to the stereotypes that battered women are unwilling or unable to seek help, in a large-scale study of battered women seeking shelter services throughout Texas, Gondolf and Fisher (1988) found that battered women tended to be active help seekers and that their efforts to obtain help increased as their batterers became more dangerous. Bowker's (1983) research also supports the view of battered women as active help seekers who use both formal and informal sources of support. However, active help-seeking behavior is undermined when the potential sources of help are unresponsive or negative, thereby reinforcing the belief that help or escape from a violent relationship is not possible. When these messages come from officially designated sources of help, such as the police, the impact can be lethal.

In a 1976 study of women incarcerated for the murder or manslaughter of their partners, 40 percent reported a previous history of abuse by that partner. In addition, those women who killed abusive partners indicated that they called the police for help at least five times before the final lethal incident and that the abuse from their mates worsened after these attempts to solicit police intervention (Lindsey, 1978). Multiple calls to the police were also made by the battered women in Browne's (1987) study. In another study of police records in domestic homicide cases in two cities, police had responded to the home of the parties at least once in the two years before the homicide in 85 percent of the cases and at least five times in slightly more than half the cases (Police Foundation, 1976). The homicide victim in most of the cases was the battered woman. The absence of earlier effective assistance may have contributed to the escalation of battering incidents to the point of partner homicide.

The failure of the police to respond effectively to domestic violence situations is well documented (Dutton, 1987; Goolkasian, 1986; Waits, 1985) and has been attributed to (1) inappropriate goals of the criminal justice system, such as reconciliation rather than arrest (Waits, 1985); (2) deference to family privacy (Soler, 1987; Waits, 1985); (3) the perception of wife abuse as a victimless crime (Dobash & Dobash, 1978; Waits, 1985); (4) the inability of legal institutions to combat complex social problems (Waits, 1985); (5) fear that the arrest of the batterer will precipitate further violence (Lerman, 1982; Waits, 1985); and (6) the lack of knowledge about the prevalence, seriousness, and patterns of battering (Frieze & Browne, 1989; Dutton & McGregor, 1992). According to Soler (1987), "[T]his stance of nonintervention indirectly condones violence and ignores the frequent escalation that all too often ends in homicide" (p. 21). The long-standing reluctance of the criminal justice system to respond effectively to domestic violence has resulted in at least two successful class-action lawsuits (*Bruno* v. *Codd* [1979]; *Scott* v. *Hart* [1976]) mandating more effective legal intervention on behalf of battered women. Such strategies may serve a preventive function by reducing the number of spousal violence cases culminating in homicide.

Support for the preventive function of legal and extralegal resources for battered women comes from the work of Browne and Williams (1989), who evaluated patterns of partner homicide committed by males and females as a function of the increased availability of resources (e.g., domestic violence legislation, shelters) for battered women. Using states as the level of analysis for the years 1980 to 1984, as contrasted with the period from 1976 to 1979, lower rates of female-, but not male-perpetrated, partner homicide were reported in states with domestic violence legislation and other resources for battered women. Browne and Williams argued that the availability of resources for battered women serves important symbolic and practical functions by promoting the social condemnation of battering and by making people aware that alternatives to remaining in violent relationships do exist.

Research on Battered Women Who Killed Their Abusers

According to the National Clearinghouse for the Defense of Battered Women, approximately 750 cases of partner homicide are committed by battered women each year (Trafford, 1991). With the goal of understanding more about the dynamics of battering relationships that culminate in the death of the abuser, Browne (1987) studied forty-two battered women charged with the murder or attempted murder of their abusive partners (the homicide group), compared with 205 battered women who had been in abusive relationships but did not commit acts of violence against their abusive partners (the control group). The women in the homicide group did not have a history of violence, and consistent differences between the two groups on background characteristics were not observed.[3] The differences that were found pertained to the behavior of the men and the escalation of violence in the relationships. The following characteristics distinguished the men in the homicide group from those in the comparison group: (1) more frequent substance abuse and intoxication, (2) a greater number of threats to harm or kill someone, (3) more assaultive behavior, (4) physical abuse of the children in the home, (5) more frequent assaults of their mates, (6) more injurious consequences resulting from assaults, and (7) an increased likelihood of sexually assaulting their mates.[4]

The violence reported by the women in the homicide group became more frequent and more severe over time, leading to major shifts in the women's behavior, from trying to understand and help their mates to developing strategies enabling them to survive the violence. Although many did try to leave their mates, these women were frequently hunted down and beaten or threatened into returning to their abusers (see also Walker et al., 1982). The escalation of violence in these relationships was reported to reach the point that the women believed their own deaths were inevitable. Fagan (1988) states: "They faced the worst of all Hobson's choices: stay and be killed, leave and be killed, or kill" (p. 172). In explaining the final lethal incident, the women in the homicide group described the last battering incident as far more severe and out of the range of violence that they had previously experienced, resulting in the woman taking an aggressive stance to protect herself and/or her children from harm. Most homicides occurred (1) during the threat but before the attack, (2) during a battering incident, or (3) in the midst of an attempt to escape. Similarly, Ewing (1985) noted that in a sample of eighty-five cases in which a battered women killed her abuser, only one-third of the homicides were committed during the battering incident, whereas two-thirds of the homicides were committed after a battering incident (a substantial number occurred while the batterer was asleep). As will be seen, the context of the homicide, including the timing of the act relative to the abusive incident, plays a critical role in the successful application of a self-defense strategy.

Legal Disposition of Battered Women Who Killed Their Abusers

In Browne's (1987) study, 56 percent of the women in the homicide group went to trial on the basis of a self-defense plea (33 percent pleaded guilty to a reduced charge in exchange for a promise of leniency in sentencing; 8 percent entered a plea of insanity or diminished capacity; the charges were dropped in one case, and self-defense arguments were rejected by the court in another case). Dispositions in the cases that went to trial were as follows: (1) Almost 50 percent received jail or prison sentences (ranging from six months to twenty-five years and, one case, fifty years); (2) 30 percent received either probation or a suspended sentence; (3) 20 percent were acquitted; and (4) the charges were dropped in one case. Ewing (1985) examined the details of eighty-five cases in which a battered woman killed her abuser. In his sample, 86 percent of the women took their cases to trial on the basis of self-defense. The dispositions were as follows: Seventy-four percent were convicted on various charges (of this group, 81 percent received sentences ranging from four years' probation to twenty-five years in prison, and 19 percent received life sentences), and the remaining 26 percent were acquitted. Based on her experience with more than 150 battered women's homicide cases, Walker (1990) reported an acquittal rate of approximately 25 percent. Despite media reports suggesting that battered women are "getting away with murder" (e.g., *Time,* November 28, 1977), these women were not subjected to exceptionally lenient treatment by the courts. Schneider and Jordan (1981) observed, that when battered women are convicted of killing their mates, they receive stiffer sentences than do men convicted of killing their female partners. In response to the high rates of conviction and severe sentences imposed on these women, Fagan (1988) commented: "Although women are the majority of victims in family violence, it is the woman who kills her husband who gets public attention and who is subject to the full force of the law" (p. 171).

Admissibility of Expert Testimony

The admissibility of expert testimony is predicated on legal standards that generally require that the testimony be "beyond the ken of the average layman" (Dyas, 1977) or that it "assist the trier of fact to understand the evidence or determine a fact in issue" (Rule 702, FRE, 1984).[5] Although the trend in admissibility rulings has been in direction of accepting expert testimony on the battered woman syndrome (for a list of cases, see Kinports, 1988), a review of admissibility rulings in sixteen states described three patterns of state rulings (Coffee, 1986–1987). Approximately 44 percent of those states admitted the testimony unconditionally, and 31 percent of the states admitted the testimony because criteria other than "beyond the ken" were satisfied. One-fourth of the states surveyed ruled against admissibility, generally on the grounds that the content of such testimony was within the province of a jury's understanding, thereby making it superfluous, or that such testimony would be unlikely to aid the jury's understanding. One New York court, for example (*People v. Torres* [1985]), issued a ruling supporting expert testimony on the grounds that most laypersons accept many myths and misconceptions regarding the behavior of victims of spousal violence. Acker and Toch (1985) argued for the exclusion of expert testimony based on their assumption that knowledge of the dynamics and consequences of violence is available to most laypersons. They based their position on the following points: (1) Because of the increasing rates of marital discord leading to divorce and separation, most people are familiar with domestic problems; and (2) because half the population is female, they are informed about the obstacles facing battered women who try to leave an abusive relationship. This is a clear example of an inferential leap based on specious assumptions. Melton (1984) similarly documented numerous examples of erroneous judicial assumptions about the "psychology of family life."

In sum, there is inconsistency in terms of both admissibility rulings and what is considered to lie within (or beyond) the understanding of jurors, even though the general trend has been to support the admission of expert testimony. Even rulings that unconditionally accept the admission of expert testimony seem to do so on the assumption that jurors are uninformed and that they believe the myths and misinformation about battered women. Empirical data showing the patterns and correlates of juror understanding of battering might help clarify this divisive issue.

Jurors' Common Understanding

The belief that laypersons endorse many myths and misconceptions about the dynamics and consequences of battering relationships has been addressed descriptively and anecdotally by several researchers (e.g., Martin, 1976; Pagelow, 1981; Walker, 1979). Using various survey and vignette methodologies, several studies report on attitudes toward battering (e.g., Ewing & Aubrey, 1987; Gentemann, 1984; Koski & Mangold, 1988). Only one published paper, however, reported on the development of a psychometrically reliable instrument to assess attitudes and beliefs about wife beating (Saunders et al., 1987). The authors of this paper offered evidence of this instrument's construct validity, although a large-scale community evaluation using the instrument has not yet been done. An examination of convergent validity demonstrated the relationship between attitudes toward wife beating and attitudes toward women and traditional sex-role stereotypes. Females presented more sympathetic attitudes toward wife beating than males did (Saunders et al., 1987). The instrument developed by Saunders and colleagues has a number of desirable properties, although it does not contain any items reflecting a knowledge of wife battering, thus resulting in a scale tapping predominantly attitudes and beliefs. Although this is useful in its own right, it is likely that the construct of jurors' understanding is not limited to attitudinal dimensions.

Greene, Raitz, and Linblad (1989) used an experimental design in two studies with a vignette methodology to assess lay knowledge of battering. In the first study, prospective jurors were asked to read a 300-word vignette describing a typical relationship involving battering. Next, the subjects were asked about the extent of their agreement with each of twelve statements about battering derived from the available research literature—for example, self-blame by battered women, feelings of helplessness, and potential for future relationship violence. The results indicated that jurors were informed about some, but not all, aspects of battering. In the second study, the socioeconomic status (SES) and age of the prototypical couple in the written vignettes were manipulated, and subjects were asked about the extent of their agreement with the same twelve statements. No differences were found for the manipulated differences in the age of the couple. But the SES did have an impact, in that the research findings were seen as fitting the low, but not the high, SES couple in the vignette. This suggests that jurors may be using SES as a schema within which their assumptions about domestic violence are organized. In subsequent work, Dodge and Greene (1991) administered their knowledge questionnaire to a group of experts in the field of domestic violence. They discovered differences between the expert and lay samples, with the experts less likely than the nonexperts to view battered women as masochistic or emotionally disturbed.

Overall, the research suggests that jurors are knowledgeable about some, but not all, aspects of battering. Moreover, the studies to date have examined either attitudes toward or knowledge about battering. Because juror understanding is probably composed of a combination of attitudes and knowledge, it might be profitable for future work to evaluate the complex interrelationships between knowledge and attitudes in lay and expert samples. This may eventually help target both large-scale educational interventions and expert testimony in accordance with the attitudes and knowledge of prospective jurors.

Legal Strategies Used on Behalf of Battered Women Who Killed Their Abuser

Self-Defense Theory

Increasingly, battered women who killed their abuser are contending that the homicide they committed was justified by self-defense. Traditionally, if one does not initiate an attack, the use of self-defensive force requires a reasonable belief that the risk of death or serious bodily injury is imminent and that the use of such force is necessary to avoid this harm (see, generally, LaFave & Scott, 1986). In addition, only a reasonable amount of force can be used to repel an attack. Justifiable use of force requires that at the time of the assault these beliefs must be either honest (as in the subjective standard used in the Model Penal Code and adopted by a minority of states) or honest and reasonable (a combination of subjective and objective standards used in most jurisdictions), although they may turn out later to be erroneous (described in Kinports, 1988). According to Kinports (1988):

> When self-defense is defined to include an objective component, courts typically instruct the jury to analyze whether a reasonable person would have felt the need to use self-defense under the same circumstances. The jurisdictions that purport to apply an entirely subjective standard of self-defense use a similar instruction: in order to acquit on grounds of self-defense, the trier of fact must find that a reasonable person in the same situation, seeing what the defendant saw and knowing what she knew, would have resorted to self-defense. (p. 318)

The subjective and objective standards differ in the extent to which the defendant's unique perception is introduced into the evaluation of her self-defensive actions (Kinports, 1988).

Expert Testimony on Battered Woman Syndrome

Defense strategies on behalf of battered women who killed their abuser frequently include attempts to introduce expert testimony on battered woman syndrome to explain how the experience of repeated violence shaped the batter woman's perceptions and judgments, leading to the perception that she was at risk of imminent death or bodily injury, even though she might have committed the homicide at a time other than in the midst of an attack. Applying self-defense theory to cases in which the battered woman killed her abuser in the midst of an attack poses fewer problems because the cases more closely parallel the requirements of traditional self-defense doctrine.

According to Blackman (1986), a psychologist and experienced expert witness on this topic,

> Expert testimony on the battered woman syndrome details psychological traits that typify battered women and their perceptions of the potential dangerousness of the abuser's violence. The components of the syndrome and the process by which violent acts become known as typical or atypical are elucidated. Illustrative examples from a particular defendant's experiences are then related to these models. (p. 228)

Blackman then describes three categories of behavioral change seen in battered women (relevant to their difficulty in leaving the abusive relationship) and a fourth characteristic pertaining to their increased ability to discern cues of violence from their mates that help explain the women's subjective perceptions of danger. These elements of expert testimony on the subject of battered woman syndrome are described in the next section.

Blackman first describes Walker's (1979, 1984a) application of the learned helplessness model to battered women, showing how repeated battering leads to isolation, shame, fear, and a diminished ability to leave the abusive relationship.[6] Second, the concept labeled "high tolerance for cognitive inconsistency" is invoked to explain contradictions or inconsistencies noted in battered women's descriptions (e.g., a report that the mate is abusive only when drunk, followed by a subsequent report of a battering incident that occurred when the mate was sober). According to Blackman (1986),

> this tolerance for inconsistency grows out of the fundamental inconsistency of a battered woman's life that the man who supposedly loves her also hurts her . . . (such contradictions) may be interpreted as signs of a generally poor memory or of a bungled attempt to be deceptive . . . these inconsistencies in no way serve the battered woman's legal interest and are best understood as the results of her efforts to make sense out of an inherently senseless situation. (p. 229)

Third, Blackman explains the battered woman's perception that her options are limited. Because battered women frequently believe that escape is impossible, their focus remains on developing strategies that will enable them to survive (or cope with) the violence. The women's perception that escape from the abuse is impossible may have been reinforced by ill-fated attempts to escape or receive help from friends, family, police, or other social service agencies (Bowker, 1983; Browne, 1987). Thus although a nonbattered individual may be able to perceive options available to the battered woman that would enable her to leave the situation, repeated victimization alters these perceptions, resulting in a complete failure to perceive any options at all or a belief that alternatives are not available to her.

Fourth, as a result of having survived repeated instances of victimization and abuse, battered women develop an enhanced acuity enabling them to detect minute deviations from their mate's typical pattern of violence. Blackman (1986) took this point further:

> For battered women, this response to the ongoing violence is a survival skill . . . they know what sorts of danger are familiar and which are novel. They have had myriad opportunities to develop and hone their perceptions of their partner's violence. And, importantly, they can say what made the final episode of violence different from the others: they can name the features of the last battering episode that enable them to know that this episode would result in life-threatening action by the abuser. (p. 229)

Although these three characteristics might be described as deficits, this enhanced perceptual acuity has been labeled an adaptive survival skill (Schneider, 1986).

The content of expert testimony in battered women's self-defense cases varies along several dimensions, depending on the particular expert's training and the basis for the admissibility ruling (Blackman & Brickman, 1984). Blackman and Brickman offered five dimensions along which this type of expert testimony varies: (1) reliance on empirical findings, (2) use of a theoretical framework to explain why battered women remain in abusive relationships (e.g., learned helplessness), (3) level of detail reported in describing the relationship between the battered woman syndrome and the life history of the defendant on trial, (4) recapitulation of the defendant's "story" by the expert, and (5) debunking of common myths and stereotypes regarding battered women (e.g., they remain in abusive relationships because they are masochistic and enjoy the abuse). Depending on the jurisdiction, the expert may be allowed to testify only about the research findings on battered women in general (including myths and stereotypes regarding battering) but not specifically about the defendant herself. In those cases, jurors must decide whether the defendant fits the depiction of battered women portrayed by the expert. In other jurisdictions, the expert is permitted to present not only the general research findings but also his or her clinical evaluation of the defendant, which frequently includes a statement to the effect that the defendant's behavior is consistent with BWS.

Posttraumatic Stress Disorder

From a clinical or diagnostic perspective, battered woman syndrome has been described as a subcategory of posttraumatic stress disorder (PTSD) (Douglas, 1987; Walker, 1984b). PTSD is a formally recognized diagnostic entity, whereas BWS is not specifically identified in the official diagnostic classification system, the *Diagnostic and Statistical Manual of Mental Disorders,* fourth edition (*DSM*-4) (American Psychiatric Association, 1994). PTSD is observed in some people who have been exposed to traumatic events including, but not limited to, combat, criminal victimization, hostage taking, and natural or human-made disasters. Not all individuals exposed to a traumatic event meet the diagnostic criteria for PTSD (e.g., Kilpatrick & Resnick, 1993; Norris, 1992). Physical assault and rape are among the traumatic events most likely to result in PTSD in women (Norris, 1992; Resnick et al., 1993). Rates of PTSD are much lower in response to noncrime traumatic events, such as accidents or disasters (Norris, 1992; Resnick et al., 1993). Among the risk factors most consistently identified for the development of PTSD are the perception of life threat and/or injury during the trauma and high levels of exposure to the trauma (e.g., Kilpatrick & Resnick, 1993; Kilpatrick et al., 1989; Cascardi, Riggs, et al., 1993; Resnick et al., 1993; Riggs et al., 1991).[7] The identification of these factors as increasing one's risk for developing PTSD is consistent across various types of traumatic events, for example, combat (Gallers et al., 1988), childhood sexual abuse (see Rowan & Foy, 1993, for a review of PTSD in child sexual abuse survivors), rape (Kilpatrick et al., 1989; Neumann, Gallers, & Foy, 1989), and domestic violence (Astin, Lawence, & Foy, 1993; Cascardi, O'Leary, et al., 1993). Repeated victimization has also been identified as a risk factor contributing to the likelihood of developing PTSD, particularly an unremitting, chronic course of PTSD (Norris & Kaniasty, 1994). This finding is important with respect to battered women because of their high frequency of exposure to repeated incidents of violence that tend to increase in frequency and severity over time (e.g., Walker, 1984a).

Battered Women and PTSD

Several studies examined the prevalence of PTSD in battered women. Housekamp and Foy (1991), Astin and associates (1993), and Dutton-Douglas (1992) found PTSD rates of 44 percent, 45 percent, and 40 percent, respectively, in samples of battered women. Kemp, Rawlings, and Green (1991) found a much higher rate of PTSD (85 percent) in their sample of battered women seeking services at a shelter. The lowest rates of PTSD (33 percent) were reported in a sample of battered women seeking treatment for martial therapy for physical aggression in marriage (Cascardi et al., 1993). Both the Astin (1993) and the Cascardi, O'Leary, et al. (1993) studies detected a significant association between higher levels of exposure to violence and increased rates of PTSD.[8] Overall, the differences in the sampling approaches, diagnostic measures, and assessment of trauma exposure in these studies probably account for the varying rates of PTSD reported.

Although Browne (1987) did not specifically evaluate PTSD in her sample, there is a stunning similarity between the relationship violence reported by the battered women with PTSD in the Cascardi et al. study and the relationship violence described by the women in Browne's study who eventually killed their abusers. In the Cascardi et al. study, the battered women with PTSD (compared with the battered women without PTSD) reported (1) more fear of their spouses, including a fear of what they might do; (2) more severe injuries; (3) more coercive behavior by their spouses; and (4) a greater incidence of spousal rape. These data underscore the connection between PTSD and evidence of severe relationship violence in battered women and point to a possible link between battering, homicide, and PTSD that invites further exploration.

Compared with other types of trauma victims, the reactions of battered women have been described as most closely paralleling those of hostages or prisoners of war (Browne, 1988). Graham, Rawlings, and Rimini (1988) and Graham and Rawlings (1991) applied the term *Stockholm syndrome* to battered women, arguing that bonding to one's tormentor "may be a universal response to inescapable violence." Similarly, Dutton and Painter (1981) proposed a "traumatic bonding theory" to explain the behavior of battered women toward their abusers. Gondolf and Fisher (1988) used an empowerment model in their empirically based portrayal of battered women's behavior as reflecting their agency and survival skills, rather than passivity and helplessness. These models frame the symptomatic reactions of battered women as *normal responses to pathological situations*. In contrast, personal pathology models conceptualize the reactions of battered women as pathological responses attributable to individual psychological vulnerabilities, flaws, or deficits. Focusing on external or situational variables as capable of producing "pathological" reactions in almost any individual exposed to the situation is far less victim blaming. More important, when problems are defined as having external rather than internal causes, the solutions are more likely to include large-scale macrolevel interventions, such as educational or social programs geared toward effecting legal, political, and systemic change. Problems framed in terms of individual frailties lead only to individual person–centered interventions, such as counseling and therapy, that do not address the social and political structures that may cause or contribute to the problem. Consistent with feminist critiques of traditional individual pathology models, these alternative constructions of battered women have profound implications for battered women seeking redress and/or justice through legal channels.

The Relationship Between Battered Woman Syndrome and PTSD

Douglas (1987) described BWS as "a collection of specific characteristics and effects of abuse that result in a woman's decreased ability to respond effectively to the violence against her." She suggested that PTSD is only one aspect of the disruption observed in women with BWS. According to Dutton-Douglas, the symptoms of BWS fall into three general categories: (1) traumatic effects of the abuse (PTSD symptoms), (2) learned helplessness deficits, and (3) maladaptive coping responses.

TRAUMATIC EFFECTS OF ABUSE

The traumatic effects of abuse refer specifically to the classic features of PTSD: symptoms of reexperiencing the trauma (e.g., intrusive memories, nightmares, flashbacks), psychic numbing and avoidance (e.g., emotional numbness, withdrawal, amnesia, avoidance of trauma-related cues), and symptoms of increased autonomic arousal (e.g., hypervigilance, excessive startle response, sleep disruption, concentration difficulties).

LEARNED HELPLESSNESS DEFICITS

Learned helplessness deficits describe the battered woman's perceptions that she is helpless to stop the abuse, as observed by Lenore Walker. This does not mean that battered women are passive. In fact, Douglas, Walker, and others argued that to the contrary, battered women actively attempt to please or placate the batterer in an effort to reduce the violence perpetrated against them. These efforts are often successful initially, leading to reinforcement of the erroneous belief that the woman can do something to stop the violence. Over time, however, as the violence escalates and the placating behavior does not reduce it, the battered woman comes to realize that there is nothing she can do to stop the violence; that is, she is helpless to stop the violence. The use of adaptive strategies for ending the violence, such as police intervention or obtaining a protective order, are frequently not tried or are given up prematurely due to a number of factors, such as (1) the belief that it would be useless, anyway; (2) an increased threat of danger from the batterer to the woman or her family; and (3) the fear that her efforts to stop the violence will result in ending the relationship, which she may have mixed feelings about. Data previously cited describing the increased risk of homicide to a battered woman when she tries to separate from the batterer, along with the documented failure of law enforcement agencies at protecting battered women, reinforce her belief that she is, indeed, "helpless." Once the battered woman learns that her own behavior cannot stop the violence, her focus shifts to survival behavior that may appear less active and may entail the use of maladaptive coping behaviors.

MALADAPTIVE COPING RESPONSES

The function of survival behavior is to minimize the impact of the violence and to find ways to cope with it. Although coping efforts may initially have an adaptive value, there is usually a long-term cost. The numbing of feelings by using alcohol or drugs is one example of a temporarily adaptive response that is maladaptive in the long run. Minimizing or denying the lethality of the violence or injuries sustained by the violence is another example of maladaptive coping. Although these behaviors may help a battered woman "survive" the abuse, they do not increase the likelihood of her successfully leaving the abusive relationship. Expert testimony in battered women's homicide cases described by Douglas would include a description of each of these components of BWS.

The Impact of Expert Testimony

Even though expert testimony on battered woman syndrome is being used in jury trials, its impact on jurors' verdicts is unknown, in part because jurors merely convict or acquit the defendant without giving reasons for their decisions (Kinports, 1988). Data reported by Ewing (1985) indicated that only 35 percent ($n = 11$) of the cases using expert testimony resulted in acquittal,[9] and Walker (1990) reported a 25 percent acquittal rate. In light of the many factors other than expert testimony that might influence a juror's decision, it is impossible to draw any conclusions regarding the effectiveness of expert testimony solely by relying on reported conviction rates collected from a diverse sample of cases. To date, a few studies have examined the impact of expert testimony on juror verdicts or juror decision making in these types of cases.

Experimental Studies of the Impact of Expert Testimony on BWS

Using written vignettes, Follingstad and colleagues (1989) evaluated the impact of expert testimony on decision making in a battered woman's homicide case. The rate of acquittals was most strongly influenced by the type of instructions given by the judge, rather than by the presence of expert testimony. Contrary to observations of actual court cases in which acquittal by reason of self-defense is infrequent, instructions regarding self-defense options produced more acquittals than did instructions for an insanity option. Even though the presence of expert testimony did not affect the verdict directly, the expert testimony may have influenced the perceptions of the facts of the case, thereby indirectly influencing the verdict. Other factors affecting mock jurors' decisions in this simulation were the perceived severity of the abuse and the level of force used by the victim in the lethal encounter.

Schuller (1992) conducted two studies to evaluate the impact of expert testimony on decision making in a battered woman's homicide case. Undergraduate students serving as mock jurors read a written trial transcript based loosely on the facts of the case, *Ibn-Tamas* v. *United States* (1979). Two different versions of expert testimony were presented, and contrasted with no expert testimony. The two types of testimony varied in only one way. In the general expert testimony condition, participants were informed only about research findings pertaining to battered women. In the specific expert testimony condition, the expert presented the same research findings, but also indicated that he had examined the defendant and found her behavior to be consistent with battered woman syndrome. Results of the study indicated that only the expert testimony that pertained to the *specific* defendant resulted in juror decision making that was more consistent with the self-defense theory presented by the defense. Greater leniency in verdicts were observed by subjects in the expert testimony condition. These findings were for individual juror verdicts only. When jurors were permitted to deliberate to a verdict as a group, both forms of testimony contributed to a shift toward leniency. It is interesting to note that the acquittal rate was not affected by the expert testimony. Instead, murder convictions were reduced in favor of manslaughter convictions.

In a recent experimental study using videotaped trial materials plus mock juror deliberations, Kasian, Spanos, Terrance and Peebles (1993) manipulated the presence of expert testimony (present versus absent), the type of plea entered by the defendant (self-defense, automatism,[10] or hypothetical psychological self-defense[11]), and the severity of the abuse suffered by the defendant (severe versus moderate). The presence of expert testimony had no direct impact on verdicts, although as in the Schuller (1992) study, expert testimony did influence the deliberation process. Acquittals were most frequently observed with the automatism plea, followed by psychological self-defense. The fewest acquittals were observed when the traditional self-defense plea was presented. In contrast with the results of Follingstad et al. (1989), the diminished mental capacity manifested in the automatism plea was more likely than the self-defense plea to result in acquittal, suggesting that mock jurors in this study were more comfortable with a pathologized construction of a battered woman that presented her as an impaired actor rather than as one behaving reasonably and justifiably in a menacing situation. In a different type of study, Finkel, Meister, and Lightfoot (1991) also found that expert testimony did not influence verdicts directly, but that it influenced reasoning about the case, leading jurors to use insanity and diminished capacity frameworks for understanding a battered woman's lethal act. When the case was a nonconfrontational situation (versus a confrontational one) between the battered woman and her abusive mate, a "guilty but mentally ill" option was favored over an acquittal.

In sum, the experimental studies reviewed have failed to find robust direct effects for expert testimony on jury decision making in battered women's homicide cases. When effects were found, they were observed to influence the process of deliberation, thereby only indirectly influencing verdicts. Moreover, preferences were evidenced across most of the studies for jurors to view the battered woman's behavior as excusable on the basis of an impaired mental state rather than as justified based on the facts. This model of impairment is clearly contrary to the strategic use of self-defense claims advocated by legal representatives on behalf of battered women who kill. With the exception of the Follingstad study, acquittal rates were not high, suggesting that regardless of expert testimony, jurors have trouble viewing most battered women's homicide cases as instances of the legitimate use of self-defensive force. Low rates of acquittal by reason of self-defense have been found in both experimental research and actual cases.

With one exception (Kasian et al., 1993), all the experimental studies described used written rather than videotaped materials, and all employed college students to serve as mock jurors. Future research should be extended to include samples that more closely approximate actual jurors and more ecologically valid methods, including the use of videotape trial materials in favor of written transcripts.

Legislative and Policy Issues

Although the trend has been to support the admission of expert testimony on BWS in state courts, several jurisdictions have excluded it, thus prompting innovative legislative action. In 1987, Missouri became the first state to provide legislative support for admitting evidence of BWS in self-defense or in defense of another. (Mo. Rev. Stat. §563,033 (Supp. 1988); see Brewer, 1988). Legislative authority for introducing evidence of abuse and BWS was enacted in both Ohio (Ohio Rev. Code Ann. §2901.06) and Maryland (Act of May 14, 1991, chapter 337, 1191 Md. Laws 2275) after the governors of these states pardoned battered women incarcerated for killing their mates. Expert testimony in Ohio and Maryland had previously been excluded in state court decisions. In 1991, the state of Texas signed into law a bill allowing the admission of evidence of violence and its effects in trials for murder and manslaughter (Senate Bill 275). California also enacted legislation establishing an evidentiary standard permitting testimony on BWS in any criminal action, in the defense of a battered woman, or in the prosecution of batterers (Bill AB 785). In the majority of states in which the admission of expert testimony is discretionary, the defense must overcome a substantial burden to justify its admission. The lack of information accessible to judges, attorneys, experts, and jurors creates an additional obstacle for battered women defendants. Thus, the creation of statutory provisions for the appropriate admission of expert testimony removes at least one of the impediments facing battered women who wish to use expert testimony in their defense.

Conclusions and Thoughts About Future Directions

Despite the fact that legal efforts on behalf of battered women who have killed their mates is to include expert testimony on BWS, the impact of such testimony on verdicts and on the deliberation process remains somewhat elusive. The small experimental literature suggests that the mechanism of influence for expert testimony is indirect, that expert testimony appears to shape the deliberation process which, in turn, affects verdicts. Although the purpose of expert testimony is to provide the judge or jury with a framework within which a battered woman's lethal actions might appear reasonable in light of her history of abuse by the victim, mock jurors seem to have trouble accepting this construction. Instead of reasonable, these lethal actions are frequently viewed as unreasonable but nonetheless excusable acts. Perhaps beliefs that it was unreasonable for the woman to have remained in an abusive relationship contributes to this reasoning.

The discrepancy between acquittal rates stemming from the use of insanity or diminished capacity versus self-defense instructions is interesting both practically and conceptually. On a practical level, competing options of acquittal by reason of insanity versus self-defense are untenable because an affirmative criminal defense requires a choice to be made in advance between these defense options. Thus even though experimental manipulations can provide mock jurors with such acquittal alternatives, the luxury of simultaneously introducing both defense options is non-existent. Conceptually, it is worth recalling that the introduction of expert testimony on behalf of battered women was spearheaded by feminist advocates who argued that without experts to provide a contextual frame of reference for battered women's perceptions and actions leading up to the homicide, they faced injustice from gender-biased courts (e.g., Schneider, 1986). Serious problems accepting the reasonableness of battered women's homicidal behavior have been demonstrated with real and mock jurors and have spawned a second generation of feminist criticism regarding the use of expert testimony on BWS.

Recent criticism by feminist legal scholars of the use of expert testimony on BWS has centered on a few key issues. First, the use of "syndrome" testimony pathologizes battered women, implicitly conveying an aura of impairment, as opposed to agency, thereby suggesting that battered women lack the capacity to act effectively, reasonably, and lawfully on their own behalf. Both the battered woman's earlier failure to leave the abusive relationship and her homicidal actions fall prey to conceptualizations based on incapacity. Such constructions of helplessness, it has been posited, make it less likely that the woman's actions will appear reasonable. In part, this is due to the dialectical conflict between behavioral extremes. It is a struggle to reconcile a description of prior behavior premised on notions of passivity—that is, learned helplessness with aggressive actions arising from agency, or, the active stance of defending oneself through the use of lethal force (Schneider, 1986). Mahoney (1991) and other feminist legal scholars point out that the use of testimony on BWS engenders a new set of stereotypes no less insidious than those that the testimony is intended to obviate. Mahoney argues that expert testimony on BWS "has through the pressures of the legal system contributed to a focus on victimization that is understood as passivity or even pathology on the part of the woman" (p. 42). Jenkins and Davidson (1990) remind us that instead of disabusing legal audiences of sexist stereotypes of battered women, when the trial process includes expert testimony on BWS, the trial is reduced to a battle of "dueling stereotypes" (p. 169).

Second, it has been argued that no one explanation of battered woman and their responses can adequately convey the diversity and multiplicity of battered women's experiences. Fearful that the use of expert testimony on BWS will result in the instantiation of a new standard, the "reasonable battered woman" standard, feminist legal scholars have admonished us that battered women who do not resemble the prototypical case may be jeopardized because their behavior may appear unreasonable vis-à-vis the "reasonable battered woman" standard.

Even more troubling is that fact that most expert testimony is based on data from Walker's (1979, 1984a) pioneering research on the experiences of predominantly middle-class, European-American battered women recruited for her research from newspapers. She did not include the experiences of women of color, non-middle-class women, and lesbians in her research, so it is not clear if and how her findings can be generalized to other populations of battered women. Thus the available empirical literature, which has been criticized on methodological grounds (Faigman, 1986), has also failed to consider the diversity of battered women. In regard to this problem, Blackman (1989) offers her personal experience as an expert witness to illustrate the dilemma she has faced when contacted by criminal defense attorneys, who told her: "My client is not a typical battered woman, but I wonder if you can help her, anyway." Blackman interprets questions like this to mean that the battered woman in question was "very poor and part of a lifestyle in which violence is rampant" (p. 205). Blackman shares the following analysis:

> To date, the work of experts in this area—my own included—has been classist and, as a result, not comprehensive or objective beyond its boundaries . . . for poor women who were fighting to stay alive in many ways and who also had to fight off abusive men, our work has not been as illuminating as it ought to be. To acknowledge this weakness is a beginning. Still, much work remains to be done with regard to very poor battered women, an undertaking that requires the most astute collaboration with the women themselves, in order to understand how chronic violence has affected their psychologies . . . future research must be designed with a view toward understanding the impact of social class on the psychology of battered women. (pp. 205–6)

Research by Gondolf and Fisher also underscores the plight of women dually afflicted by abject poverty and battering. Clearly, social-change efforts need to be geared not only toward the eradication of violence against women but also toward eliminating the social conditions that compromise the possibilities for personal well-being and social justice.

Finally, I must offer a cautionary note: A sobering and painful reality in our culture is that battered women are at highest risk of being killed by their abusive mates, and this risk increases dramatically when they try to end the relationship. The small but significant minority of battered women who find themselves in the unenviable position of having to defend their own homicidal actions against their victimizers to a generally unsympathetic legal system has been the focus of this chapter. Despite my choice to do experimental and survey research on this intellectually stimulating and important topic, I ardently believe that our long-term goals should not be to discover how to contextualize battered women's lethal actions against their abusers so that courts are able to see these acts as justifiable and reasonable given the backdrop of violence permeating the women's lives. I am unable to imagine a more tertiary response to this devastating social ailment. Rather, the problem of spousal violence demands immediate attention focused upon the primary and secondary prevention of relationship violence, particularly in young people. Relationship violence among teens in dating relationships is on the rise, and this does not bode well for the future generation of our society.

In a recent issue of *Time* (July 4, 1994), Jill Smolowe lamented: "Suddenly, domestic abuse, once perniciously silent, is exposed for its brutality in the wake of a highly publicized scandal" (p. 19). Although I find little consolation in the fact that battering has been ignored as a social problem by the lay public until the downfall of an idealized American sports "hero," the window of opportunity to make changes has been nudged open by the public airing of the Simpson tragedy. In this spirit I would like to reiterate and underscore the excellent "policy recommendations for stopping wife abuse" that Gondolf and Fisher identified in their 1988 book *Battered Women as Survivors: An Alternative to Treating Learned Helplessness*. These recommendations, include the following general provisions: (1) expanded shelter funding; (2) prioritized funding to support services to battered women and their children; (3) coordinated interventions among existing social services; (4) a national campaign to send the message that abusive behavior is unacceptable and will have severe consequences; (5) legislation to ensure the prompt legal investigation and processing of spouse abuse; (6) antipoverty programs; (7) legal change in the area of women's rights in the contexts of divorce, employment, and abuse; (8) education aimed at preventing male violence; and (9) long-term treatment programs for batterers that progress from incarceration through community education and self-help programs. It is abundantly clear that reactive efforts alone will fail to promote the long-term solutions that are urgently needed. I am optimistic that proactive attempts to provide readily accessible resources, both tangibly and symbolically, will ebb the flow of intimate violence and forestall its deadly eruption in homicide.

Notes

1. Walker (1988) describes battered woman syndrome as an identifiable symptom pattern "diagnosed in the ICD-9 as its own separate category and in DSM-IV under Post Traumatic Stress Disorder. The clinical syndrome includes features of both anxiety and affective disorders, cognitive distortions including dissociation and memory loss, reexperiencing traumatic events from exposure to associated stimuli, disruption of interpersonal relationships, and psychophysiological disturbances. A hypersensitivity to potential violence occurs that creates an expectation of harm and a readiness to protect and defend oneself. If actual defense is seen as impossible, then the best coping skills are developed to keep the potential harm at a minimum level. For some, it is seen as an impossible task and a passive, helpless reaction is adopted. Such intense concentration on manipulating the environment to keep as safe as possible sets abused persons apart from others who believe their world is a relatively safe place" (p. 143).

2. Throughout this chapter, the terms *battering, spouse abuse, domestic* (or *intimate*) *violence*, and *assault* are used interchangeably to refer to women who have been subjected to physical and/or sexual

assault by a man with whom they have (or have had) an intimate relationship, whether or not they are legally married.

3. High rates of exposure to childhood violence (as either a witness or a victim) and sexual victimization during childhood were reported by both groups of women.

4. These data were self-reported by the women after the homicide occurred; thus the men could not be interviewed for corroborative evidence. In order to enhance the reliability of the self-reported data, Browne obtained all available police and hospital records (including those from prior battering incidents), in addition to testimony by family members and other witnesses. Reports on the men were obtained from former employers, past acquaintances, and service providers. Browne notes that when there were discrepancies between the women's reports and those from other sources, the women typically minimized (rather than overstated) the extent of the problems.

5. Note that the other admissibility criteria pertain to the specific expert's qualifications to testify (Dyas, 1977; FRE 702) and to whether the state-of-the-art knowledge in the subject area permits an expert opinion to be drawn (Dyas, 1977). Although both of these criteria have been subject to varied rulings, they will not be addressed further in this chapter. (For a critique of the use of expert testimony on battered woman syndrome, based on scientific grounds, see generally Faigman, 1986.)

6. This model is based on research originally done by Seligman (1975) with dogs that were exposed to uncontrollable electric shocks. Later, these dogs were unable to remove themselves from the aversive situation even when they were given an opportunity to do so. Walker applies this theory to battered women by arguing that once these women experience uncontrollable beatings, they learn that their behavior will not change the situation, and so they become depressed and unable to leave the abusive relationship. Although Walker's application of learned helplessness is frequently invoked with respect to battered women, the empirical support for this position is limited.

7. Although the presence of life threat or injury increased the likelihood of PTSD, the presence of both factors was responsible for the highest rates of PTSD (Resnick et al., 1993).

8. The rates of lifetime PTSD were 32 percent for completed rape and 39 percent for physical assault in a large national probability sample of women. In the presence of both life threat and injury, PTSD rates increased to 45 percent. These characteristics were present most often in physical assault (61 percent) and rape (36 percent) (Resnick et al., 1993).

9. Only 20 percent ($n = 17$) of the cases in the entire sample ($n = 85$) used expert testimony. Because the selection criteria for the inclusion or exclusion of cases from the Ewing study were not reported, it is impossible to know why expert testimony was presented in only 20 percent of the cases.

10. In the automatism condition, the battered woman was described as being in a dissociated state as a result of a head injury, and so she was unable to form intent or understand the consequences of her actions.

11. The hypothetical psychological self-defense pleas is based on the work of Ewing (1987), who argued that women should be able to defend themselves against threats to the "psychological self," not only their physical selves. This position has not been accepted by any court. For a critique of the concept of psychological self-defense, see Morse (1990). See Greenwald, Tomkins, Kenning, and Zavodny (1990) for another experimental evaluation of psychological self-defense instructions.

References

Acker, J. R., and H. Toch. 1985. "Battered Women, Straw Men, and Expert Testimony: A Comment on State vs. Kelly." *Criminal Law Bulletin* 21: 125–55.

Astin, M. C., K. J. Lawerence, & D. W. Foy. 1993. "Risk and Resiliency Factors Among Battered Women." *Violence and Victims* 8: 17–28.

Blackman, J. 1986. "Potential Uses for Expert Testimony: Ideas Toward the Representation of Battered Women Who Kill." *Women's Rights Law Reporter* 9: 227–38.

Blackman, J. 1989. *Intimate Violence: A Study of Injustice*. New York: Columbia University Press.

Blackman, J., and E. Brickman. 1984. "The Impact of Expert Testimony on Trials of Battered Women Who Kill Their Husbands." *Behavioral Sciences and the Law* 2: 413–22.

Bochnak, E. 1981. *Women's Self-Defense Cases*. Charlottesville, Va.: Michie Press.

Bowker, L. H. 1983. *Beating Wife-Beating*. Lexington, Mass.: Lexington Books.

Brewer, M. 1988. "Missouri's New Law on Battered Spouse Syndrome: A Moral Victory, a Partial Solution." *St. Louis Law Review* 33: 227–55.

Browne, A. 1987. *When Battered Women Kill*. New York: Free Press.

Browne, A. 1988. "Family Homicide: When Victimized Women Kill." In *Handbook of Family Violence*, ed. V. B. Van Hasselt, R. L. Morrison, A. S. Bellack, and M. Hersen, pp. 271–89. New York: Plenum.

Browne, A., and K. R. Williams. 1989. "Exploring the Effect of Resource Availability and the Likelihood of Female Perpetrated Homicides." *Law and Society Review* 23: 76–94.

Bureau of Justice Statistics. 1991a. *Female Victims of Violent Crime*. Special report, NCJ 126826. Washington, D.C.: Department of Justice.

Bureau of Justice Statistics. 1991b. *Women in Prison*. Special report, NCJ 127991. Washington, D.C.: Department of Justice.

Cascardi, M., K. D. O'Leary, K. A. Schlee, and E. Lawerence. 1993. "Prevalence and Correlates of PTSD in Abused Women." Paper presented at the twenty-seventh annual conference of the Association for the Advancement of Behavior Therapy, Atlanta.

Cascardi, M., D. S. Riggs, D. E. Hearst, and E. B. Foa. 1993. "Assault Characteristics as Predictors of Crime Related PTSD: The Role of Severity, Location, and Identity of the Perpetrator." Paper presented at the ninth annual meeting of the International Society for Traumatic Stress Studies, San Antonio, Texas.

Chimbos, P. 1978. *Marital Violence: A Study of Interspousal Homicide*. San Francisco: R & E Research Associates.

Clarke, C. Unpublished data. "Domestic Violence: A Community Survey." University of Illinois, Champaign-Urbana.

Coffee, C. 1986–1987. "A Trend Emerges: A State Survey on the Admissibility of Expert Testimony Concerning Battered Woman Syndrome." *Journal of Family Law* 25: 611–15.

Daniel, A., and P. W. Harris. 1982. "Female Homicide Offenders Referred for Pretrial Psychiatric Examination: A Descriptive Study." *Bulletin of the American Academy of Psychiatry and the Law* 10: 261–69.

Dobash, R. E., and R. P. Dobash. 1978. "Wives: The 'Appropriate' Victims of Marital Violence." *Victimology* 2: 426–42.

Dodge, M., and E. Greene. 1991. "Jurors and Expert Conceptions of Battered Women." *Violence and Victims* 6: 271–82.

Douglas, M. A. 1987. "Battered Woman Syndrome." In *Domestic Violence on Trial*. ed. D. J. Sonkin, pp. 39–54. New York: Springer.

Dutton, D. G. 1987. "The Criminal Justice Response to Wife Assault." *Law and Human Behavior* 11: 189–206.

Dutton, D. G. 1988. *The Domestic Assault of Women: Psychological and Criminal Justice Perspectives*. Boston: Allyn & Bacon.

Dutton, D. G., and B. S. McGregor. 1992. "Psychological and Legal Dimensions of Family Violence." In *Handbook of Psychology and Law*, ed. D. K. Kagehiro and W. S. Laufer, pp. 318–40. New York: Springer-Verlag.

Dutton, D. G., and S. L. Painter. 1981. "Traumatic Bonding: The Development of Emotional Attachments in Battered Women and Other Relationships of Intermittent Abuse." *Victimology: An International Journal* 6: 139–55.

Dutton-Douglas, M. A. 1992. "Treating Battered Women in the Aftermath Stage." *Psychotherapy in Private Practice* 10: 93–98.

Ewing, C. P. 1985. "Battered Women Who Kill: Psychological Defense as Legal Justification." Paper presented at the annual meeting of the American Psychological Association, Los Angeles.

Ewing, C. P. 1987. *Battered Women Who Kill: Psychological Defense as Legal Justification*. Lexington, Mass.: Heath.

Ewing, C. P., and M. Aubrey. 1987. "Battered Women and Public Opinion: Some Realities About the Myths." *Journal of Family Violence* 2: 257–64.

Fagan, J. 1988. "Contributions of Family Violence Research to Criminal Justice Policy on Wife Assault: Paradigms of Science and Social Control." *Violence and Victims* 3: 159–86.

Faigman, D. L. 1986. "The Battered Woman Syndrome and Self-Defense: A Legal and Empirical Dissent." *University of Virginia Law Review* 72: 619–47.

Finkel, N. J., K. H. Meister, and D. M. Lightfoot. 1991. "Self-Defense and Community Sentiment." *Law and Human Behavior* 15: 585–602.

Follingstad, D. R., D. S. Polek, E. S. Hause, L. H. Deaton, M. W. Bulger, and Z. D. Conway. 1989. "Factors Predicting Verdicts in Cases Where Battered Women Kill Their Husbands." *Law and Human Behavior* 13: 253–69.

Frieze, I. H. 1987. "The Female Victim of Rape, Wife-Beating and Incest." In *Cataclysms, Crises, and Catastrophes: Psychology in Action*, ed. G. R. Vandenbos and B. K. Bryant, pp. 109–46. Washington, D.C.: American Psychological Association.

Frieze, I. H., and A. Browne. 1989. "Violence in Marriage." In *Family Violence*, ed. L. Ohin and M. Tonry, pp. 163–218. Chicago: University of Chicago Press.

Gallers, J., D. Foy, C. P. Donohoe, Jr., and J. Goldfarb. 1988. "Post-Traumatic Stress Disorder in Vietnam Combat Veterans: Effects of Traumatic Violence Exposure and Military Adjustment." *Journal of Traumatic Stress* 1: 181–92.

Gentemann, K. M. 1984. "Wife Beating: Attitudes of a Non-Clinical Population." *Victimology: An International Journal* 9: 109–19.

Gillespie, C. K. 1989. *Justifiable Homicide*. Columbus: Ohio State University Press.

Gondolf, E. W., and E. R. Fisher. 1988. *Battered Women as Survivors: An Alternative to Treating Learned Helplessness*. Lexington, Mass.: Lexington Books.

Goolkasian, G. A. 1986. *Confronting Domestic Violence: A Guide for Criminal Justice Agencies*. Washington, D.C.: Department of Justice, National Institute of Justice.

Graham, D. L., and E. Rawlings. 1991, November. "Stockholm Syndrome in Abused Women." *American Psychological Association Monitor* 22: 31.

Graham, D. L., E. Rawlings, and N. Rimini. 1988. "Survivors of Terror: Battered Women, Hostages, and the Stockholm Syndrome." In *Feminist Perspectives on Wife Abuse*, ed. K. Yllo and M. Bograd, pp. 217–23. Newbury Park, Calif.: Sage.

Greenblat, C. S. 1983. "A Hit Is a Hit Is a Hit . . . Or Is It? Approval of the Use of Physical Force by Spouses." In *The Dark Side of Families: Current Family Violence Research*, ed. D. Finkelhor, R. Gelles, G. Hotaling, and M. A. Straus, pp. 235–60. Beverly Hills, Calif.: Sage.

Greenblat, C. S. 1985. "'Don't Hit Your Wife . . . Unless': Preliminary Findings on Normative Support for the Use of Physical Force by Husbands." *Victimology: An International Journal* 10: 221–41.

Greene, E., A. Raitz, and Linblad. 1989. "Jurors' Knowledge of Battered Women." *Journal of Family Violence* 4: 105–25.

Greenwald, J. P., A. J. Tomkins, M. Kenning, and D. Zavodny. 1990. "Psychological Self-Defense Jury Instructions: Influence on Verdicts for Battered Women Defendants." *Behavioral Sciences and Law* 8: 171–80.

Housekamp, B. M., and D. W. Foy. 1991. "The Assessment of Post-Traumatic Stress Disorder in Battered Women." *Journal of Interpersonal Violence* 6: 367–75.

Jenkins, P., and B. Davidson. 1990. "Battered Women in the Criminal Justice System: An Analysis of Gender Stereotypes." *Behavioral Sciences and the Law* 8: 161–70.

Jurik, N. C., and R. Winn. 1990. "Gender and Homicide: A Comparison of Men and Women Who Kill." *Violence and Victims* 5: 227–42.

Kalmus, D. 1979. "The Attribution of Responsibility in a Wife-Abuse Context." *Victimology: An International Journal* 4: 284–91.

Kasian, M., N. P. Spanos, C. A. Terrance, and S. Peebles. 1993. "Battered Women Who Kill: Jury Simulation and Legal Defenses." *Law and Human Behavior* 17: 289–312.

Kemp, A., E. I. Rawlings, and B. L. Green. 1991. "Post-Traumatic Stress Disorder (PTSD) in Battered Women: A Shelter Sample." *Journal of Traumatic Stress* 4: 137–48.

Kilpatrick, D. G., and H. S. Resnick. 1993. "PTSD Associated with Exposure to Criminal Victimization in Clinical and Community Populations." In *PTSD in Review: Recent Research and Future Directions*, ed. R. T. Davidson and E. B. Foa, pp. 113–43. Washington, D.C.: American Psychiatric Press.

Kilpatrick, D. G., B. E. Saunders, A. Amick-McMullan, C. L. Best, L. J. Veronen, and H. S. Resnick.

1989. "Victim and Crime Factors Associated with the Development of Crime-Related Post-Traumatic Stress Disorder." *Behavior Therapy* 20: 199–214.

Kinports, K. 1988. "Defending Battered Women's Self-Defense Claims." *Oregon Law Review* 67: 301–73.

Koski, P. R., and W. D. Mangold. 1988. "Gender Effects in Attitudes About Family Violence." *Journal of Family Violence* 3: 225–37.

LaFave, W., and A. Scott 1986. *Handbook on Criminal Law*. St. Paul: West.

Lerman, L. G. 1982. "Expansion of Arrest Power: A Key to Effective Intervention." *Vermont Law Review* 7: 59–70.

Lindsey, K. 1978, September. "When Battered Women Strike Back: Murder or Self-Defense?" *Viva*, pp. 58–59, 66–74.

Mahoney, M. 1991. "Legal Images of Battered Women: Redefining the Issue of Separation." *Michigan Law Review* 90: 1–111.

Martin, D. 1976. *Battered Wives*. San Francisco: Glide.

Maryland Special Committee on Gender Bias in the Courts. 1989. "Domestic Violence and the Courts: Maryland Special Joint Committee on Gender Bias in the Courts." *Response to the Victimization of Women and Children* 12: 3–6.

Melton, G. B. 1984. "Family and Mental Hospital as Myths: Civil Commitment of Minors." In *Children, Mental Health and the Law*, ed. N. D. Repucci, L. A. Weithorn, E. P. Mulvey, and J. Monahan, pp. 151–67. Beverly Hills, Calif.: Sage.

Morse, S. J. 1990. "The Misbegotten Marriage of Soft Psychology and Bad Law: Psychological Self Defense as a Justification for Homicide." *Law and Human Behavior* 14: 595–618.

Newman, D. A., J. Gallers, and D. Foy. 1989. "Traumatic Violence and PTSD in Rape Victims." Paper presented at the annual meeting of the Society for Traumatic Stress Studies, San Francisco.

Norris, F. H. 1992. "Epidemiology of Trauma: Frequency and Impact of Different Potentially Traumatic Events on Different Demographic Groups." *Journal of Consulting and Clinical Psychology* 60: 409–18.

Norris, F. H., and K. Kaniasty. 1994. "Psychological Distress Following Criminal Victimization in the General Population: Cross-Sectional, Longitudinal, and Prospective Analyses." *Journal of Consulting and Clinical Psychology* 62: 111–23.

Pagelow, M. D. 1981. *Woman-Battering: Victims and Their Experiences*. Beverly Hills, Calif.: Sage.

Pagelow, M. D. 1992. "Adult Victims of Domestic Violence: Battered Women." *Journal of Interpersonal Violence* 7: 87–120.

Police Foundation. 1976. *Domestic Violence and the Police: Studies in Detroit and Kansas City*. Washington, D.C.: Police Foundation.

Resnick, H. S., D. G. Kilpatrick, B. S. Dansky, B. E. Saunders and C. Best. 1993. "Prevalence of Civilian Trauma and Post-Traumatic Stress Disorder in a Representative Sample of Women." *Journal of Consulting and Clinical Psychology* 61: 984–91.

Riggs, D. S., E. B. Foa, B. O. Rothbaum, and T. Murdock. 1991. "Post-Traumatic Stress Disorder Following Rape and Non-Sexual Assault: A Predictive Model." Unpublished manuscript.

Rounsaville, B. 1978. "Theories in Marital Violence: Evidence from a Study of Battered Women." *Victimology: An International Journal* 3: 11–31.

Rowan, A. B., and D. W. Foy. 1993. "Post-Traumatic Stress Disorder in Child Sexual Abuse Survivors: A Literature Review." *Journal of Traumatic Stress* 6: 3–20.

Saunders, D. G. 1986. "When Battered Women Use Violence: Husband-Abuse or Self-Defense?" *Violence and Victims* 1: 47–60.

Saunders, D. G., A. Lynch, M. Grayson, and D. Linz. 1987. "The Inventory of Beliefs About Wife-Beating: The Construction of a Measure of Beliefs and Attitudes." *Violence and Victims* 2: 39–57.

Schneider, E. 1986. "Describing and Changing: Women's Self-Defense Work and the Problem of Expert Testimony on Battering." *Women's Rights Law Reporter* 9: 195–222.

Schneider, E., and S. B. Jordan. 1981. "Representation of Women Who Defend Themselves in Response to Physical or Sexual Assault." In *Women's Self-Defense Cases: Theory and Practice*, ed. E. Bochnak, pp. 119–43. Charlottesville, Va.: Michi Press.

Schuller, R. 1992. "The Impact of Battered Woman Syndrome Evidence on Jury Decision Processes." *Law and Human Behavior* 16: 597–620.

Schulman, M. 1979. *A Survey of Spousal Violence Against Women in Kentucky.* Washington, D.C.: Department of Justice, Law Enforcement Assistance Administration.

Seligman, M.E.P. 1975. *Helplessness: On Depression, Development and Death.* San Francisco: Freeman.

Simon, R. J., and L. Landis. 1991. *The Crimes Women Commit, the Punishment and Death.* San Francisco: Freeman.

Smolowe, J. 1994, July 4. "Domestic Abuse Hits Home." *Time,* pp. 19–25.

Soler, E. 1987. "Domestic Violence Is a Crime: A Case Study—San Francisco Family Violence Project." In *Domestic Violence on Trial,* ed. D. J. Sonkin, pp. 21–35. New York: Springer.

Stark, E., A. Flitcraft, and W. Frazier. 1979. "Medicine and Patriarchal Violence: The Social Construction of a Private Event." *International Journal of Health Services* 9: 461–63.

Straus, M. A., R. J. Gelles, and S. Steinmetz. 1980. *Behind Closed Doors: Violence in American Families.* Garden City, N.Y.: Doubleday/Anchor.

Taylor, S. E. 1983. "Adjustment to Threatening Events: A Theory of Cognitive Adaptation." *American Psychologist* 38: 1161–73.

Thyfault, R. K., C. E. Bennett, and R. B. Hirschorn. 1987. "Battered Women in Court: Jury Trial Consultants and Expert Witnesses." In *Domestic Violence on Trial,* New York: Springer.

Trafford, A. 1991, February 26. "Why Battered Women Kill: Self Defense, Not Revenge, Is Often the Motive." *Washington Post,* pp. 71–83.

Totman, J. 1978. *The Murderess: A Psychological Study of Criminal Homicide.* San Francisco: R & E Research Associates.

U.S. Department of Justice, Federal Bureau of Investigation. 1991. *Crime in the United States, 1991.* Washington, D.C.: Government Printing Office.

Waits, K. 1985. "The Criminal Justice Response to Battering: Understanding the Problem and Forging the Solutions." *Washington Law Review* 60: 267–329.

Walker, L.E.A. 1979. *The Battered Woman.* New York: Harper & Row.

Walker, L.E.A. 1984a. *The Battered Woman Syndrome.* New York: Springer.

Walker, L.E.A. 1984b. "Battered Women, Psychology and Public Policy." *American Psychologist* 39: 1178–82.

Walker, L.E. 1988. "The Battered Woman Syndrome." In *Family Abuse and Its Consequences,* ed. G. T. Hotaling, D. Finkelhor, J. T. Kirkpatrick, and M. A. Straus, pp. 139–48. Beverly Hills, Calif.: Sage.

Walker, L. E. 1990. *Terrified Love: Why Battered Women Kill and How Society Responds.* New York: Harper & Row.

Walker, L., and J. Monahan. 1987. "Social Frameworks: A New Use of Social Science in Law." *Virginia Law Review* 73: 559–98.

Walker, L. E., R. K. Thyfault, and A. Browne. 1982. "Beyond the Juror's Ken: Battered Women." *Vermont Law Review* 7: 1–14.

Wilbanks, W. 1983a. "The Female Homicide Offender in Dade County, Florida." *Criminal Justice Review* 8: 9–14.

Wilbanks, W. 1983b. "Female Homicide Offenders in the U.S." *International Journal of Women Studies* 6: 302–10.

Wolfgang, M. E. 1958. *Patterns in Criminal Homicide.* New York: Wiley.

Wolfgang, M. E. 1967. "A Sociological Analysis of Criminal Homicide." In *Studies of Homicide,* ed. M. E. Wolfgang, pp. 15–28. New York: Harper & Row.

Zimring, F. E., S. K. Mukherjee, and B. Van Winkle. 1983. "Intimate Violence: A Study of Intersexual Homicide in Chicago." *University of Chicago Law Review* 50: 910–43.

III

Assessment, Intervention, and Specialized Programs

10

Shelter-Based Crisis Intervention with Battered Women

Sophia F. Dziegielewski, Cheryl Resnick, and Nora B. Krause

Current estimates of victims of spouse abuse are that 2 million women are battered each year (Council on Scientific Affairs, 1992; Novella, 1992; Roberts & Roberts, 1990) with more than 1 million women annually seeking medical care for injuries due to spouse battering (Schecter, 1987; Wodarski, 1987). Twenty-two to 35 percent of hospital emergency room visits were by women whose injuries were directly related to abuse by their partner. Even so, Lenore Walker (1984) estimated that no matter how extreme the violence was, 50 percent of abused women still did not receive the medical and psychological help that they needed.

Although the term *spouse abuse* has been redefined by some researchers to include incidences of females abusing males, most research shows that 95 percent of assaults are directed against females (Schecter, 1987). In this chapter, the term *spouse abuse* refers only to women who are assaulted by a male partner, regardless of whether or not they are married.

The diagnostic assessment and treatment of women abused by their partners is a fairly recent area of interest for researchers and clinicians. Indeed, from 1939 through 1969, the *Journal of Marriage and the Family* made literally no reference to violence (Schecter, 1982), and in the twenty-five years following this period, only about thirty articles were published that covered the area of family violence, with the majority of them (twenty-one articles) coming after 1986.

In order to understand the plight of battered women and to establish effective interventions, we must view the problem from a feminist perspective. Societies that believe that what happens in the family is a private matter, that a man should "rule" his partner, that women want to be dominated, and that men need to keep their women in line hinder women trying to escape from an abusive situation (Schecter, 1982). The treatment of the abused partner must consider these cultural influences, but of course, they, combined with the unresponsiveness of the society's institutions, often limit the treatment options for abused women.

Shelters and Safe Houses

Today, many women are treated through shelter programs, which offer a wide range of services. Erin Pizzy, who is credited with establishing one of the first women's shelters, began the Women's Aid Project in England by setting up a "refuge home" for women with personal problems, but within three years this refuge home was filled to capacity with battered wives. Currently, the shelter setting still remains the primary recourse available to women and children fleeing abusive situations. It is important to note that approximately one-third to two-thirds of women who remain in shelters for several weeks do not return to their abusive partners. The women in shelters also report less depression and a greater feeling of independence.

Unfortunately, the safety and security of the shelter are only temporary. Upon discharge, working-class women often have few options available to them: getting a poorly paid job, collecting welfare, living off the kindness of families and friends, finding another relationship, or depending once again on their abuser. Indeed, Davidson and Jenkins (1989) believe "that a woman might not find that her partner's violence is her first concern nor her worst oppressor" (p. 494). Because the shelter provides a haven from domestic violence, it is important that it not make the women's battering experience worse. Thus programs to help women escape abuse must in no way revictimize those they seek to serve (Srinivasan & Davis, 1991), which makes building and running ethnically, racially, and socioeconomically equitable shelters a necessity (Coley & Beckett, 1988). The role of the social worker becomes crucial to establishing equality for all involved.

Social Work Treatment in the Shelter

It is seldom recognized that social workers have been working with abused women since the early twentieth century. These early social workers addressed their needs for shelter, food, clothing, advocacy, and legal assistance, with the provision of housing and employment services serving as the means for keeping these women away from their abusive partners (Edelson, 1991).

Spouse abuse occurs in 20 to 30 percent of families (Geffner & Pagelow, 1990). Although not all victims seek treatment, the number is growing, but the funding available is not keeping pace. Shelters provide safety and security for the abused client, yet few shelters receive government funding (Gelles & Cornell, 1990). This lack of funds limits the number of days that women can spend in the shelter and the services the shelter can offer. As Roberts and Roberts (1990) noted, the severe violence that prompts women to seek help is likely to have occurred late at night, on weekends, or during holidays, and often during these hours the shelter is minimally staffed. Also, McDonald (1989) found that 34 percent of women in shelters are from out of town and so have no local family support. Furthermore, because of the limited funds and overcrowding, there is often little privacy. Crisis intervention is a short-term treatment, and its emphasis on limited time and concrete goals is well suited for use in the shelter.

Often, abused women leave their homes in a rush and arrive with few resources of their own. Although they need a great deal of help, neither they nor the shelter usually has enough time and money for a prolonged treatment. In addition, the abusive situation is generally multiproblematic, and so the solution cannot be simple.

When treatment is provided at the shelter, research has found that once a woman has received help and support, she is less likely to return to her abuser. According to McDonald (1989), there is empirical support for the shelter's role in ending battering, but as Schecter (1982) explained,

> [T]he issues facing many battered women are so overwhelming, medical problems, loneliness, children with emotional scars, poor housing and jobs, that they may decide to go back to their husbands. Many women want to reunite with their husbands for emotional, as well as, economic reasons and they hope the violence will cease. (p. 283)

There also appears to be a pattern in the lifestyle that the battering relationship creates, which is characterized by intense love–hate interactions. Once a woman has decided to try to survive in this chaotic relationship, it is difficult for her to relinquish this survival mechanism. Because the characteristic lows and highs cease once the client is no longer in the household, the transition to the shelter environment becomes even more difficult, because the old patterns of "survival" coping still remain. It thus is during these first critical days that the battered woman is most likely to return to the environment from which she came.

In addition, the amount of time that a qualified counselor can spend with the client and the number of sessions available may also be limited by the client's decision to return to her spouse. This makes effective short-term treatment essential to help bring the battered woman out of a crisis state, to establish a safety plan, and to give her needed referrals.

Victims of spouse abuse often deny the abuse (Geffner & Pagelow, 1990; Walker, 1984). Bolton and Bolton (1987) described victims as wanting direction and information and typically not being "verbal," and so the traditional insight therapies are not helpful. The treatment must therefore be highly structured and short term, avoiding long-term introspective efforts. Costantino (1981) discovered that counseling was most effective when it was short term and focused on solving immediate problems. A study of battered women coming to a hospital emergency room where immediate consultation by a psychiatrist or social worker was available found that their initial response to the emergency room contact was extremely positive. Unfortunately, however, most of the women did not seek further treatment. Issues regarding employment and resources were major factors in the women's ability to follow through with the counselor's recommendations (Rounsaville, 1978).

The Theoretical Model

The theoretical model recommended for this kind of short-term treatment is based on crisis intervention and cognitive–behavioral techniques.

The major conceptual development of crisis theory is attributed to Dr. Eric Lindemann, Gerald Caplan, Reuben Hill, and Lillian Rappaport. *Crisis* is identified as an upset in a steady state that creates disequilibrium. The occurrence of a hazardous event disturbs the homeostasis of the individual person (or family) and creates a vulnerable state, and so formerly effective problem-solving strategies no longer work. A crisis generally entails a period of transition or a turning point during which there is a confrontation with an unfamiliar obstacle. Familiar resources and past experiences are tested and may be found wanting.

The crisis paradigm implies that passing through maturational crises and confronting sudden, accidental crises are common to all and exemplify normal life circumstances. Maturational crises characterize a person's expected adaptation to life's transitional phases (e.g., starting school, leaving home, getting married, retiring), whereas sudden or accidental crises are those unexpected or unplanned events in life for which there is little or no preparation.

In a crisis, a person responds according to his or her own personality traits and coping patterns, and so crisis intervention focuses on the person's ability to regain his or her equilibrium and to learn new coping mechanisms and problem-solving skills. The emphasis is on the person's strong, healthy aspects and not on the pathological traits. This model suggests that during critical situations people are more open to change and that crisis need not be viewed negatively. Crisis intervention is short term, with the focus on the here and now. With the increasing demand for mental health services, crisis theory has gained popularity as an effective, brief method of treatment. The emotional and physical abuse that constitutes battering is an example of such a crisis.

Roberts and Roberts (1990) believe that the clinician in a shelter must have "an understanding of crisis theory and the techniques of crisis intervention" in order to meet the client's needs. Most spouse abuse victims have been repeatedly abused, with a recent severe attack, and therefore enter the shelter in a crisis state. The crisis state is caused by a "precipitating or hazardous event" followed by a time of tension and distress. The three most common precipitating events that bring abused women into the shelter for treatment are (1) acute battering resulting in severe injury, (2) serious injury inflicted on the woman's child or children, and (3) the temporary impairment of hearing, vision, and/or thought processes resulting from the battering (Stith, Williams, & Rosen, 1990). According to Roberts and Roberts (1990), the precipitating event(s) is generally viewed as the last straw. When the precipitating event takes place, the client tries her usual coping methods, and when they fail, a crisis state results (Roberts, 1990).

In crisis theory, it is necessary that the atmosphere surrounding the therapy be one of respect for the client. The goal of crisis work is to enable her to regain the "capacity to deal effectively with the crisis" and "to increase his/her mastery over his/her own behavior and gain greater self awareness" (Getz et al., 1974, p. 43). Whereas interventions based on crisis theory seek to restore the client to the level of functioning that existed before the crisis, Roberts and Roberts (1990) see the end result for the domestic violence victim as a "person returning to [her] pre-crisis state or growing from the crisis intervention so that she learns new coping skills to utilize in the future" (p. 27). This type of crisis intervention usually requires from one to six sessions (Puryear, 1979), and because of the time and goal-limited focus, it can provide an excellent therapeutic milieu for a woman living in a shelter.

Another form of brief short-term treatment that has been shown to be effective for victims of domestic violence is cognitive-behavioral therapy. As Webb (1992) explained, "distorted beliefs interfere with the abused women's ability to manage their lives effectively" (p. 206). These beliefs may arise from efforts to cope with the abusive situation, from an abusive childhood, and/or from societal norms affecting gender roles and expectations.

From a cognitive-behavioral perspective, the "assumption that maladaptive behaviors are learned and maintained in accordance with principles of conditioning" is emphasized (Getz et al., 1974, p. 7). In cognitive-behavioral therapy, the causal relationship of thinking, feeling, and behaving is highlighted, on the belief that people experience emotional distress as a result of faulty thinking (Webb, 1992).

Researchers specializing in the treatment of domestic violence victims agree that these women have distorted beliefs about both themselves (including their self-worth, ability to survive on their own, and responsibility to an abusive partner) and others (Bolton & Bolton, 1987; Webb, 1992; Wodarski, 1987). Walker (1984) sees these women as demonstrating Seligman's "learned helplessness" and wrote that cognitive-behavioral techniques are especially suited to treating phobic responses conditioned during violence. According to Walker (1984) the use of cognitive therapy is appropriate for most abused women because they have a need to regain control over their own minds.

Albert Ellis's rational emotive therapy (RET), which is based on cognitive therapy, is a form of short-term treatment that can be used with domestic violence victims. Geffner and Pagelow (1990) described the use of RET to reduce irrational beliefs such as the idea that "violence, intimacy, love, sex, and affection are intermingled" (p. 129). RET techniques can be useful in conjunction with crisis intervention, for example, when a client is "catastrophizing" (Getz et al., 1974). In RET, irrational unrealistic thoughts are identified, and the client is taught how to extinguish them (Ellis & Grieger, 1977). It is a short-term procedure, which "begins to work promptly" in most cases only oriented toward homework assignments" and other active–directive techniques such as role playing, assertion training, and conditioning and counterconditioning procedures (Ellis, 1979, p. 44).

When using RET with abused women, the ABCDE format is followed. That is, A is the activating experience, B is the belief about A, and C is the consequence (emotional, behavioral, or both). It is the irrational or faulty belief that causes C, not the activating experience. The treatment also includes D, which is the disputation of distorted beliefs, and E, the new effect or philosophy that evolves from the rational belief that replaces the faulty belief (Ellis & Grieger, 1977). RET sees behavior as "habituated" and "irrational" thoughts as present in all people. As a treatment model, RET is relatively confrontive yet respectful of the client, and it works to increase the client's independence and positive self-regard.

Implementation of Treatment

As described earlier, treatment is initiated when the victim is in a crisis state, and the techniques used are from a time-limited crisis-intervention model and cognitive–behavioral therapy. The focus of the beginning phase is the condition of the client upon her arrival at the shelter. Often the abuse has taken one or more forms, including physical, emotional, sexual, and economic (Schecter, 1988). The victim probably has medical injuries. Examples of physical abuse run the gamut from pinching to hitting, burning, choking, mutilating, and destroying a beloved pet (Schecter, 1988). Several studies show that pregnant women are more likely to suffer abuse, perhaps because they are more vulnerable while pregnant (Geffner & Pagelow, 1990; Walker, 1984; Wodarski, 1987). The victim is likely to have suffered a sexual assault, and the negligence of a sexual assault could result in serious consequences for the women based on the implementation of inadequate or incomplete treatment plans (Geffner & Pagelow, 1990).

The incident of abuse that prompts the victim to go to a shelter averages several hours in length, and physical abuse is coupled with psychological and emotional abuse (Walker, 1984). The victim may also be dealing with psychiatric difficulties and alcohol and/or drug abuse and may be suffering posttraumatic stress disorder or a dissociative reaction in response to pain (Geffner & Pagelow, 1990, p. 117; Walker, 1984, p. 25). Some researchers compare the victim's behavioral and emotional reactions with those of hostages. Those exhibiting symptoms of the Stockholm syndrome react with "frozen fright" and "psychological infantilism," in which the victims suppress their rage for survival purposes and suffer a "traumatic depression" after their escape. To do this, the victim takes the perspective of the victimizer (Graham, Rawlings, & Rimini, 1988). The victim's behavior may be characterized by low self-esteem, denial of the abuse, an inability to trust, and dependence on the victimizer (Bolton & Bolton, 1987).

Because of all the things that may have happened to the victim, it is important to assess him or her for the possibility of suicide. One-half of all battered women have considered suicide, and one-fourth of all suicide attempts are directly related to abuse (Geffner & Pagelow, 1990). Many times these women view suicide as a permanent solution to a seemingly unsolvable problem.

Those principles that need to be observed in the treatment's first session are

1. The intervention must be immediate (deal with the victim immediately, in the hospital or police station if necessary).
2. It must be action oriented.
3. It must set limited goals.
4. It must offer support to the victim.

5. It must assist with focused problem solving.
6. It must begin to assess and help the client increase her self-image.
7. It must assign to the woman as much independence and responsibility for her own actions as possible.

According to Walker (1984), the first interview usually takes one-half to two hours. The social worker should take a brief history, work to build trust, evaluate the risks of further danger, and help the client devise an "escape plan." The victim will be terrified and overwhelmed, and the social workers must focus only on immediate problems and bring her to a point that they can more objectively view her situation. It is important to note, however, that although a great deal of information needs to be obtained and transmitted during this session, the therapeutic time allotted for this session should not be rushed or reduced. Taking time to establish a rapport and to reach the client's agreement and cooperation in the treatment process is essential.

Roberts and Roberts (1990) pointed out that an overriding goal of crisis intervention in this phase of work is to make certain that the woman and her children are safe. The clinician must assess the safety of the victim while she is in the shelter, reassuring her while respecting her fears. Geffner and Pagelow (1990) explained that battered women sometimes have developed a fear so great that they believe their abusers are almost omnipotent. These fears should be addressed and not ignored.

The victim often may try to deny or minimize the violence and can be helped to attain a more realistic perspective by acknowledging the particular injuries she has suffered. According to the cognitive-behavioral approach, the denial of violence is a learned behavior. Walker (1984) commented that battered women often are not believed when they talk about the details of violence, and thus when they discuss the events they act as if they do not remember them. But if the discussion focuses on such details as "Tell me how you got the bruises on your arms," the victim will be capable of remembering and will feel more comfortable talking in a safe, nonjudgmental environment.

Even if the victim is currently in a "safe" place such as a shelter, her treatment must include an evaluation of risk and the joint development of a safety plan. This is a crucial step to take in the first session, given the possibility that the victim may return to her batterer. The clinician can evaluate the risk to the victim by asking her if the abuser is suicidal or homicidal or if he has a weapon and what it is (Schecter, 1987). Questions should also focus on how obsessive the abuser is regarding the victim, his access to her, and the presence of rage, depression, drug and alcohol dependence, or abuse in the abuser (Hart, 1988).

The social worker must assess the victim's condition—whether she needs medical care, psychiatric care, or entry into a drug and alcohol treatment program, depending on the shelter's policy. Tests to determine the possibility of suicide and level of depression can be administered. If the client presents suicidal ideation and plans to complete the suicidal act, hospitalization will be required. The development of a safety plan is an important portion of the beginning phase, and it can also serve as an intervention that empowers the victim by offering her options.

Work with the victim should be immediate and action oriented. The clinician should create an atmosphere in which the client feels that the therapist believes her and is capable of helping. As the client begins to return to the level of her precrisis functioning, the therapist should begin to outline the treatment program and set the number of sessions (generally six to eight sessions are recommended). At the end of each session, the social worker should have the victim verbally review the safety plan.

The safety plan should be developed during the first three sessions of the treatment program. One portion of the plan must deal with the safety of the victim should she return to her abuser or come into contact with him under other circumstances. The plan should focus on how the victim can escape, where she can go, and who can help her. This should be laid out in terms of very specific behaviors, including such items as which phone she would use and where she could keep some clothes, an extra set of car keys, and the like.

The second part of the safety plan is to supply the victim with information. Hart (1988) wrote that men who batter often withhold information or manipulate and distort it in order to control their battered partner. The clinician must work through several sessions to teach the victim about the causes and effects of battering, legal services, government benefits, and treatment programs for batterers. Indeed, Schecter (1982) noted that abused women "lack the information or freedom of movement that most people take for granted" (p. 223). Such abuse often includes social and financial isolation (Walker, 1984), and so information can be a powerful form of intervention, by helping the victim make changes in her life. Referrals given to the victim may include legal aid, medical care, careers for homemakers, day-care programs, low-cost housing, shelter in another state, Big Brothers, drug and alcohol treatment programs, and general equivalency diploma (GED) programs (Roberts & Roberts, 1990). The power and control issues of abuse and Walker's (1984) cycle theory of battering can be taught to the client using handouts explaining the dynamics.

Guidelines for treatment of the domestic violence victim include a focus on what Schecter (1987) calls an "empowerment process." All phases of the counseling should involve tasks of validating experiences, exploring options, building on the client's strengths, and respecting her right to self-determination. All questions about the abuse should be direct and concise (Rodenburg & Fantuzzo, 1993). The clinician must emphasize to the victim that the abuse was not the victim's fault and should also make statements similar to the following: The abuse is criminal and wrong; many times, leaving an abuser is the only way to end the abuse; a family staying together simply to be together is not always best (Follingstad et al., 1991; Schecter, 1987). This is often a delicate balancing act for the clinician because the client must make her own decisions. The client is likely to express a sense of ambivalence about her relationship with the victimizer. But the clinician must give the victim a sense of her own strength and at the same time ensure that the victim recognize that the relationship is not healthy.

The middle phase of the treatment, the fourth through the sixth sessions, is based on both crisis intervention and cognitive–behavioral therapy during which the social worker and client decide on goals and objectives. The goals must be stated in measurable terms, and a way to evaluate progress must be established. One of goals should be development and enacting of an action plan for the victim. It is vital that the social worker make the victim aware of the danger that could result from her returning to her abuser, yet it is important for the victim to participate in establishing her own plan of action. According to Walker (1984), "[I]t is crucial for the woman to understand that the purpose of therapy . . . is to help her grow and regain her emotional strength" (p. 122). An overall goal may be simply "the client will regain her sense of self-worth," and one of the objectives to help her achieve this would be "not returning to the abuser." The victim may need assistance in getting help from various organizations and institutions, including obtaining government benefits and going to court.

In the middle phase of treatment, it is important that the social worker introduce the client to the principles of cognitive-behavioral therapy. This could include a simple statement to the client that sometimes we "learn" things that are incorrect and that incorrect thoughts can lead to certain unwanted emotional reactions. The therapist should take some time to find out whether the client subscribes to any illogical beliefs and to point them out to her. One irrational belief we mentioned earlier is that violence, intimacy, and love are all of a piece. Another distorted idea for the victim is the belief that she can maintain a stress-free world for . . . [her] abuser (Walker, 1984). Other irrational or illogical beliefs may include the victim's idea that the abusive situation is her fault, that violence is a normal part of relationships, and that she cannot leave the abusive situation (Finkelhor, 1988). Webb (1992) explained that battered women "learn a host of mistaken beliefs about themselves and others that cause them significant emotional distress and behavioral disorders" (p. 208).

Treatment must include intervention to enhance the victim's assertiveness and promote her self-esteem. A focus on strengths and assets helps offset the strong dependency and feeling of worthlessness that have been conditioned as part of the battering cycle (Geffner & Pagelow, 1990). When teaching assertiveness, it is important for those who work with victims of domestic violence to caution the women that their new assertiveness may, in some cases, make the batterer angrier and even more volatile than he was before. (Geffner & Pagelow, 1990; Walker, 1984).

After introducing the client to the basic premises of RET and beginning to assess her illogical beliefs in reference to herself and others, the clinician can give her daily assignments to carry out in the shelter. The client is taught to observe and record irrational thoughts and then to replace them with more realistic ones. Ellis and Grieger (1977) regard irrational beliefs as including overgeneralizations, "shoulds" and "musts" ("I must stay in this relationship"), "awfulizing" ("it would be awful if I left him"), and "damning" of the self.

The client can begin to examine her own thoughts in several ways. She can be asked to keep an "emotional diary" for a few days, noting any changes in her feelings and in what was going on at the time of her abuse (Wessler & Wessler, 1980). The client can record, using a triple-column technique, an event associated with an unpleasant mood on the left side, actual cognitions in the middle column, and a blank on the right side for the clinician and client to comment on the validity of the cognitions while in session (Shaw & Beck, 1977). Another intervention, rational self-analysis, requires that the client record facts and events in part A and self-talk in part B. For part C, the client asks whether her thinking is factual, whether the thinking will help her protect herself, and whether the thinking will help her feel the emotions that she wants to feel. Next the client should works on part D, which is the debate about part B, and part E, which is the way she wants to think and act (Maultsby, 1975).

Rational–emotive imaging (REI) can also be used during the middle phase. REI is based on the same principles as RET is but adds the "use of imagination" to "pattern nerve impulses." For ten minutes at a time, four times a day, the client writes out her ABC analysis and then comes up with a rational response. She learns relaxation techniques, including deep breathing with a mental rehearsal of the event with a rational response (Maultsby, 1975). This is a skill that the victim can learn and generalize to areas of difficulty in her life.

Other cognitive-behavioral techniques used with battered women are modeling, thought stopping, cognitive restructuring, reframing, and stress inoculation (Webb, 1992). Retribution techniques (Shaw & Beck, 1977), which challenge the assumption that the victim is responsible for the abuse, can also be used. Alternative techniques (Mancoske, Standifer, & Cauley, 1994; Shaw & Beck, 1977) can be used to generate a range of solutions or interpretations of events. Behavioral-change tasks must be small and should increase in difficulty as the client progresses. These might include contacting a lawyer or calling a family member to ask for support.

In working with the client to collect, examine, and replace illogical cognitions, it is important to tread carefully in areas where anger may erupt. In order to survive, abused women often repress their anger toward the batterer and those people or organizations who were unwilling or unable to help her. Walker (1984) warned that feelings of anger should not be unleashed too quickly. Rather, anger-management techniques should be taught while acknowledging the victim's right to live without abuse (Geffner & Pagelow, 1990).

An ongoing component of the treatment program should be a group program for the victim to attend while at the shelter (Roberts & Roberts, 1990) and perhaps to continue after discharge. The same techniques used in the shelter (e.g., RET and REI) can also be used in group work to help victims find options, learn to protect themselves, and keep away from abusive relationships.

In the final sessions, or ending phase of treatment—the seventh and eighth sessions—the client's overall progress should be summarized at the end of each session, with an emphasis on her empowerment. The client's practical concerns in regard to resources are discussed in an atmosphere that engenders hope and fosters independence. In the final stage, if the client's progress toward these goals has been hampered, a new contract for additional sessions may need to be established.

The lack of funding and the possibility of the battered victim's returning to her abuser often limit the time of treatment. When the treatment is completed, the social worker and client should measure the progress made toward the client's goals. During the final session they should review the safety plan, along with the progress made toward modifying distorted thoughts. The client should end the treatment with information about the resources available to both her and the batterer in the community, an understanding of the dynamics of abuse, and knowledge of techniques that enable her to examine her unrealistic thinking and explore her options.

If the client has elected to leave the abusive relationship, a portion of the final sessions should be spent making sure that the client has been able to obtain needed services such as housing and government benefits. It is the victim's choice as to whether or not she will return to her abuser. The social worker may be tempted to evaluate the treatment in terms of the victim's leaving her abuser, but successful treatment can also be measured in the client's increased self-esteem and ability to judge her situation objectively. It is crucial to let the client know that if she does return to the abuser, she will be in danger but at the same time convey to her that the clinician and agency will be available to her should she need further help.

In determining the effectiveness of the treatment method, the social worker should decide whether the client has returned to her precrisis level of functioning although, this level of functioning may well have been characterized by low self-esteem and fearfulness. The effectiveness of the treatment should be gauged by some type of objective measure (e.g., a depression and/or a self-esteem measurement scale). For a list of such scales in the behavioral sciences, the reader is referred to Corcoran and Fischer (1988). These scales should be administered before the treatment is begun and again when it is completed (Webb, 1992). If treatment has been effective, the client should be able to explain to the social worker the dynamics of abuse and should leave armed with information, including referrals. The victim's experience should have been validated by the shelter. The treatment also can be judged to have been effective if the victim is able to identify her own core strengths in a final session.

Future Directions

Society has tended to uphold the historical conviction of the sanctity of the family's right to privacy in cases of wife battering (Costantino, 1981). Society has traditionally also been reluctant to incarcerate abusive men and to force them to receive help. Accordingly, spousal abusers have been reluctant to seek assistance in resolving the problem (Finkelhor, 1988). There must be stronger social sanctions against domestic violence, and these must be reflected in both the penal system and the legal system.

Broader social issues relating to sex and gender stereotyping and unfair practices of sexism must be addressed. Recognizing the problem of abuse as a widespread social issue is a first step toward remedying it. Although battered women may call their local police department two to five times over a six-month period, the record of those calls will be lost if each incident is managed as a new case.

The police are frequently the first place to which battered women turn. As a result of the *Thurman* case in Torrington, Connecticut (in which a battered woman filed suit against the police for failing to protect her and was awarded $2.3 million), several police departments have established interdisciplinary crisis teams that include professional social workers (Stith et al., 1990). The responsibilities of these crisis teams (working in groups of two) are: advocacy, counseling, transportation to and from the shelter and/or medical centers, and referrals to appropriate social service agencies. (For a more detailed description of the collaboration needed between police and social workers, see Chapter 6.)

Walker (1984) stated that the "ultimate goal of therapy is to become a survivor, putting the effects of victimization in the past and getting on with life" (p. 128). In considering the ways in which the shelter programs can better meet the needs of abused women, a great part of the answer is increased funding, as the economic resources that offer a woman with children the option of leaving an abusive partner are severely limited.

Despite the growing attention to spouse abuse on a community and national level, there is still a stigma attached to the woman who leaves her partner, even if he is abusive. As Schecter (1982) explained, "[B]attered women are victims of sexist economic, political and social institutions" (p. 26). Treatment models that advocate a feminist perspective are vital to the shelter setting. The fact that male violence is supported by our society and that domination is part of the abuse gives women a broader understanding of their situation.

Treatment in a shelter setting based on crisis intervention and cognitive–behavioral therapy appears to be an effective and efficient way to serve abused women. They have learned not to act and that trying to escape does not reap rewards. They have accepted their abuser's distorted perspective and so must learn a more stable and healthy view of reality. By learning cognitive–behavioral therapy, they find out that they do have choices.

Finally, one way in which treatment for abused women needs to be expanded is to include the almost always forgotten victims, the children. These children need to continue to be incorporated into some portions of the treatment process, perhaps using a family system framework. Although the literature reveals that more and more researchers are demonstrating a concern for these children, relatively little has been done to develop a comprehensive treatment program for them. For a review of shelter-based programs and group counseling (on a limited scale) for children see Chapter 11.

References

Bolton, F., and S. Bolton. 1987. *Working with Violent Families: A Guide for Clinical and Legal Practitioners*. Newbury Park, Calif.: Sage.

Coley, S. M., and J. O. Beckett. 1988. "Black Battered Women: Practice Issues." *Social Casework* 69: 483–90.

Constantino, C. 1981. "Intervention with Battered Women: The Lawyer–Social Worker Team." *Social Work* 26: 456–60.

Corcoran, K., and J. Fischer. 1987. *Measures for Clinical Practice—A Source Book*. New York: Free Press.

Council on Scientific Affairs, American Medical Association. "Editorial." 1992. *Journal of the American Medical Association* 267: 3184–89.

Davidson, B. P., and P. J. Jenkins. 1989. "Class Diversity in Shelter Life." *Social Work* 34:491–95.

Edelson, J. L. 1991, June. "Note on History: Social Worker's Intervention in Women Abuse: 1907–1945." *Social Service Review*, pp. 304–13.

Ellis, A. 1979. "The Theory of Rational Emotive Therapy." In *Theoretical and Empirical Foundations of Rational-Emotive Therapy,* ed. A. Ellis and J. M. Whitely, pp. 33–60. Monterey, Calif.: Brooks/Cole.

Ellis, A., and R. Grieger, eds. 1977. *Handbook of Rational–Emotive Therapy.* New York: Springer.

Finkelhor, D. 1988. *Stopping Family Violence.* London: Sage.

Follingstad, D. et al. 1991. "Factors Moderating Physical and Psychological Symptoms of Battered Women." *Journal of Family Violence* 6: 81–95.

Geffner, R., and M. Pagelow. 1990. "Victims of Spouse Abuse." In *Treatment of Family Violence: A Source Book,* ed. R. Ammerman and M. Hersen, pp. 113–35. New York: Wiley.

Gelles, R. J., and P. Cornell. 1990. *Intimate Violence in Families.* London: Sage.

Getz, W., A. Wiesen, S. Sue, and A. Ayers. 1974. *Fundamentals of Crisis Counseling.* Lexington, Mass.: Heath.

Graham, D., E. Rawlings, and N. Rimini. 1988. "Survivors of Terror—Battered Women, Hostages and the Stockholm Syndrome." In *Feminist Perspectives on Wife Abuse,* ed. K. Yllo and M. Bograd, pp. 217–33. Newbury Park, Calif.: Sage.

Hart, B. 1988. "Beyond the Duty to Warn." In *Feminist Perspectives on Wife Abuse,* ed. K. Yllo and M. Bograd, pp. 234–48. Newbury Park, Calif.: Sage.

Mancoske, R. J., D. Standifer, and C. Cauley. 1994. "The Effectiveness of Brief Counseling Services for Battered Women." *Research On Social Work Practice* 4: 53–63.

Maultsby, M. C., Jr. 1975. *Help Yourself to Happiness.* New York: Institute for Rational Living.

McDonald, P. 1989. "Transition Houses and the Problem of Family Violence." *Interviewing with Assaulted Women: Current Theory Research and Practice,* ed. B. Pressman, G. Cameron, and M. Rothery, pp. 111–23. Hillsdale, N.J.: Erlbaum.

Novella, A. C. 1992. "From the Surgeon General: U.S. Public Health Service." *Journal of American Medical Association* 267: 3132.

Puryear, D. 1979. *Helping People in Crisis.* San Francisco: Jossey-Bass.

Roberts, A. 1990. *Crisis Intervention Handbook: Assessment, Treatment and Research.* Belmont, Calif: Wadsworth.

Roberts, A., and B. Roberts. 1990. "A Comprehensive Model for Crisis Intervention with Battered Women and Their Children." In *Crisis Intervention Handbook: Assessment, Treatment and Research,* ed. A. Roberts, pp. 106–23. Belmont, Calif.: Wadsworth.

Rodenburg, F., and J. Fantuzzo, 1993. "The Measure of Wife Abuse: Steps Toward the Development of a Comprehensive Assessment Technique." *Journal of Family Violence* 8: 203–27.

Rounsaville, B. J. 1978. "Battered Wives: Barriers to Identification and Treatment." *American Journal of Orthopsychiatry* 48: 487–94.

Shaw, B. F. and Beck, A. T. 1977. "The Treatment of Depression with Cognitive Therapy." In *Handbook of Rational Emotive Theory and Practice,* ed. A. Ellis and R. Grieger. New York: Springer.

Schecter, S. 1982. *Women and Male Violence.* Boston: South End Press.

Schecter, S. 1987. *Guidelines for Mental Health Practitioners in Domestic Violence Cases.* Washington, D.C.: National Coalition Against Domestic Violence.

Schecter, S. 1988. "A Framework for Understanding and Empowering Battered Women." In *Abuse and Victimization Across the Life Span,* ed. M. Straus, pp. 240–53. Baltimore: John Hopkins University Press.

Srinivasan, M., and L. V. Davis. 1991. "A Shelter: An Organization Like Any Other?" *Affilia* 6: 38–57.

Stith, S. M., M. Williams, and K. Rosen. 1990. *Violence Hits Home: Comprehensive Treatment Approaches to Domestic Violence.* New York: Springer.

Walker, L. 1984. *The Battered Woman Syndrome.* New York: Springer.

Webb, W. 1992. "Treatment Issues and Cognitive Behavior Techniques with Battered Women." *Journal of Family Violence* 7: 205–17.

Wessler, R. A., and R. L. Wessler. 1980. *The Principles and Practice of Rational–Emotive Therapy.* San Francisco: Jossey-Bass.

Wodarski, J. 1987. "An Examination of Spouse Abuse: Practice Issues for the Profession." *Clinical Social Work Journal,* 15: 172–79.

11

Children of Battered Women: Research, Programs, and Services

Bonnie E. Carlson

As awareness of the prevalence and impact of domestic violence has grown, professional attention has shifted from the affected adults to the children who are exposed to abuse between their parents. During the 1980s, research on such children proliferated so that we now have enough information to begin to understand the impact on children of observing interparental violence.

A Review of the Research

Since the early 1980s, research on the impact on children of witnessing violence or abuse between their parents has grown in both quantity and quality. More controlled studies have compared children who have witnessed abuse with matched control or contrast group children who have not witnessed abuse. In addition, controls have been introduced for several factors, including age, gender, the effects of maternal stress, and the effects of also being the victim of physical abuse by a parent. Increasingly, these factors have been conceptualized as mediating variables that can amplify or buffer the impact of abuse. The findings of these research studies are summarized in this chapter.

The major conclusion to emerge from the research is that children exposed to marital violence tend to exhibit elevated levels of at least some of the measured symptoms (Christopoulous et al., 1987; Davis & Carlson, 1987; Fantuzzo et al., 1991; Holden & Ritchie, 1991; Hughes, 1988; Hughes, Parkinson, & Vargo, 1989;

Jaffe et al., 1986; Jouriles, Murphy, & O'Leary, 1989; Kempton, Thomas, & Forehand, 1989; Stagg, Wills, & Howell, 1989). Thus it can be concluded generally that observing marital violence is associated with diminished well-being in children. The characteristics of these studies are summarized in Table 11.1.

The effects of witnessing marital violence were found in at least three areas of functioning. First, the evidence indicates elevated levels of *internalizing behavior problems,* such as depression, anxiety, and withdrawal (Christopoulous et al., 1987; Davis & Carlson, 1987; Fantuzzo et al., 1991; Jaffe et al., 1986). These children present with problems such as manifest sadness, excessive worrying, detachment, or somatic difficulties like sleeping or eating problems. *Externalizing behavior problems,* such as aggression, acting out, misbehavior, or uncooperativeness also was found to be elevated compared with those in groups of children who had not witnessed domestic violence (Davis & Carlson, 1987; Fantuzzo et al., 1991; Jaffe et al., 1986). Some studies found internalizing problems more common (Christopoulous et al., 1987; Hughes et al., 1989), whereas others reported that externalizing problems tended to predominate (Holden & Ritchie, 1991). Finally, evidence of *impaired social competence* (a measure of social adjustment, such as participation in social activities and involvement with age mates) was found in children who had witnessed domestic violence (Davis & Carlson, 1987; Fantuzzo et al., 1991; Jaffe et al., 1985).

The relationship between observing marital violence and child distress was even stronger in the case of children who had also been physically abused by their parent(s). Abused children constitute a significant but varied subgroup of children found in domestic violence shelters, comprising as few as one-fourth of one sample to as many as 91 percent of another sample (Christopoulous et al., 1987; Hughes, 1988; Hughes et al., 1989; Jouriles, Barling, & O'Leary, 1987; Layzer, Goodson, & DeLange, 1986). Some studies found that being the direct victim of physical abuse had a more detrimental impact on children than did observing abuse between parents (Jouriles et al., 1987). Based on the research findings, we can conclude that physical abuse and witnessing interparental abuse appear to contribute independently to difficulties in children and thus to have an additive effect on them (Jouriles et al., 1989).

Most studies found, based on age and gender, variation in the symptoms manifested by different subgroups of children who observed marital violence (Christopoulous et al., 1987; Davis & Carlson, 1987; Holden & Ritchie, 1991; Hughes, 1988; Jaffe et al., 1985; Jouriles et al., 1989). Most designs compared younger and older schoolage children with one another and with preschoolers and examined the findings separately by gender.

Few studies examined adolescents exposed to domestic violence, who tend not to stay with their mothers in shelters as frequently as younger children do. This is unfortunate insofar as exposure to abuse is increasingly considered to vary as a function of developmental level and duration of exposure, both of which would be different in adolescents compared with younger children. One study of adolescents in residential placement found that males exposed to domestic violence were more likely to have run away from home and consider suicide than were males not exposed to marital abuse but that witnessing domestic violence was not related to

Table 11.1. Comparison of Empirical Studies of the Impact of Domestic Violence on Children

	Age	Dependent variables	Control group	Sample size	Mediating variables
Carlson, 1991	13–18	Attitudes, substance abuse peer relationships, self-esteem, depression, violent behavior, running away, destructive behavior	No	101	None
Christopoulous et al., 1987	5–13	CBCL[a]: internalizing and externalizing behaviors	Yes (40)	80	None
Davis & Carlson, 1987	4–16	CBCL: social competence internalizing and externalizing behaviors, depression, somatic complaints, aggression	No	78	Yes, physical abuse
Fantuzzo et al., 1991	3–6	CBCL	Yes	107	Yes, shelter residence, verbal abuse
Hughes, 1988	3–12	Self-esteem, anxiety, depression, behavioral problems	Yes (83)	178	Yes, physical abuse
Hughes et al., 1989	4–12	Anxiety, depression	Yes (66)	150	Yes, physical abuse
Jaffe et al., 1986b	4–16	CBCL: social competence, internalizing, and externalizing	Yes	50	No
Jouriles et al., 1987	5–13	Maternal perceptions of child behavior problems	No	45	Yes, physical abuse
Jouriles et al., 1989	5–12	Child behavior problems	No	87	Yes, age and gender
Kempton et al., 1989	11–15	Conduct problems, anxiety, withdrawal, cognitive and prosocial functioning	No	48	None
Stagg et al., 1989	4–6	CBCL: total problems, internalizing and externalizing problems, social competence	No	26	Yes, ethnicity
Wildin et al., 1991	9 mos.–13 yrs.	School behavior (attendance, aggression, and other problem behaviors), suicidal ideation	No	76	None
Wolfe et al., 1985	4–16	CBCL: social competence, internalizing, externalizing	Yes	102	Yes, maternal stress, negative life events, family crises

[a]Child Behavior Checklist (Achenbach & Edelbrock, 1982).

girls' well-being (Carlson, 1990). Among those subjects who had both been physically abused and observed marital violence, compared with those who had experienced only one type of abuse or no abuse at all, well-being was lower (Carlson, 1991).

Only one study considered ethnic variations and concluded that white boys were at higher risk for developing behavioral problems than were African-American boys or were girls of either race (Stagg et al., 1989). Clearly, the area of ethnic effects needs further research.

Although many studies found age and gender differences, those differences tend not to be consistent across studies, so it is difficult to draw conclusions regarding age or gender effects. We could tentatively conclude that younger children appear to be more symptomatic than older children do and that boys are somewhat more symptomatic than girls, especially with respect to externalizing behavior problems.

These findings are consistent with other research in the mental health field that found boys to be more symptomatic than are girls exposed to the same stressors. It is also possible that nonsymptomatic girls may experience deferred effects that manifest at later developmental stages (this could also be true for nonsymptomatic boys). Younger children might be expected to be more symptomatic than older children are, because they are more dependent on the family for development and have fewer nonfamily resources to use for coping than older children do. On the other hand, based on what we know about the chronicity of domestic violence, older children are likely to be exposed over a much longer period than younger children are, possibly leading to more serious effects. Perhaps there is a bimodal distribution of negative outcomes, with very young children and adolescents more adversely affected than schoolage children. Studies comparing children from all three age groups would be necessary to confirm such a suspicion.

Relatively few studies have considered the impact of exposure to marital violence on children's school performance. There is every reason to assume, however, that given the pervasiveness of the effects of exposure to abuse, school behavior and performance would be affected. The research findings of at least one study are consistent with that prediction. The children of thirty-nine battered women in one shelter, most of whom were nonwhite, were found to be experiencing a number of school-related problems. These included developmental delays in 39 percent of the twenty-eight preschoolers studied, academic problems (such as being held back) in almost half the forty-six schoolage children studied, behavior problems in 30 percent of the schoolage children serious enough to warrant a phone call from school to the child's mother, and missing an average of 3.6 days from school because of the mother's victimization (Wildin, Williamson, & Wilson, 1991). The researchers acknowledge that the "low educational level in some mothers and low socioeconomic status may have played a significant role in the poor academic achievement in this sample" (Wildin et al., 1991, p. 303). Further research is needed on school performance in a more varied sample of children exposed to domestic violence.

The impact of witnessing abuse may extend to less obvious domains as well, such as the attitude and personal responsibility for the violence or self-blame. Because it is arguments about children that often precede violence (Straus, Gelles, & Steinmetz, 1980), it is not surprising that some children believe themselves to be the cause of their parents' abuse. This in part appears to be a developmental phenomenon. That is, as children grow older, they become less egocentric and better able to attribute correctly the causes of the abuse to their parents rather than themselves (Jaffe, Hurley, & Wolfe, 1990; Jaffe, Wilson, & Wolfe, 1988; Jaffe, Wolfe, & Wilson, 1990). Studies of schoolage children indicate greater approval of violence among those exposed to marital abuse (Jaffe et al., 1988; Jaffe, Wolfe, & Wilson, 1990). However, one study of a clinical sample of adolescents did not find that youths exposed to physical abuse, marital violence, or both were more likely to approve of interpersonal violence, compared with those not exposed to abuse (Carlson, 1991).

In addition to age and gender mediating the relationship between witnessing parental violence and child dysfunction, maternal stress has been found to play an intervening role (Holden & Ritchie, 1991; Moore et al., 1990). Mothers who are functioning well and adequately performing their roles as parents can buffer some of the potentially adverse effects of children's exposure to marital violence. But women in these circumstances are often under extreme duress themselves because of the abuse they are experiencing and thus may not be able to perform well as a parent. Children are thus at greater risk for dysfunction under these circumstances (Wolfe et al., 1985).

Little has been written about how children cope with the experience of witnessing abuse between their parents and related stresses, such as being the victim of physical abuse, having parents who are divorcing, or testifying in court against a parent on another's behalf (Davis, 1988). These related stresses appear to contribute independently to behavioral problems in children (Jaffe et al., 1985; Jouriles et al., 1987). For some children exposed to parental violence, traumatization is the result. This is manifested as a sense of fear and helplessness, accompanied by symptoms of depression, psychic numbing, self-blame, and withdrawal (Silvern & Kaersvang, 1989), most of which have been discussed earlier. In fact, some children exposed to domestic violence may meet the criteria for posttraumatic stress disorder (PTSD), although this conceptual framework has not been widely used to view the problems of children exposed to marital violence. On the other hand, it could be argued that violence between parents is sufficiently common that it is not "outside the range of usual human experience," which is one criterion for PTSD (American Psychiatric Association, 1987). And yet observing interparental violence would certainly meet the criterion of being "markedly distressing to almost anyone," "is usually experienced with intense fear, terror, and [is probably experienced by children with a sense of] helplessness" (American Psychiatric Association, 1987, p. 247).

Is witnessing abuse inevitably harmful to children? Controlled research studies show that not all children who are exposed to domestic violence are more symptomatic than nonexposed children are (Carlson, 1990; Jaffe et al., 1988; Jouriles et al., 1989). This could be attributed to methodological limitations of the research; that is, perhaps we are not studying the right variables or in the right way. Or it may be that some children exposed to marital violence have resources that enable them to survive the experience without becoming symptomatic. On the other hand, of those who are not symptomatic at the time they are studied but continue to be exposed to violence between their parents, some additional percentage will undoubtedly develop difficulties over time. And interestingly, among those who are affected, not all are affected in the same way. Whereas one child may act out behaviorally and present control problems, another may become withdrawn and depressed or develop interpersonal difficulties.

Among those children who are harmed by exposure to parental abuse, an important question is, what is it about that experience that is distressing to them? The answer to that question may have as much to do with events associated with domestic violence, such as multiple parental separations or residential moves or chronic marital discord than it does with the actual observation of acts of aggression between the parents. As mentioned earlier, a large subgroup of child witnesses to domestic violence are also abused and/or neglected by their parents. Many, if not most, children who stay in domestic violence shelters are also poor. In addition, verbal abuse directed at the victimized parent or the children may contribute to an unhealthy environment. That these multiple stressors have a cumulative effect is supported by research indicating that child witnesses who had more stressors in their lives were likely also to have more behavioral problems (Jaffe et al., 1985). This brings to mind Rutter's (1980) work on the impact of multiple stressors on children. Often when domestic violence is present, we also see a number of marker variables that accompany it and place additional stress on family members, including children. Thus, the factors associated with domestic violence may harm children as much as the direct effects of witnessing abuse do (Jaffe, Wolfe, & Wilson, 1990).

Methodological Issues

Numerous methodological problems plague the research on child witnesses to domestic violence. First, most of the samples studied were relatively small; in light of the need to consider separately children of different ages and genders, this means that most groups on which the generalizations were based were small in size. For the most part, the studies used similar instruments, but not always. In some cases, mothers or teachers provided information about the children's functioning, whereas in other cases children reported on their own emotional states and behaviors. The results from different categories of reporters, therefore, were often inconsistent.

Almost all the information comes from mothers staying temporarily in domestic violence shelters who are reporting on their children. But information on child functioning in these circumstances may be fraught with biases and other problems that lead us to question its validity. That is, mothers under such stress may have difficulty being objective about their child's functioning. In addition, children's behavior is influenced by being in unfamiliar surroundings, away from familiar possessions and people, in the aftermath of what has probably been, for most, a crisis. There may be uncertainty about the future, specifically where the family will be going next and when, and who will be there. This situation can give rise to intense emotional reactions that young children in particular have difficulty describing accurately and that may be only indirectly related to the parental abuse they have witnessed (Hughes, 1988), and yet such emotional states can easily contaminate measurements intended to assess the impact of observing abuse. At least one study found that being in a shelter contributed independently to internalizing and social competence problems in children even when parental discord and other variables were statistically controlled (Fantuzzo et al., 1991).

It is also important to keep in mind that since most women who experience marital violence do not stay in a domestic violence shelter, the children studied there are undoubtedly not a cross section of all children who witness violence between their parents. Instead, the children studied in shelters are likely to be those who observed the most chronic and severe violence, who are poor, and whose mothers have the fewest resources with which to cope with such abuse. Thus, it is likely that the children evaluated in most of these studies not only witnessed the most extreme forms of marital violence but also experienced many of the accompanying stressors.

Programs and Services

There is a limited but growing literature on programs and services for children who have observed domestic violence between their parents, who may number one in ten of all children (Jaffe, Wolfe, & Wilson, 1990). Most of the existing services appear to be offered almost exclusively within and under the auspices of domestic violence shelters, although only a fraction of children exposed to marital violence ever stay in such a shelter (Jaffe et al., 1988; Moore et al., 1989). Thus although shelters may be more likely to provide special programming for children than they did previously, such programming is undoubtedly missing the majority of exposed children who never stay in a shelter. In addition, the transient nature of the shelter population of children presents major challenges for programming (Moore et al., 1989).

Elements of a Comprehensive Program

Based on the research examining the impact on children of witnessing violence between their parents and on the literature on programs and services, a comprehensive model program is proposed that includes the following components:

1. *Individual assessment.* Each child should be evaluated individually by staff with training in child development, through observations and interviews with the child and his or her mother.
2. *Individual counseling* for children who exhibit serious emotional or behavioral problems or disorders. This is indicated based on research showing that substantial numbers of children seen in shelters are in the clinical range for externalizing and internalizing behavior problems or both (Davis & Carlson, 1987; Jaffe, Hurley & Wolfe, 1990). These services can be provided by program staff or contracted out; volunteer professionals might also be used to provide counseling if no other alternatives are available.
3. *Referral* for services, such as medical treatment, educational services, child care (e.g., Head Start), or counseling. Referral to mental health services is extremely important with so many child witnesses expected to be in clinical ranges, especially for those shelters that do not provide individual assess-

ment and counseling. Since most shelters have limited resources and wish to avoid duplicating services available in the community, this is a practical approach when child mental health services are available in the community. Referral for health screening is also indicated insofar as most children who stay in shelters are poor or near-poor and often lack regular health evaluations and preventive health-care services such as immunizations.

4. *Advocacy* with agencies from which child witnesses to domestic violence might need services, such as schools and educational programs, mental health agencies, and medical clinics or physicians. This is necessary because many of these children come from underserved, low-income families and have mothers who are overwhelmed by the abuse in their lives and feel stigmatized by it.

5. *Group work* for children residing temporarily in domestic violence shelters or residing in the community but living in homes where the violence is occurring or has occurred, either with peers or siblings.

6. *Regular, structured recreational activities* for children of all ages that take place both inside and outside the shelter, such as games (inside or outdoors if it is safe), trips to shopping malls, museums, restaurants, sports events, or movies. Although informal or spontaneous recreational activities are enjoyable, the temporary and unstable living situation in which child witnesses find themselves necessitate planned, structured activities that they can count on.

7. *Aftercare* or follow-up services to monitor how children are faring after they leave the shelter to return home or relocate. Often the circumstances of these children's lives remain chaotic and unstable, necessitating ongoing monitoring and services such as counseling, or medical care.

8. *Prevention services,* such as presentations at local schools to discuss dating violence in teen relationships or talks or workshops in the community on domestic violence. Such educational efforts are essential to assist the general public and professionals in understanding domestic violence in general and its impact on children in particular.

9. *Parenting education and support groups* that offer information about parenting and also encourage mothers to ventilate and share with others the joys and frustrations of parenting. Both empirical research and clinical reports from shelters indicate that battered women are frequently depressed, anxious, and overwhelmed and so would benefit from social support and information on how to be better parents.

10. *Evaluation* that systematically assesses the impact and effectiveness of all aspects of the program. Unless children's programs are evaluated systematically, the programs' sponsors and funding sources cannot be certain that they are effective and, if they are, which components are most valuable and cost effective.

The Research

A qualitative research project was conducted to study children's programming in New York State's domestic violence shelters. Three types of information were used:

1. A directory of domestic violence programs compiled by the New York State Coalition Against Domestic Violence, entitled *1992–1993 New York State Directory of Services for Victims of Domestic Violence.*
2. Brief telephone interviews with shelter staff members who were responsible for children's programming. All twenty-one domestic violence shelters listed as having a children's program were contacted about the content of their program as well as staffing patterns and funding, the number and age distribution of children, and referral patterns. Fifteen programs (71 percent) were reached and agreed to provide information; none refused to cooperate.
3. Documents and materials provided by the shelters to describe and support their children's programs.

Children's Programs in New York State's Domestic Violence Shelters

Overview

The New York State Department of Social Services (DSS) defines four categories of residential domestic violence programs, of which there were a total of seventy-three in 1991. Not all are funded by DSS, but in 1992 and 1993, most (61 percent) were.

In the twenty-seven *domestic violence shelters,* defined by DSS regulations as "congregate facilities with a capacity of 10 or more persons serving exclusively domestic violence victims," twenty-one (78 percent) reported that they offered a children's program. In contrast, none of the four *domestic violence programs,* defined as "facilities which would meet the definition of domestic violence shelter except they serve a mixed population—70% must be victims of domestic violence," offered a special program for children. Finally, there were forty-two *safe home networks* ("organized network[s] of private homes offering temporary shelter and emergency services domestic violence to victims") and *domestic violence sponsoring agencies* (offering temporary shelter at safe dwellings and emergency services exclusively to victims of domestic violence," with a capacity of fewer than ten people), nineteen of which (45 percent) were listed as having a children's program.

Thus formal children's programs were most likely to be offered in large shelters and were least likely to be available in the few shelters that served primarily (but not exclusively) domestic violence victims.

Survey Results

The average number of program components per shelter was 3.8, with a range of one to seven. The most common program components were parenting education and/or support groups for mothers (50 percent), which were seen as interventions on behalf of children. The next most common components were child care (33 percent), individual counseling (33 percent), and group counseling for children (33 percent). Formalized recreation programs (27 percent), and prevention programs (27 percent) carried out in the community also were utilized. Forty-seven percent also included other programs such as having an art therapist work with children weekly, ensuring that all children see a pediatrician, and visiting the children at home after their departure from the shelter.

In regard to staffing, two-thirds of the programs had the equivalent of at least one full-time staff person devoted to children's programming, and 33 percent had more than a full-time staff member. Generally these positions carried titles such as children's coordinator, children's advocate, or youth services coordinator, but also more generic titles such as administrative assistant and shelter coordinator. Typically the positions were funded by a variety of sources, most commonly the Division for Youth or DSS (New York State funds) or private funds from organizations such as the United Way, as well as donations. Most children's programs were funded by at least two sources. In some cases, the person responding to the survey did not know how the position was funded.

Regarding referrals, all fifteen shelters said they made referrals as needed, on a case-by-case basis, and named a mean of 3.6 sources. The most common types of referrals made were for medical care, educational reasons (e.g., to get a child in school or Head Start), or mental health reasons.

Model Programs

The survey identified two exemplary programs offering numerous elements of a comprehensive program for children.

Domestic Violence Services of Saratoga, New York, is a relatively young program, beginning in 1987. The children's program, Kidstuff, has six components: three for children and three for mothers. All paid staff are encouraged to assume responsibility for the children, in contrast with many shelter programs that employ child development specialists who are responsible for children's services. In addition, numerous volunteers are utilized. Ten-week closed groups called Kidsafe are offered regularly for children at four developmental levels (preschool, six- to eight-year-olds, nine- to twelve-year-olds, and adolescents) who have lived in an abusive family environment. Kidwreck is an organized program of recreational activities such as art and movement exercises and special holiday celebrations, as well as respite child care. Against the Grain is a prevention program of educational presentations offered to the schools and community groups regarding the cycle of abuse, violence in dating relationships, and the impact of exposure to domestic violence on children.

For mothers, Kidstuff offers a weekly, open, Mothers' Group that provides support and addresses parenting skills, especially discipline, stress management, and issues of single parenting. It is offered collaboratively with the Saratoga Task Force on Child Abuse. A six-session closed group called Coping with Custody is offered to mothers who are dealing with custody and visitation issues with a former abusive partner. It addresses the impact of domestic violence and separation and divorce on children, legal issues, and parent–child power struggles. Finally, Time Together, a program of organized, supervised visitation is offered jointly with the Saratoga Task Force on Child Abuse for families referred by a family court.

Another model children's program is located in the Rockland Family Shelter in

Spring Valley, New York. The majority of child clients in residence are quite young, and the number of children staying at the shelter at any one time is relatively low, seven to eight on average. But the program also serves mothers and children who are victims of domestic violence but do not necessarily need or desire shelter. The program is multifaceted, including one full-time staff member and two part-time, master's degree-level social workers. When the children enter the shelter, a case aide helps orient them, encouraging them to express their feelings about their experience. All children are formally assessed and evaluated by a pediatrician. Groups for children are held daily. In addition, a weekly parenting group for mothers emphasizes empowerment and parenting skills, especially discipline.

Examples of other model shelter programs that effectively address children's needs can be found in Roberts and Roberts's *Crisis Intervention Handbook* (1990).

Intervention with Children of Battered Women

Assessment

The research literature just summarized indicates that substantial numbers of children who observe domestic violence are in the clinical range for externalizing and internalizing behavior problems as well as social competence. Thus, all three areas should be assessed while children are living in domestic violence shelters or in other community settings.

It may be difficult, for several reasons, to obtain an accurate assessment of children's functioning during a shelter stay. First, the setting is generally unfamiliar, and the children have been displaced from their homes. Typically, they have just experienced a family crisis, insofar as a serious violent incident usually precipitates a shelter stay. In addition, they have been separated from their fathers and sometimes other siblings as well. Often they have ambivalent feelings toward one or both parents during this time. Ambivalence toward their father is understandable because he hurt their mother and may have frightened or abused them. But a mixture of confusing feelings toward the mother is also not uncommon because she has decided to leave the family home and that has disrupted their life. Thus, children may be frightened, angry, confused, and/or relieved about being at the shelter. For all these reasons, assessment should not be attempted in the first few days of a child's stay, in order to permit him or her an opportunity to settle in.

If as many as 10 percent of all children have been exposed to domestic violence, the percentage among clinical populations of children is likely to be even higher. This has led to the recommendation that clinicians who work with children routinely explore for information about whether a child has been exposed to parental violence (Jaffe, Wolfe, & Wilson, 1990).

Treatment

In addition to treating behavioral, emotional, and interpersonal problems in children exposed to domestic violence, the literature suggests that clinical attention focus on three other issues. First, we must address the child's safety. Second, we must consider the child's feelings about what he or she has experienced. Finally, we must focus on the child's sense of guilt or responsibility for what has happened between the parents (Jaffe, Wilson, & Wolfe, 1990; Silvern & Kaersvang, 1989).

Treatment can be on an individual basis or in a group format. The lack of professional staff can limit a shelter's ability to provide individual counseling, whereas offering activity or support groups for children is more feasible and does not require a high level of professional expertise. Professional counseling of children and youth exposed to marital violence thus may take place more often in community agencies and also in residential treatment facilities serving adolescents.

Little has been written about offering individual counseling to youngsters who have witnessed a parent behaving abusively toward the other, although Jaffe, Wolfe, and Wilson's (1990) advice regarding important issues for shelter staff to be aware of is a useful starting point. They noted that they staff should be aware that (1) children can be in a posttraumatic state while in a shelter (and should be treated accordingly); (2) children in a shelter may feel insecure about what is likely to happen next to their family, which is frightening and leaves them with a higher-than-average potential for aggressive behavior; and (3) these children have a greater need for a sense of trust and security than other children do.

Group Work

Several descriptions exist of groups for children who have witnessed domestic violence (Frey-Angel, 1989; Grusznski, Brink, & Edelson, 1988; Ragg, 1991; Wilson et al., 1989). Frey-Angel (1989) describes a sibling group at a shelter that met at the same time a mother's group was being held. This is a common practice that alleviates the need for child care while the mother is busy while also offering programming for children. Frey-Angel's approach takes into account that children in the same family may respond differently to violence. As an indicator of its success, Frey-Angel (1989) reports sharing even among siblings for whom this had not been the norm. This was accomplished by focusing on social skill development, problem solving, and communication.

Grusznski and colleagues (1988) and Wilson and colleagues (1989) described similar groups for schoolage children aged six to twelve or thirteen. Wilson and colleagues noted that such groups are needed because children learn several lessons from violent parents, such as that violence is an acceptable way to resolve disagreements or deal with stress or that victims have no choice but to tolerate abusive behavior.

Both the Grusznski and the Wilson models recommend ten-session groups with male and female co-leaders and with each session focused on a particular topic. Both models discuss the following issues: feelings of responsibility for the parents' abuse; labeling and expressing feelings like shame and anger; safety or protection skills, such as the ability to call 911 for help; traditional gender roles; and self-esteem or self-concept. Both use substantial education about domestic violence to help children feel better about themselves. Neither reports the results of a controlled evaluation of the groups' impact, but anecdotal reports suggest that the participants in one group seemed to be better able to admit domestic violence in their family, to know how to keep themselves safe if abuse occurred again in the future, and to feel less responsible for the abuse occurring between their parents (Grusznski et al., 1988).

Discipline

A major challenge for all shelter programs is how to address misbehavior, especially aggressive misbehavior, by the children in residence. Such behavior is extremely common for many of these children, as documented by both empirical research and the clinical observations of the shelter staff. Taken from their homes and staying temporarily in unfamiliar surroundings, many children in shelters imitate what they have seen modeled in their families. This in turn creates the need for discipline and limit setting by parents and shelter staff. Since most shelters have rules against using any form of violent behavior and most parents rely to at least some extent on physical discipline, a problem ensues. The standard response of shelters to this common situation is to try to improve parenting skills with a focus on nonviolent forms of discipline. The staff explains the importance of setting firm limits and how to do so, even though this might make one's children temporarily unhappy or angry. They also discuss the importance of consistency in limit setting and discipline, as well as the possible consequences of inconsistency, including such behaviors as continually testing limits and not complying with parents' or staff requests. Most important, the staff point out alternatives to physical discipline, such as time out, in the context of both formal parenting groups and individually and informally.

The Long Island Women's Coalition shelter in Islip, New York, provides an example of such an approach. In mandated groups on parenting, the shelter staff provide handouts and assignments for mothers that (1) ask them about their views on punishment and discipline; (2) explain why spanking is ineffective and can perpetuate the cycle of violence; (3) provide information about alternatives to physical discipline such as ignoring misbehavior (when possible), explaining expectations for children's behavior, using positive reinforcement and follow-through; and (4) giving examples of ineffective "discipline" (which would be considered by some to be psychological or emotional abuse), such as threatening, frightening, or humiliating children.

Resources

A number of resources have been developed that can be useful for programs serving children of battered women. For example, Family Communications, Inc., which produces *Mister Rogers' Neighborhood,* has produced two videotapes and a book for children in collaboration with the Pennsylvania Coalition Against Domestic Violence. One video program is aimed at young boys and another at young girls who are staying in domestic violence shelters with their mothers. The book *I Do, and I Don't,* by Fred Rogers with Hedda Sharapan, is designed to be used with children of both genders. It addresses the children's ambivalence toward the experience of observing violence between their parents. These materials are available from the Pennsylvania Coalition Against Domestic Violence, 2505 N. Front St., Harrisburg, Pa. 17110; (800) 537-2238; the cost is $75 for domestic violence programs and $150 for nondomestic violence programs.

Another useful resource is a book entitled *Children of Domestic Violence: Healing the Wounds,* by Judith McDermott and Frances Wells. It is a guide for mothers that addresses child development, parenting issues, children's feelings about violence between their parents and how to deal with such feelings, and how to obtain help for family violence. It also includes a reading list for mothers and for children on domestic violence, divorce, and related topics. It can be obtained for $5.95 from the Rockland Family Shelter, 300 N. Main St., Spring Valley, N.Y.; (914) 425-0112.

Several shelters also use other materials such as coloring books that they create for children. Or they use existing coloring books like *I Wish the Hitting Would Stop: A Workbook for Children Living in Violent Homes,* published by Red Flag Green Flag Resources, Rape and Abuse Crisis Center, Box 2984, Fargo, N.D. 58108; (800) 627-3675. An accompanying facilitator's guide is also available, oriented toward working with schoolage children who have lived in a home where their mother has been physically abused. According to the introduction, it is designed to help such children cope with the stress of living in a violent home environment. It addresses issues of trusting parents, self-protection, feelings about living in an abusive home, and how to feel happy in such an environment.

Conclusions

The domestic violence service community widely recognizes the potential negative effects on children of observing abuse between their parents. If New York State is typical of other states in the country, this recognition is reflected in the many programs for children in shelters for battered women. Unfortunately, since most children who are exposed to marital violence never go to a domestic violence shelter, they cannot receive the benefits of these services. This means that the broader mental health community will need to become more educated about the pervasiveness of this problem and to offer appropriate services to these children. The domestic violence movement can play an invaluable role in helping educate these community-based professionals as well as advocating the more widespread availability of services designed to meet the special needs of this population, such as the groups described by Grusznski and associates (1988) and Wilson and associates (1989).

References

Achenbach, T., and C. Edelbrock. 1982. *Manual for the Child Behavior Checklist and Child Behavior Profile.* Burlington: University of Vermont Press.

American Psychiatric Association. 1987. *Diagnostic and Statistical Manual (DSM-III-R).* Rev. ed. Washington, D.C. American Psychiatric Association.

Carlson, B. E. 1990. "Adolescent Observers of Marital Violence." *Journal of Family Violence* 5: 285–99.

Carlson, B. E. 1991. "Outcomes of Physical Abuse and Observation of Marital Violence Among Adolescents in Placement." *Journal of Interpersonal Violence* 6: 526–34.

Christopoulous, C., D. A. Cohn, D. S. Shaw, S. Joyce, J. Sullivan-Hanson, S. P. Kraft, and R. E. Emery. 1987. "Children of Abused Women: I. Adjustment at Time of Shelter Residence." *Journal of Marriage and the Family* 49: 611–19.

Davis, K. E. 1988. "Interparental Violence: The Children as Victims." *Issues in Comprehensive Pediatric Nursing* 11: 291–302.

Davis, L. V., and B. E. Carlson. 1987. "Observation of Spouse Abuse: What Happens to the Children?" *Journal of Interpersonal Violence* 2: 278–91.

Fantuzzo, J. W., L. M. DePaola, L. Lambert, T. Martino, G. Anderson, and S. Sutton. 1991. "Effects of Interparental Violence on the Psychological Adjustment and Competencies of Young Children." *Journal of Consulting and Clinical Psychology* 59: 258–65.

Frey-Angel, J. 1989. "Treating Children of Violent Families: A Sibling Group Approach." *Social Work with Groups* 12: 95–107.

Gruszinski, R. J., J. C. Brink, and J. L. Edleson. 1988. "Support and Education Groups for Children of Battered Women." *Child Welfare* 67: 431–44.

Holden, G. W., and K. L. Ritchie. 1991. "Linking Extreme Marital Discord, Child Rearing and Child Behavior Problems: Evidence from Battered Women." *Child Development* 62: 311–27.

Hughes, H. M. 1982. "Brief Interventions with Children in a Battered Women's Shelter: A Model Preventive Program." *Family Relations* 31: 495–502.

Hughes, H. M. 1988. "Psychological and Behavioral Correlates of Family Violence in Child Witnesses and Victims." *American Journal of Orthopsychiatry* 58: 77–90.

Hughes, H. M., D. Parkinson, and M. Vargo. 1989. "Witnessing Spouse Abuse and Experiencing Physical Abuse: A 'Double Whammy?'" *Journal of Family Violence* 4: 197–209.

Jaffe, P. G., D. J. Hurley, and D. Wolfe. 1990. "Children's Observations of Domestic Violence: I. Critical Issues in Child Development and Intervention Planning." *Canadian Journal of Psychiatry* 35: 466–70.

Jaffe, P., S. K. Wilson, and D. Wolfe. 1986. "Promoting Changes in Attitudes and Understanding of Conflict Resolution Among Child Witnesses of Family Violence." *Canadian Journal of Behavior Science* 18: 356–66.

Jaffe, P., S. K. Wilson, and D. Wolfe. 1988. "Specific Assessment and Intervention Strategies for Children Exposed to Wife Battering: Preliminary Empirical Investigations." *Canadian Journal of Community Mental Health* 7: 157–63.

Jaffe, P., P. Wolfe, and S. K. Wilson. 1990. *Children of Battered Women*. Beverly Hills, Calif.: Sage.

Jaffe, P., D. Wolfe, S. K. Wilson, and L. Zak. 1985. "Critical Issues in the Assessment of Children's Adjustment to Witnessing Family Violence." *Canada's Mental Health* 33: 15–19.

Jaffe, P., D. Wolfe, S. K. Wilson, and L. Zak. 1986. "Similarities in Behavioral and Social Maladjustment Among Child Victims and Witnesses to Family Violence." *American Journal of Orthopsychiatry* 56: 142–46.

Jouriles, E. N., J. Barling, and K. D. O'Leary. 1987. "Predicting Child Behavior Problems in Maritally Violent Families." *Journal of Abnormal Child Psychology* 15: 165–73.

Jouriles, E. N., C. M. Murphy, and K. D. O'Leary. 1989. "Interspousal Violence, Marital Discord, and Child Problems." *Journal of Consulting and Clinical Psychology* 57: 453–55.

Kempton, T., A. M. Thomas, and R. Forehand. 1989. "Dimensions of Interparental Conflict and Adolescent Functioning." *Journal of Family Violence* 4: 297–307.

Layzer, J. I., B. D. Goodson, and C. Delange. 1986. "Children in Shelters." *Response* 9: 2–5.

Moore, T. E., D. Pepler, R. Mae, and R. Kates. 1989. "Effects of Family Violence on Children." In *Intervening with Assaulted Women: Current Theory, Research, and Practice*, ed. B. Pressman, G. Cameron, and M. Rothery, pp. 75–91. Hillsdale, N.J.: Erlbaum.

Moore, T., D. Pepler, B. Weinberg, L. Hammond, J. Waddell, and L. Weiser. 1990. "Research on Children from Violent Families." *Canada's Mental Health* 38: 19–23.

Ragg, D. M. 1991. "Differential Group Programming for Children Exposed to Spouse Abuse." *Journal of Child and Youth Care* 5: 59–75.

Roberts, A. R., and B. S. Roberts. 1990. "A Comprehensive Model for Crisis Intervention with Battered Women and Their Children." In *Crisis Intervention Handbook: Assessment, Treatment and Research,* ed. A. R. Roberts, pp. 106–23. Belmont, Calif.: Wadsworth.

Rutter, M. 1980. "Protective Factors in Children's Responses to Stress and Disadvantage." In *Primary Prevention of Psychopathology.* Vol. 3: *Promoting Social Competence and Coping in Children,* ed. M. W. Kent and J. E. Rolf, pp. 49–74. Hanover, N.H.: University Press of New England.

Silvern, L., and L. Kaersvang. 1989. "The Traumatized Children of Violent Marriages." *Child Welfare* 68: 421–36.

Stagg, V., G. D. Wills, and M. Howell. 1989. "Psychopathology in Early Childhood Witnesses of Family Violence." *Topics in Early Childhood Special Education* 9: 73–87.

Straus, M. A., R. J. Gelles, and S. K. Steinmetz, 1980. *Behind Closed Doors: Violence in the American Family.* Garden City, N.Y.: Doubleday/Anchor.

Wildin, S. R., W. D. Williamson, and G. S. Wilson. 1991. "Children of Battered Women: Developmental and Learning Profiles." *Clinical Pediatrics* 30: 299–304.

Wilson, S. K., S. Cameron, P. Jaffe, and D. Wolfe. 1989. "Children Exposed to Wife Abuse: An Intervention Model." *Social Casework* 70: 180–84.

Wolfe, D. A., P. Jaffe, S. K. Wilson, and L. Zak. 1985. "Children of Battered Women: The Relation of Child Behavior to Family Violence and Maternal Stress." *Journal of Consulting and Clinical Psychology* 53: 657–65.

12

Mental Health Interventions with Battered Women

Patricia A. Petretic-Jackson and Thomas Jackson

This chapter is designed to provide a format for mental health professionals in their work with women who have been victims of violence in their adult intimate relationships. The assessment and intervention strategies reviewed in this chapter are limited to measures and techniques that have been empirically demonstrated to be effective with battered women. Although this chapter addresses concerns specific to battered women, many of the assessment and intervention strategies discussed may be applicable to other trauma/victim populations. In addition, since many battered women have experienced a variety of past and current life stressors besides the actual battering episodes (Foy, 1992), we examine assessment and treatment concerns related to these compounding stressors.

This chapter also explores issues relevant to clinical work with battered women: current research findings; theoretical conceptualizations of the battered woman; the cognitive, interpersonal, physiological, emotional, and behavioral sequelae of battering; public and professional attitudes and their role in help seeking and treatment outcome; and program evaluation.

Philosophy

As do the majority of clinicians and researchers working with battered women, we believe that violence in the context of an adult intimate relationship cannot be viewed as simply another symptom of a dysfunctional relationship. A clinician who views violence as "just a symptom" in the context of a distressed relationship and not as a problem in itself that necessitates specific attention and intervention may be subscribing to the often false assumption that improving the relationship will alleviate the violence. A similar misperception is that violence is caused by alcohol or substance misuse and that treating the substance problem will "take care of" the violence. Because of the serious risk of severe injury or death to a woman as a result of battering, such violence needs to be addressed directly, candidly, and as an issue separate from that of the relationship. It is not ultimately in the best interests of the woman for a clinician to be unwilling to discuss relationship violence, even when a woman may be reluctant to do so. We agree with the philosophy espoused by Walker (1987). That is, a clinician's failure to address assaultive behavior directly and promptly in effect sends a message to the client that the status quo (i.e., continuation of the violent behavior) is insignificant and/or acceptable when it occurs in the context of a continuing intimate relationship.

We also recommend that clinical interventions with battered women be guided by the following principles:

1. *Intervention goals should be appropriate to the needs of the client and reflect her right to self-determination.* To that end, the clinician must be noncontrolling and flexible in interactions with the battered client. At the same time, the clinician must evaluate all actions taken in the therapeutic relationship to ensure that interventions "pass the litmus test," by examining three areas of concern: increasing the client's personal safety; increasing her sense of empowerment, esteem, and control; and reducing the psychological trauma resulting from the violence.

2. *Assessment and treatment protocols should be developed that best meet the identified needs of battered women, and clinicians should employ empirically proven and psychometrically sound methods and measures that permit the objective assessment of a client's unique constellation of presenting problems, as well as the effectiveness of clinical interventions.* Given the specific symptoms that characterize a woman's response to battering, problem-specific assessment and interventions are most useful. Cognitive-behaviorally oriented crisis intervention and time-limited treatment approaches appear to be the most appropriate intervention options (see also Chapters 9 and 10). Within such a framework, battering is conceptualized as a form of trauma, and the woman's symptomatic response to the battering is viewed as a reaction to a situational event or trauma rather than as an indication of personality deficits that somehow caused the battering (Walker, 1979, 1984). In addition, when planning assessment and intervention strategies, clinicians must be aware of the range of symptoms that may occur and be prepared for such diversity in their clients' expression of problems related to the battering experience.

3. *A contextual perspective must guide assessment and intervention.* Clinicians must recognize and not underestimate the impact of situational and cultural variables on the battered woman's response to battering and her recovery. For example, it has been documented that cultural considerations can significantly influence a battered woman's likelihood to seek treatment (Constantine, 1992; de las Fuentes, 1992; McKee, 1992). Although clinicians should not engage in stereotyping or overgeneralizing when working with battered women from different cultural backgrounds, they must be aware of the impact of cultural and other situational factors

on a particular woman and their influence on the therapeutic relationship. In addition, the attitudes toward domestic violence held by the woman, the community at large, the woman's support system, and the legal and health professionals she may encounter influence her likelihood to seek mental health services.

4. *Clinicians must engage in on-going monitoring of their own attitudes, feelings, and behaviors.* This self-monitoring refers to both client and clinician care. Ideally, clinicians should examine their personal values concerning battering and adopt a treatment philosophy before beginning any intervention with battered women. They then should continue to examine these values and feelings, as clinicians may experience countertransference reactions involving overidentification or emotional detachment, either of which may adversely affect their clients' therapeutic progress. Of particular concern are the clinicians' expectations for the women's change or action. Often clinicians become frustrated when working with women who seek services and have not yet decided to terminate the battering relationship. If the clinicians perceive that the women do not share their own intervention goals, the clinicians may begin to feel helpless and/or develop a victim-blaming attitude.

Working with battering victims, particularly when they are in a state of crisis, is highly stressful. Clinicians may experience psychological distress, commonly expressed as posttraumatic symptoms. McCann and Perlman (1990) used the term *vicarious traumatization* to describe such consequences of a clinician's exposure to the experiences of a trauma victim. They also found alterations in the cognitive schemas of clinicians who work with trauma victims. Cognitive schemas related to issues of trust/dependency, safety, power, independence, esteem, intimacy, and frame of reference may be affected and contribute to a clinician's emotional distress. We believe that continuing attention to self-care, the impact of any personal victimization history, and the use of a supportive professional network is critical to reduce the clinicians' burnout.

5. *The impact of clinical interventions must be evaluated.* Our empirically based understanding of assessment and treatment issues related to battered women is relatively meager compared with our knowledge of victims of other forms of trauma. Therefore, there is a need for continuing empirical research in this area, particularly with regard to program evaluation and treatment efficacy. Additionally, the clinician should be aware that specific assessment or treatment methods have the potential to retraumatize the battered woman and must assess for this possibility.

6. *Clinicians must develop and use a conceptual framework to guide assessment and treatment.* During the past two decades, several explanatory models have been developed that describe the nature of response to traumatic events. Clinicians and researchers have more recently used such models to explain the psychological response of a battered woman to her battering experience. Such models conceptualize the battered woman's symptoms as a traumatic response to stress. Therefore, it is hypothesized that in the process of her postassault adjustment, a victim of battering will experience many of the same reactions and employ many of the same coping mechanisms used by individuals responding to other types of life crises (Follingstad, Neckerman, & Vormbrock, 1988; McCann, Sakheim, &

Abrahamson, 1988). Researchers have compared the reactions of battered wo-men with those of other types of victims, including victims of acute and chronic traumas.

Using this trauma framework, a clinician can estimate the severity of a client's response to trauma by assessing four variables: (1) the specific nature of the trau-matic experience, including the extent of physical injuries and the amount of per-ceived threat or danger; (2) the victim's adjustment before her most recent traumatic episode, including her social, intellectual, and occupational adjustment, as well as her previous exposure to physical, psychological, and sexual victimization or other trauma; (3) the response of the victim's social support system; and (4) the victim's coping and response strategies and skills.

Assault by an intimate partner creates specific circumstances that distinguish battering from other forms of trauma (Stark & Flitcraft, 1988). Several issues are particularly salient to the battering trauma. First, the clinician must recognize that battering is a recent event for most women seeking clinical assistance. Thus ensur-ing the victim's physical safety is paramount. Battered women frequently have life-threatening experiences (Dutton, 1992a). Battering is often a chronic problem, characterized by multiple incidents over a long period of time. In many instances, the response to battering may also be compounded by previous exposure to other forms of trauma, such as childhood abuse or earlier adult sexual and physical assaults (Foy, 1992). A final consideration is that the consequences of an assault that occurs in the context of an intimate relationship are different from those that occur when one is assaulted by a stranger. That is, when the abuse occurs in a "safe" intimate relationship, the meaning of the event is altered (Foa, Steketee, & Roth-baum, 1989). The relationship between the victim and her offender is particularly important because it determines the battered woman's ability to deal with her battering on a cognitive level. Also, unlike child victims of familial violence, an adult woman who has been battered by an intimate partner has the element of social evaluation with which to contend. She may be perceived as contributing to the cause and maintenance of her status as a victim, more so than are victims of other forms of violence. Such victim-blaming perceptions are commonly expressed directly to a battered woman by her abusive partner. Similar perceptions, however, may be shared by many friends, family members, helping professionals, and the commu-nity at large and ultimately may be incorporated into the woman's cognitive sche-ma. Thus battering can be distinguished from other forms of trauma based on the continuing threat of traumatization, its repetitive nature, and the ongoing relation-ship between the woman and her battering partner.

Review of Current Research

Although a comprehensive review of the literature on battered women is beyond the scope of this chapter, we have identified two areas relevant to clinical assessment and treatment: (1) definitions, and (2) the impact of attitudes and beliefs on assess-ment and treatment. The reader is referred to Chapters 4 through 8 for a synopsis of the literature concerning such issues as theories of the etiology of women battering, law enforcement responses, and legal remedies; homicide; marital rape; and the debunking of myths and stereotypes.

Definitions

Walker (1987) defined the *battered woman* as "any woman who is repeatedly abused physically, sexually, and/or psychologically by a man with whom she is intimate in order for him to get what he wants without any regard for her needs" (p. 132). She defined *battering acts* as behaviors exhibited by a batterer directed toward an intimate partner that

> typically include slapping, hitting, punching, shaking, shoving, pushing; throwing into furniture, across the room, or down the stairs; kicking (with shoes on or off); pulling and dragging by the hair; shaving genital areas, mutilating sexual areas of the body; biting, burning, cutting, stabbing, shooting; hitting with objects, hurting with an automobile; and threats with guns, knives, and other weapons. Forced oral, anal, and vaginal intercourse frequently occurs. (p. 132)

In addition to these actions, other commonly reported acts of physical violence are choking, holding hands over the victim's mouth, and pinching.

Whereas the early descriptions and definitions of battering reported in the clinical literature detailed physically abusive incidents, more recent definitions have broadened the scope of battering behaviors. For example, whereas Walker (1987) focused on physical acts in defining battering, she also expanded the definition to incorporate sexual and psychological abuse. Within this broader scope, *battering* is defined as an *intentional act that is used to gain power and control*. Therefore, physical abuse is only one part of a system of abusive behaviors used by the batterer against a partner, and it rarely occurs in isolation (Follingstad et al., 1990). This increasing emphasis on the psychological consequences of battering trauma reflects a shift away from medical–legal definitions of battery.

Follingstad and colleagues (1990) examined the relationship between emotional and physical abuse in interviews with 234 battered women. They identified six types of emotional abuse: threats of physical harm, ridicule, jealousy, threats to change marriage, restriction, and damage to property. Virtually all the women reported having experienced at least one episode of emotional abuse, with ridicule being the most commonly reported form of emotional abuse. Interestingly, two-thirds of the women believed that emotional abuse had a more severe impact on them than did physical abuse. Consistent with reports in the clinical literature, threats of abuse, jealousy, and restriction were more characteristic of long-term abusive relationships.

Thus, in addition to physical acts, the batterer may use isolation, emotional abuse, economic abuse, sexual abuse, manipulation of the children, intimidation, and other coercive behaviors (Pence & Paymar, 1986; Tolman, 1992; Walker, 1987; Webb, 1992) to control the victim's behavior. It is imperative that clinicians inquire about these additional forms of coercive control when interviewing victims about their battering experiences.

However assessing the abuse to which a woman is exposed requires more than "tallying up" the acts of violence or coercion. The clinician must also consider the battered woman's cognitions regarding the abuse, including such aspects as her appraisal of the severity of past abuse, the probability of continued abuse and its lethality, attributions of causality for the abuse, and judgments about her safety (Dutton, 1992b). We now turn to an issue that affects how definitions of abuse are perceived and distorted: attitudinal biases.

Attitudes Toward Battering and Their Impact on Assessment and Treatment

The investigation of attitudes toward domestic violence has been a research area of growing interest in the last several years. For example, Ewing and Aubrey (1987) examined whether 108 males and 108 females in a community sample held erroneous beliefs about battered women (e.g., beliefs that battered women are masochists who are somehow responsible for the battering they suffer and could avoid being battered by simply leaving their batterers). The results suggest that many community members hold erroneous, stereotypical beliefs about battered women and that women are more likely than men to subscribe to these stereotypes.

Although professionals in the health and mental health fields are now more aware of the problem of battering, the responses of service providers to battered women may play a significant role in either ameliorating or compounding the problems. The research we discuss addresses the development and use of a standardized measure of blame distribution regarding a specific form of battering, wife abuse. One purpose of this research was to investigate the attitudes held by medical and mental health professionals concerning the perceived causes of wife abuse and to determine the impact of such professionals' beliefs on the nature and quality of professional services offered to both victims and offenders.

In the rape victimization literature, Brodsky (1976) hypothesized that the offender was not the only party blamed for the act. He maintained that in the minds of the general public, societal attitudes, situational variables, and even the victim herself should also be held partly accountable for the rape. Even though this argument seemed logical, Brodsky offered no empirical support. Then Ward and Resick (1980) standardized and cross-validated a twenty-item scale based on Brodsky's conceptualization. The resulting scale, the Attribution of Rape Blame Scale (ARBS), was found to be factor analytically sound, and it distributed the blame for the occurrence of rape across offender, societal, situational, and victim blame dimensions. In subsequent studies of mental health professionals (Resick & Jackson, 1981), rural and urban college women (Kenning & Jackson, 1984), Native Americans (Jackson & Plane, 1987), incarcerated sex offenders (Jackson and Eck, 1987), attorneys and judges (Morris & Jackson, 1989), and college student athletes (Jackson, 1991), a similar pattern of blame distribution was obtained. In all these studies, the offender was blamed the most for the rape. Societal variables, such as the amount of sex and violence in the media, were usually held the second most responsible for rape. Situational variables, such as poorly lit areas, were held somewhat accountable for rape. The victim, although blamed the least, was not considered completely blameless. Another, perhaps more important, finding in these studies involved gender effects. Consistently, in all studies that sampled both males and females, the male respondents held the victim significantly more at fault for her own rape than did the female respondents. Furthermore, the offender was blamed significantly more by female than by male respondents for the occurrence of rape.

A second series of victimization blame attribution studies adapted the rape blame scale for use with the crime of incest. The Jackson Incest Blame Scale (JIBS; Jackson & Ferguson, 1983) was developed to parallel the dimensions represented on the ARBS. Like the ARBS, the JIBS was a factor analytically sound, twenty-item Likert scale. Blame for incest was distributed across offender, societal, situational, and victim factors. The findings from a series of studies of mental health professionals (Jackson & Fischer, 1982), attorneys and judges (Jackson & Sandberg, 1985), metropolitan police officers (Prentice & Jackson, 1984), and incest victims (Ferguson & Jackson, 1986) replicated the original standardization results. In studies sampling both males and females, victims of incest were blamed significantly more by the male respondents, and the offenders were blamed significantly more by the female respondents.

In an effort to assess whether the established order and gender effects obtained with rape and incest blame would generalize to wife abuse, Sandberg, Petretic-Jackson, and Jackson (1985) developed the Domestic Violence Blame Scale (DVBS), a twenty-three-item Likert scale that assesses attributional blame for wife abuse accorded to situational, societal, victim/wife, and offender/husband causes. Using a sample of midwestern college students, Sandberg and colleagues found that as with rape and incest, wife abuse was perceived by adults in the college population as having several causes. Although the victims were blamed least for their victimization, they were not perceived as blameless. However, in contrast with other forms of assault (e.g., incest, rape, child physical abuse), the offenders in cases of wife abuse were not assigned the most blame for the abuse to their partners. Situational determinants, including a number of factors in the external environment, were believed to "stress the dyad" to the point of abuse. Included among the situational factors were the abuser's use of drugs and/or alcohol. Societal attitudes toward acceptable relationship violence and gender roles were thought to play a contributory role as well in the etiology of wife abuse. Thus laypersons were found to perceive wife abuse as a unique form of interpersonal violence. Would professionals hold similar perceptions, and if so, what would be the implications for intervention? The DVBS was subsequently administered to regional and national samples of health and mental health professionals to determine those salient respondent characteristics that might influence attributional biases in treatment.

To study the attributions of wife abuse in health professionals, the DVBS was administered to both practicing physicians and medical students. In a study of 145 midwestern physicians, Tarver and Jackson (1992) found a rank ordering of factors identical to that of the college standardization sample. A significant gender effect was obtained, with male physicians blaming female victims to a greater extent than did female physicians. Male and female physicians also differed in their referrals to mental health practitioners, with male physicians making fewer mental health referrals. In addition, physicians with higher victim blame scores were less likely to suggest mental health interventions or to develop a protection plan to ensure the victim's safety. Work setting or personal experience with violence did not affect the blame scores. It appears that physicians' attitudes toward blame affect their use of the mental health network. Such findings have implications for the modification of physicians' educational and training programs.

Whereas Tarver and Jackson (1992) sampled practicing physicians, Noonan (1989) sampled 230 physicians in training at three medical schools, in part to identify whether the current training programs had incorporated knowledge about domestic violence. If such training was offered, did it have a positive impact on attitudes? Noonan's findings mirror those of Tarver and Jackson and suggest that recent physician training has not incorporated adequate information about wife abuse. Although the medical students' victim blame scores were lower than those of the physicians in Tarver and Jackson's study, this may be attributed in part to sampling differences. Interestingly, the medical school respondents regarded as inadequate their training with respect to the problem of wife abuse. Those students who reported having had such training in other settings (i.e., not medical) had lower victim blame scores.

Although it appears that training programs in the mental health professions have been more successful at incorporating such information into their training programs, there appears to be considerable variability in practitioners' attitudes according to gender, theoretical orientation, and other therapist characteristics. For example, the initial survey of licensed psychologists in three midwestern states indicated that practicing psychologists had the same overall blame scores as did the college standardization and physician samples (Sandberg & Jackson, 1986a). Male psychologists, like male physicians, had higher victim blame scores than did female practitioners. It also appeared that the practitioner sample as a whole conceptualized cases of wife abuse from a systemic approach (Sandberg & Jackson, 1986b). The more a wife was blamed, the more often systemic treatment was advocated. And the more societal factors that were blamed, the more individual treatment approaches were endorsed.

White and Petretic-Jackson (1992) then surveyed a stratified random national sample of 437 licensed psychologists listed in the National Register of Health Service Providers in Psychology. They used a modification of the DVBS, the Modified Domestic Violence Blame Scale (MDVBS), a forty-eight-item scale developed from the original item pool of the Domestic Violence Blame Scale (DVBS). A fifth independent blame dimension, relationship blame, was added to the scale. This decision was based on the salience of items that assessed husband–wife interactions within the DVBS situational factor and the finding that many psychologists in the Sandberg and Jackson (1986b) study preferred a couples approach to conceptualizing and treating wife abuse. Even though we do not recommend this conceptualization and approach to treatment, given the likelihood that many would adhere to such a model, we judged this dimension to be worthy of further study.

As with physicians, their differences in conceptualizing abuse as a "couple" or an "individual" problem influenced clinicians' use of other support services for the battering victim (e.g., legal remedies, shelter). Analyses yielded five independent attribution dimensions: relationship blame, societal blame, situational blame, wife blame, and internal dispositional blame for both husband and wife. Husband blame items were found to be interrelated with wife blame items (e.g., self-defeating personality; passive, dependent traits). The resulting factor, consisting of items describing characterological attributes of both the husband and wife, was labeled the *internal disposition* (i.e., personality) *blame dimension.* The personalities of both the husband and the wife were blamed most, followed by relationship blame, situational blame, and societal blame.

Therapist gender, therapeutic orientation, and marital status were found to influence significantly the degree and type of attributional blame. Female therapists blamed societal causes and the husband's and the wife's internal dispositional causes much more than did male therapists, whereas male therapists attributed blame to the wife far more than did female therapists. Compared with psychodynamic, cognitive-behavioral, and feminist therapists, systems therapists blamed relationship causes more. These findings suggest that gender-related beliefs and theoretical biases may systematically influence psychologists' attributions regarding wife abuse. Furthermore, married or previously married subjects attributed a much higher degree of blame to relationship causes than did single subjects. Thus therapists' personal experiences in a marital relationship may also influence blame attribution for wife abuse to favor "couple" causal factors.

As Roberts (1984) noted, traditional mental health professionals (e.g., psychiatrists, social workers, and psychologists) may have limited knowledge of the attitudes of paraprofessional and volunteer workers who staff community intervention programs for battered women. Similarly, they may lack information about the attitudes of alcohol and chemical dependency workers who, in the course of their addiction counseling, often encounter both husbands and wives involved in battering situations.

Using the DVBS, Parsons, Yutrzenka, and Jackson (1987) found that the patterns of attribution of blame in these groups were similar to those found with other health and mental health professional samples. They also found that victims were blamed the least and situational factors were blamed the most by their sample of mental health professionals and trained volunteers working in mental health centers, drug and alcohol treatment programs, and women's shelters. The female staff in these settings rated victims as less blameworthy, but the male staff blamed situational factors to a greater extent. Interestingly, chemical dependency workers blamed both offenders and societal factors more than did workers in traditional mental health centers. Furthermore, no differences emerged between staff who treated only female clients and those who worked with both male and female clients involved in wife abuse situations. This finding suggests that staff in mental health, shelter, and chemical dependency settings who shared an individual treatment orientation preference also shared a philosophy that endorses the offenders' personal responsibility for their problematic behaviors.

In these samples, a subset of the professionals seemed to have victim-blaming attributional biases. These findings, together with the lack of adequate training concerning wife abuse, point to the need for educational efforts regarding victim treatment directed at both students enrolled in professional training programs and practicing professionals (Tarver & Jackson, 1992).

Knowledgeable mental health professionals can play an important role in educating physicians and other health personnel concerning mental health referrals. Mental health professionals should look at their personal biases and their implications for differential case management as it relates to their clients' safety. A strong systemic bias in conceptualizing wife abuse may result in the neglect of necessary individual intervention and other services. This, of course, is related to our original philosophical premise that violence in intimate relationships must be viewed as a problem which needs to be assessed and treated in itself, rather than merely a symptom of a dysfunctional dyad.

Assessment

Assessment must focus on (1) the nature of the woman's battering experiences and (2) the consequences of the battering as reflected in the woman's current psychological functioning. In part, the clinician's choice of methods and measures is determined by the purpose of the assessment: court evaluation, determination of trauma, or program evaluation.

For practical reasons, the use of multiple, brief, problem-specific standardized measures is advisable. If the battered woman has a history of psychopathology or of multiple traumas, a more comprehensive assessment of global functioning may be warranted. The goal for most clients is to select those instruments or methods that will provide relevant information without taking too much time to be completed.

Clinicians must also be sensitive to the stress inherent in the assessment process. Often they forget that the battered woman is a survivor as well as a victim. The focus on her experience during the assessment may thus intensify the woman's distress, and the clinician may forget to identify her existing skills and strengths. *The assessment process should identify client strengths, which can be used to formulate intervention strategies for intervention and promote change. Thus examination of the woman's coping and survival skills is a crucial area which must not be omitted in the assessment process.*

Assessing the Violence

When assessing the dimensions of the traumatic event or battering episode and obtaining a history of battering, clinicians have a choice of several methods. We recommend a multimodal assessment of battering, using a combination of structured interviews, open-ended interviews, and standardized scale/questionnaire methods.

Interviews

Most clinicians begin with an open-ended interview, allowing the woman to "tell her story." This format makes it easier for the clinician to build a rapport with the woman and to establish the woman's prioritization of issues. A second option is to use a structured interview instead of the open-ended format. The structured interview permits contextual issues to be examined in more detail. A third option, which we recommend, is to begin with an open-ended interview and follow it with a structured interview.

The clinician must obtain information about the last few battering incidents, about the first incident of abuse, and a representative incident. This will help determine the pattern of the abusive cycle and the potential for escalation over time. The clinician should ascertain the sequence of events, but without phrasing the questions to appear to blame the victim.

One structured interview that clinicians may want to consider, primarily for use in forensic evaluations, is the Battered Woman Syndrome Questionnaire (BWSQ) (Walker, 1984). Used in a major research study by Walker, the highly comprehensive interview requires eight hours of face-to-face interviewing by a trained interviewer. Although its length makes impractical the routine administration of this measure, clinicians may consider this measure as a model from which to derive their own clinical interview protocol. In the Appendix at the end of this chapter, we offer an interview guide to be used with battered women.

Standardized Measures and Questionnaires

Originally, self-report questionnaires assessing battering experiences were designed to identify the nature of abusive incidents to which the battered woman was exposed in a battering relationship. The earliest measures (e.g., Conflict Tactics Scales; Straus, 1979) concentrated on physically abusive acts, with a minimal focus on sexually and psychologically abusive acts. Later questionnaires incorporated more information regarding these other forms of abuse. Most recently, attention has shifted to more detailed assessment of psychological abuse in the battering relationship.

The clinician has several measures from which to choose when assessing psychological abuse. The need for a detailed analysis of psychological maltreatment will guide the selection of the most appropriate questionnaire for a particular client. If a highly detailed measure of psychological abuse is desired, the Psychological Maltreatment of Women Inventory (PMWI) (Tolman, 1989) is recommended. The thirty-item Index of Spouse Abuse (ISA) (Hudson & McIntosh, 1981) would also be an appropriate choice if a general assessment of both physical and psychological abuse is desired in a single measure. The ISA has adequate psychometric properties and discriminates between battered and nonbattered women. Its wording is designed for female victims; no version for male self-report is available. Both of these scales are preferable to the Conflict Tactics Scale (Straus, 1979) if the clinician wants a comprehensive assessment of the dimension of psychological abuse. Only six items are used to measure verbal and symbolic aggression in the original version of the CTS, although recent variations of it (Brekke, 1987) have expanded the questions on psychological abuse. A final measure still being developed is the Severity of (Physical) Violence Against Women Scales (Marshall, 1992), in which forty-six events involving threats and actual violent acts are rated according to seriousness, aggressiveness, and physical and emotional harm. Marshall suggests both clinical and research applications for the scale, and community and student norms are available.

Thus in order to determine the nature of the abuse, a clinician may select 'rom several measures. When selecting a measure, the clinician should decide whether it provides specific information regarding the forms of abuse experienced by a particular client. Possible options are the following:

CONFLICT TACTICS SCALE

In its original form, the Conflict Tactics Scale (CTS) (Straus, 1979) is not generally recommended if a comprehensive assessment of sexual and psychological abuse is desired, although the measure does sample a wide range of physically abusive acts and a number of verbal abuse items. There have been several modifications of the original CTS (Brekke, 1987) that have added questions regarding psychological and sexual abuse. Straus has developed several methods of combining items into different indices of family violence. [1]

If the clinician is interested in a brief screening measure of psychological and physical abuse that can be used to supplement information from the primary interview, the CTS has the advantage of a large clinical database. A review of the strengths and weaknesses of the CTS can be found in Schumm and Bagarozzi (1989).

THE ABUSIVE BEHAVIOR OBSERVATION CHECKLIST

The Abusive Behavior Observation Checklist (Dutton, Freeman, & Stumpff, 1988) assesses the frequency of specific acts of physical, sexual, and psychological abuse. [2] The time periods and/or relationships considered include the last year with the abusive partner, the years before that with the abusive partner, and any previous time with any partner.

PSYCHOLOGICAL MALTREATMENT OF WOMEN INVENTORY

The Psychological Maltreatment of Women Inventory (PMWI) (Tolman, 1989) is a fifty-eight-item scale that samples a wide range of behaviors. Parallel forms for men and women determine the relative frequency of abusive behaviors. The PMWI yields two subscales, measuring dominance–isolation and verbal–emotional abuse. Preliminary validation research indicates that the scale does discriminate between battered and nonbattered women based on the number of acts endorsed and the two factor sum scores (Tolman, 1991).

Assessing Danger

Danger Assessment Scale

The Danger Assessment Scale (Campbell, 1986) was designed for use in the initial screening of battered women to determine their danger of homicide. The most recently revised version includes fifteen yes–no items. Either the woman herself or a health/mental health professional can administer the scale. The total assessment takes approximately ten minutes, and the follow-up with the woman to discuss her risk takes approximately five minutes. The scale is based on a match with demographic factors associated with increased risk of homicide, such as the presence of firearms in the home, sexual abuse, use of drugs or alcohol by the batterer, high level of control, violent jealousy, abuse during pregnancy, violence toward children, and attempts or threats of suicide by the woman. This measure is recommended for its short administration time, empirical underpinnings, and ability to give the woman a concrete measure of her risk of danger. Since informed decision making is an important goal in working with battered women, this quick measure will permit her to make an informed decision about her safety or risk of danger. (For an examination of the latest study of battered women who kill and the causal links of homicide to dropping out of high school, being on welfare, cohabiting with the abusive partner, and suicide attempts, see Chapter 2.)

Assessing Prior Attempts at Avoidance, Escape, or Protection from Abuse

Most clinicians assess the battered woman's prior use of specific coping strategies in response to the abuse in the context of the clinical interview. However, Dutton developed a written questionnaire to measure this dimension: the Response to Violence Inventory (Dutton, Hass, & Hohnecker, 1989). The measure assesses the nature and frequency of use of specific strategies in the past, perceived effectiveness in regard to protection from danger at the time, and rationale for not using particular strategies. The measure is designed to be followed by an interview with the clinician to provide clarification and greater detail. A copy of this inventory can be found in Dutton 1992b. Dutton also stresses the importance of giving an opportunity to the battered woman, using an unstructured interview format, to describe the means she has employed in the past to protect herself and others.

Assessing PTSD Symptoms

There is little literature reporting on the use of psychometric measures to look at symptoms of intrusion, avoidance, and arousal in battered women (Dutton, 1992a). Administering the Structured Clinical Interview (SC!D) for the *DSM*-III-R is one option (Spitzer & Williams, 1986), but some level of training is required for its administration. Another measure that assesses intrusion and avoidance symptoms is the Impact of Events Scale (IES) (Horowitz, Wilner, & Alvarez, 1979). This fifteen-item scale has the advantage of being used in several empirical studies of battered women. Scores on the measure are correlated with the PTSD subscale of Keane, Malloy, and Fairbank (1984), which was derived from the Minnesota Multiphasic Personality Inventory (MMPI), and the Crime-Related Post-Traumatic Stress Disorder Scale (CR-PTSD) (Saunders, Arata, & Kilpatrick, 1990), which is a modification of the SCL-90-R (Dutton et al., 1990). We believe that if the IES is used to determine PTSD symptomatology, it should be supplemented by a measure that assesses arousal symptoms, such as the SCL-90-R.

In addition, assessing PTSD symptoms is complicated by the difficulty of differentiating between posttraumatic responses to trauma and the traumatic responses by which the woman copes with battering. For example, if a woman is abusing substances in an attempt to cope with the stresses of battering, although substance use may be considered a form of avoidance, other intrusion and/or avoidance symptoms may not be evident in the assessment. Therefore, any assessment of trauma symptoms must consider the moderating effects of both threats of abuse and actual substance abuse, both of which may mask signs of PTSD (Dutton, 1992a). As with the assessment of preexisting personality disorders, an accurate assessment of PTSD symptoms may not be possible until the woman has been in a safe environment for a period of time (Horowitz, 1986).

Assessing Other Psychological Symptoms

Depression

BECK DEPRESSION INVENTORY

The Beck Depression Inventory (BDI) (Beck et al., 1979) is a twenty-one-item scale that examines cognitive and somatic components of depression. One question specifically assesses level of suicidal risk. BDI scores of 11 to 20 indicate mild to moderate depression, and scores over 20 point to severe depression.

The BDI is recommended, for a number of reasons, as a means of monitoring depression in battered women. First, the BDI has been used widely in both research and clinical practice with battered women, which gives the clinician a normative standard of comparison. The measure is also highly sensitive to change in mood, which enables monitoring fluctuations in self-reported depression levels over time. Its brief administration time makes it less intrusive and provides a consistent, standardized objective measure of depressive symptomatology over the course of intervention. Research with battered women suggests considerable variability in levels of reported depression, although women in shelter samples appear to have greater elevations on the BDI than comparison groups do.

Trauma Symptoms

DEROGATIS SYMPTOM CHECKLIST-90-REVISED

The Derogatis Symptom Checklist-90-Revised (SCL-90-R) (Derogatis, 1977) is a ninety-item scale in which symptoms are rated for the severity of discomfort that they have caused in the past week. The test yields separate scores for somatization, obsessive-compulsiveness, interpersonal sensitivity, depression, anxiety, hostility, phobic anxiety, paranoid ideation, and psychoticism. Advantages include the correspondence between item content and common trauma sequelae and the scale's utility as a screening device for more severe problems associated with compounded trauma response.

Saunders, Arata, and Kilpatrick (1990) derived the Crime-Related Post-Traumatic Stress Disorder Scale (CR-PTSD) from the SCL-90-R. Although data on the clinical use of the CR-PTSD are limited, the normative information provided for crime victims may provide a useful standard of comparison of trauma effects.

TRAUMA SYMPTOM CHECKLIST-33, TRAUMA SYMPTOM
CHECKLIST-40, AND TRAUMA SYMPTOM INVENTORY

Particularly relevant to battered women who report a history of early childhood assault, the Trauma Symptom Checklist (TSC) (Briere & Runtz, 1988, 1989; Elliott & Briere, 1992) assesses current emotional, behavioral, and somatic symptoms associated with childhood assault history. Although scores are not yet available for women whose assault experience is limited to adult violence, norms for both abused and nonabused clinical, community, and college samples have been published. Given the multiple trauma history of many battering victims, the scale may be appropriate, and the overlap of its items with the SCL-90-R permits the multiple assessment of such common sequelae as depression and anxiety. The forty-item version is particularly useful in assessing current sexual problems. The scales yield both a total trauma score and scores on five symptom subscales that measure depression, anxiety, dissociation, sleep disturbance, and post–sexual abuse trauma. Briere (1991) is in the process of publishing a 117-item version of this trauma scale, renamed the Trauma Symptom Inventory (TSI).[3] The TSI expands the clinical symptom list, includes nine clinical scales, and provides norms on various trauma groups, including victims of adult interpersonal victimization (Briere, Elliott, & Smiljanich, 1994). However, the TSI was not designed to confirm a diagnosis of PTSD.

Assessing Attitudes

Domestic Violence Blame Scale and Modified Domestic Violence Blame Scale

The Domestic Violence Blame Scale (DVBS) (Sandberg, Petretic-Jackson, & Jackson, 1985) and the modified version developed for administration to clinicians (MDVBS) (White & Petretic-Jackson, 1992) are clinical research scales designed to assess multidimension blame attribution concerning domestic violence in professional, public, and clinical groups. The DVBS provides four blame scores, consisting of offender, societal, situational, and victim blame attribution. The MDVBS provides five blame scores, assessing victim, internal disposition (personality) of both victim and offender, societal, situational, and relationship blame. Norms are available for physicians, psychologists, lawyers, shelter workers, mental health professionals, and college students. The scale can be used to examine attitude change following educational programming or training. It also can be a means of clinician self-assessment, as patterns of blame scores have been found to be related to clinicians' theoretical orientation and recommendations for treatment. Although clinical norms for battered women using the DVBS are now being developed, the scale can be used to identify salient attributional issues that would be a focus of treatment with battered women, such as the degree of self-blame versus perpetrator blame. In the clinical administration, the woman is asked to complete the scale twice, once as it applies to battered women in general and then as it applies to her own situation.

The Inventory of Beliefs About Wife Beating

The Inventory of Beliefs About Wife Beating (Saunders et al., 1987) contains the norm-based responses of 675 students, 94 community respondents, 71 batterers, and 70 advocates for battered women. The measure yields five reliable subscales. Sympathetic attitudes toward battered women are correlated with liberal views of women's roles and sympathetic attitudes toward rape victims. Abusers and advocates differ the most in their attitudes, and male and female students also obtain significantly different scores.

Assessing Global Personality Functioning

Given the varied emotional and behavioral sequelae associated with battering, serious consideration should be given to routinely administering a global measure of personality functioning.

Minnesota Multiphasic Personality Inventory-2

Clinicians are strongly encouraged to consider the routine use of the Minnesota Multiphasic Personality Inventory-2 (MMPI-2) (Butcher et al., 1989) with battered women, particularly those with a suspected or confirmed compounded rape reaction or history of psychiatric care. Its clinical utility makes it a worthwhile assessment tool, despite its lengthy administration time (one to one and one-half hours). The test is also particularly useful in detecting underlying anxiety and depression in women whose behavioral coping style may mask such problems.

Variability in profiles may reflect differences in premorbid adjustment, time since assault, type of assault, and overall level of posttraumatic stress. Rosewater's (1982, 1985, 1987, 1988) study of MMPI profiles of battered women suggested that clinical scales on the MMPI are often highly elevated, indicating high levels of distress. The profiles of women still in a battering relationship or those only recently removed from one differ from the profiles of women who have been out of the battering relationship for a year. Analysis of the Harris–Lingoes subscales (Harris & Lingoes, 1968) is recommended to interpret more accurately any clinical scale elevations. The MMPI-2 also has two PTSD subscales.

Millon Clinical Multiaxial Inventory

The Millon Clinical Multiaxial Inventory (MCMI) (Millon, 1983) is designed to differentiate between acute psychopathology (e.g., *DSM*-IV Axis I disorders) and chronic, pervasive interpersonal personality dysfunction (e.g., *DSM*-IV Axis II disorders). The 175-item measure consists of twenty clinical scales, and its administration time is approximately fifteen to twenty-five minutes. The original MCMI (now referred to as the MCMI-I) has been recently revised (MCMI-II) (Millon, 1987). But because of problems reported with the reliability and validity of the diagnostic profiles obtained when the MCMI was administered to battered women, no empirical research using the MCMI-II with this population has been available to date. Walker (1987) believes that the MCMI cannot accurately differentiate BWS from serious personality disorders. In our clinical work, we have found that a diagnosis of borderline personality disorder is frequently obtained based on MCMI test results for battering victims who have both problems of substance abuse and a history of childhood abuse, although interview information and behavioral observation often do not confirm such a diagnosis. Along similar lines, clinical research has indicated that when the MCMI is used to assess battered women in a crisis situation, Axis II personality disorders appear to be overdiagnosed, and the reliability of such diagnoses proves to be poor in subsequent retesting. The presence of preexisting personality disorders is often more accurately assessed when the MCMI is administered at least six months after a woman has left the battering relationship.

Problems Complicating Clinical Interventions with Battered Women

The intervention process with battered women can be complicated by many factors. Issues on the part of the battered woman or the clinician can interfere with the therapeutic process. If these issues relate specifically to the client, they should be addressed directly and nonjudgmentally. Any attitudes or behaviors of the clinician that interfere with treatment should be modified.

Client Issues

Walker (1987) identified five problem areas that she believes should be addressed in work with battered women. These behaviors reflect learned coping strategies that the battered woman has used so as to survive in the abusive relationship. But she may also employ these strategies outside the abusive relationship, and they may become problematic when used in other interpersonal relationships. In fact, it is not uncommon for her to use such strategies even after she is no longer in the battering relationship. The problem areas are manipulation, expression of anger, dissociation, denial and minimization of violence, and compliance.

MANIPULATION

Working under the assumption that she can control her unstable world, a battered woman often develops a manipulative style. She may be unwilling to believe that anyone else can protect her, and so she does not allow help from others. She may believe that she alone can control her environment to keep the batterer calm and herself safe. One client commented on her attempts to control everyone and everything while she was in her battering marriage in her unsuccessful effort to stop the battering:

> I got to the point that I was only sleeping three or four hours a night. The rest of the time I was trying to figure out how to get the house and the kids perfect so that he wouldn't beat me again for something that was wrong at home. I was always alert. . . . All my energy went into planning every little detail so it would be perfect. I thought I could stop it [the abuse] by myself.

Battered women develop unrealistic expectations of themselves; they expect perfection and are critical of their failures to control things. Because of their impaired trust, they rely on no one. Clinicians should recognize the potential for power struggles to emerge in therapy and act to label and defuse them quickly. Communicating openly in therapy, sharing treatment goals, and asking the client to identify potential problems with suggested treatment recommendations all help reduce manipulation.

ANGER EXPRESSION

Many clinicians report that battered women express their anger directly only infrequently while still in the battering relationship. Hilberman (1980) suggests that the woman may be anxious about her ability to control her feelings after observing her partner's loss of control and expression of anger through aggressive acts. Follingstad and associates (1988) believe that battered women express their anger by means of quiet resignation, depression, grotesque self-imagery, alcoholism, self-mutilation, and suicide attempts.

According to Walker, particularly with the validation of their battering experiences, battered women may begin to feel anger and, in some cases, rage. Battered women often express their anger indirectly, through general hostility, gossip, sarcasm, and passive–aggressive behavior. Sometime within the first six months to a year in treatment, when the battered woman is beginning to establish a sense of trust, her anger may surface, and her expression of angry feelings is often frightening to both her and the clinician. Walker (1987) comments that sometimes inexperienced clinicians become concerned that the woman will "remain an angry, bitter woman" (p. 139).

Nonetheless, anger is a common and legitimate response to perceived injustice or mistreatment. Rather than being fearful or critical of anger expression, the clinician needs to label these feelings as normal and identify the appropriate expression of such feelings as a therapeutic goal. One can think and feel at the same time; anger does not necessarily lead to unavoidable aggression. Even though the batterer may have used the excuse of being unable to control his actions because of overwhelming anger, a more constructive and realistic anger-management approach is desirable. The clinician should provide a framework for appropriate anger expression and discuss the need for a nondestructive expression of anger.

DISSOCIATION

Out-of-body dissociative experiences, frequently reported by child sexual abuse victims, may also be experienced by battered women. Such experiences are used to make the abuse more tolerable. With severe battering, the dissociative episodes may become more frequent and last longer. Walker (1987) reported that partial psychogenic amnesia may occur with life-threatening abuse and that such memory loss is common in battered women who engage in self-defense–motivated injury to the abuser. Such experiences make the battered woman wonder whether she is "crazy," and clinicians may want to relabel dissociativelike episodes as mild hypnotic trancelike states. Walker also suggested that guided imagery exercises be used to deal with dissociative images and recommended that hypnosis and relaxation techniques be used to teach self-control over such hypnoticlike trances. Body awareness techniques and physical exercise are valuable in facilitating a battered woman to reclaim her body. Walker recommends strategies as simple as taking a bubble bath or using body lotion.

DENIAL AND MINIMIZATION

Denial and minimization appear to develop over the history of abuse and are used to establish some type of meaning for the victimization (Follingstad et al., 1988) and to keep depression under control. Unfortunately, the result is lowered self-esteem. Denial may be expressed by any of the rationalizations commonly used by battered women that Ferraro and Johnson (1983) identified:

1. Denial of injury (failure to acknowledge being hurt)
   Example:
       He wasn't really abusive. He just shoved me.
       He didn't hurt me that bad. Just a few bruises.
2. Denial of the victimizer (blame on external factors beyond the control of either partner)
   Example:
       His boss had been picking on him.
       His mother keeps getting involved and criticizing the way the kids behave.
3. Denial of options (both practical and emotional)
   Example:
       I couldn't make it on my own. I don't have the skills.
       No one else would want me.
4. Denial of victimization (victim self-blame)
   Example:
       If I just wouldn't have picked on him.
       I knew better than to go out.

Related to such examples of denial and minimization are two other rationalizations identified by Follingstad and colleagues (1988). Since these rationalizations are considered more central to the woman's identity, their presence makes it much more difficult to leave the relationship. They include

1. Appeal to the salvation ethic (help him overcome his problem; abuse is to be endured until that time)
   Example:
       I know he is basically a good man. I'm sure with a little time and understanding I can get him to . . .

2. Appeal to higher loyalties (endure violence for a "higher purpose," such as religion or tradition)
   Example:
   As a good Christian, I must stay for the sake of the children. They need a father.

Therapeutically, it is advisable to ask the woman to keep a "paper trail" to identify and challenge any minimization related to injury. A woman may be asked to keep a log of details of the battering incidents or to use photographs to document bruises. Since telephone harassment is common, the woman can use an answering machine to record his remarks to her. Logs, journals, or diaries can be used to identify other cognitive distortions reflecting other forms of denial. Such statements can then be challenged, replacing victim-blaming statements with those blaming the abuse on the batterer.

COMPLIANCE AND A WILLINGNESS TO PLEASE

Compliance is demonstrated by the woman's willingness to engage in placating behavior with the batterer. Such behavior is similar to that identified in other types of trauma victims (e.g., the Stockholm syndrome). In therapeutic interactions, compliance may be evident in "yes, but" behavior; the woman appears overly compliant with the therapist's suggestions for changing or terminating the relationship but then fails to carry out these "seemingly agreed upon" suggestions for change. Although such behavior is often bewildering to the clinician, the battered woman may view continued contact with the batterer or returning to live with him as less threatening. Such traumatic bonding, in which the woman has learned to please the batterer, may motivate her return to the battering relationship. A variety of "rescuing behaviors" directed toward the batterer could also fall under this category.

The Clinician's Roles and Skills

The clinician should create an environment that is a "safe place" for the client to express her emotions and thoughts (e.g., the concept of containment). The clinician should be alert to and avoid such responses that imply avoidance, attack, indifference, or overprotection. It is imperative that the clinician be familiar with medical, police, and judicial procedures in his or her city, county, and state and be aware of the attitudes held by the medical and law enforcement professionals in the community who are likely to be working with battered woman in a professional capacity. Educating a victim about what to anticipate in her interactions with professionals in these disciplines helps her reduce her anxiety and make decisions. When the attitudes of professionals in legal or medical fields are not supportive or even blaming of the victim, it is the responsibility of mental health professionals to take the lead in educating allied health and legal professionals.

The clinician should also help the battered woman's adoption of an adaptive perception of her battering experience. This may be done by reframing the battering in terms of societal issues and shifting the blame to the batterer. Her past coping strategies should be examined to identify those that are effective and those that are problematic. For example, since many battered women use alcohol and prescription drugs to self-medicate, relabeling such behavior as an attempt at coping with the stress of continuing in a battering relationship and at the same time providing education regarding alternative means of stress reduction may be useful.

Making decisions and solving life problems are important to a battered woman, apart from the status of her relationship. Although the client may have to make many decisions, the one decision that will have the greatest effect on her is whether or not to leave the relationship. A basic goal of crisis intervention is assisting the battered woman in making decisions that reflect her own informed choice (Dutton, 1992b). Although this does not mean that the clinician should ignore or minimize the issue of risk or lethality, it does mean that the client has a right to choose what she will do in regard to the relationship, independent of the clinician's feelings. Dutton believes that clinicians who refuse to treat women who will not leave the abusive relationship are coercive, thereby negating the assumption of the client's self-determination.

Specific task-oriented strategies include

1. Progress from a general to a more specific focus when gathering information during the interview.

   Be a good listener. Use open-ended questions. Validate her feelings and thoughts. Stress that action and self-disclosure facilitate the recovery process. Avoid emotionally charged words or double-edged questions (e.g., "Don't you . . . ?") Put potentially embarrassing questions in context (e.g., I need to know about . . . because. . . ."). Probing questions should be avoided except those dealing with issues of suicide, depression, psychiatric history, and her ability to control her own behavior.

2. Assess psychosocial functioning and, take a crisis history in order to help the victim anticipate possible reactions.

   Consider the life stage and the nature and specifics of her assault. Determine the potential for lethality.

3. Be a good observer, and document your impressions and findings.

   Include the victim's comments and such nonverbals as appearance, facial expression, characteristic communicative style, and all physical findings, like bruises. Notes provide a baseline on the victim's behaviors and may be useful if you are subpoenaed for court proceedings at a later date.

4. Educate the victim regarding

   A. The available community resources, the authority of law enforcement, and various legal options open to her, so as to allow her to consider alternatives and make informed decisions. The range of physiological, behavioral, cognitive, interpersonal, and psychological/emotional sequelae she may experience. Bibliotherapy may be useful (Walker, 1978).

   B. Common myths concerning batterers and battered women.

   C. For her, a positive attitude and, for her abuser, appropriate blame attribution. Maladaptive coping responses should be identified as both problematic to her and a response to coping as opposed to stable personality traits.

5. Use anticipatory guidance and rehearsal to reinforce educational principles. In this way the client can anticipate, plan for, and better cope with many postassault situations and problems. This is particularly true for developing an escape plan. Have the woman "rehearse" mental-escape drills in the therapy session, delineating each of the steps she will take, and then conduct an actual escape drill in her home, in which she "walks through" the steps when the batterer is absent.

6. Be problem oriented.

    List the various options open to the client and the things to which she must attend in the near future. Safety is always the first priority. The clinician should develop a written protocol to assist in devising a safety plan for a woman. Identify all basic needs that must be met to allow the woman to escape successfully in the event of a dangerous battering incident. A checklist of necessary items to take with her should be made. Identify the step-by-step sequence of behaviors she must follow to get out of the house. Encourage her to prioritize events. Partialization—in which the totality of the assault is divided into manageable parts to facilitate task identification, evaluation, prioritization, and management—is a useful technique.

7. Be future oriented.

    In the initial session, encourage the client to make a schedule or a detailed plan of her activities for the next several days, scheduling them hour by hour if necessary. Also offer hope and realistic reassurance. Suggest that she will feel in greater control of her life as time progresses and she acquires skills to ensure her safety and improve her decision-making ability. Remind her that, like other women who have experienced battering, she can also return to normal functioning.

8. Identify and use the victim's social network to facilitate her recovery.

    Remember that even though the victim may have a social network, these people may not be readily able or willing to support her by validating her experience and facilitating her change. Offer services and information to concerned and supportive family members and friends.

9. Set the stage for the development of a "survivor" mentality.

    Share strategies used by other women who successfully coped with battering. Remind the client that while she has experienced legitimate trauma, she also used a variety of coping skills that enabled her to survive. These skills demonstrate that she possesses many strengths. Emphasize that she did "right" and that her survival skills will allow her to achieve recovery goals of autonomy and control.

Short-Term Therapy

Short-term therapy using either an individual or a group format may be beneficial to the battered woman. The therapist should be supportive and emphasize educational and decision-making skills, as well as symptom alleviation, using directive techniques. In the past several years, many clinicians have published guides to cognitive-behaviorally oriented short-term treatment that are designed specifically to address the concerns of battered women. Such techniques include modeling, thought stopping, cognitive restructuring, reframing, and stress inoculation (Webb, 1992).

The treatment emphasis in this area has followed the direction taken with other victim populations, focusing on the cognitive aspects of functioning. Topics in decision making include financial, legal, and educational issues. Many therapists emphasize the value of a feminist orientation, which places the abuse in a social context and stresses the woman's empowerment.

The focus of intervention in short-term therapy for a woman who has ended a battering relationship should still evaluate continuing concerns for safety, decision-making skills, and symptom relief strategies. It should also help the woman regain a sense of autonomy and control over her life and develop and identify a personal social support network.

Those therapeutic tasks that have been identified in the clinical literature (Courtois, 1988; Dutton, 1992a, 1992b; Follingstad et al., 1988) as important to treating PTSD symptoms in various trauma groups are

1. Integration of the traumatic experience by reexperiencing the traumatic event.
2. Management of subsequent stress.
3. Facilitation of affective expression.
4. Determination of the meaning of victimization.

For the battered woman, the therapeutic task of reexperiencing the traumatic event must be approached with caution and sensitivity. Two problems are possible. The first can occur when the clinician inadvertently creates a retraumatization experience—as opposed to a therapeutic experience—by asking the woman to reexperience the battering event. Before beginning this task, it is necessary to create a therapeutic environment that is safe for the woman. Reexperiencing the trauma is best done by having the woman tell her story. Although flooding and other techniques have been employed with victims of other forms of trauma to facilitate the reexperiencing of the traumatic event, this technique is not recommended for battered women. If avoidance is the primary presenting problem, the clinician may have to facilitate the storytelling process through the use of experiential techniques and documents, photographs, police reports, and the like.

Stress-management techniques are used to regulate the responses when the reexperiencing trauma leads to excessive arousal or spontaneous intrusions, such as thoughts, nightmares, and flashbacks. Techniques to manage stress include refocusing attention on external reality; using relaxation techniques; employing "dosing" (a technique discussed by Courtois [1988] in which attention is alternately shifted toward and away from the traumatic experience); time-management skills; personal self-care in terms of nutrition, rest, and reduced activity; development of a support system; and discrimination skills to evaluate prior and current situations.

Since many battered women have learned to suppress affect, a therapist-guided expression of emotions in the therapeutic relationship is critical. As mentioned earlier, suppressed anger may emerge as rage and other intense emotions long after the woman has left the relationship. Affective expression can take many forms (e.g., spoken words, journal entries, poetry, songs, art, and dramatizations or plays). It is important to remember that affective expression should be considered as an ongoing process and not a single exercise planned for a particular therapeutic session.

Posttraumatic therapy also emphasizes the importance of finding meaning from traumatic events. One must somehow regain a sense of control and predictability in one's life and rebuild shattered cognitive assumptions about one's world, others, and one's place in the world.

A sophisticated, time-limited, behavioral treatment package appropriate for use with a wide variety of sexual dysfunctions, which was originally designed to treat victims of incest and rape (Becker & Skinner 1983, 1984), may be employed if warranted. This approach is highly flexible, can be used in individual or group formats, and appears to be effective in relieving symptoms.

A Case Vignette

A case vignette illustrates a cross section of a victim's experiences, symptom patterns, adjustment level, and social support network.

Mary was a forty-three-year-old woman with a high school education who had recently remarried. Her first marriage had been highly abusive. She met her first husband while they both were in high school. She described the relationship as "very intense and exciting." They married when she was eighteen and he was nineteen. She was pregnant with their son at the time. He began to hit her during this pregnancy. He pulled her by the hair and threw her down the stairs on one occasion (she was seven months pregnant at the time), because she had failed to clean out the ashtrays, which was "her job as his wife." The battering was episodic and increased in intensity and frequency over the next several years. A second child, a daughter, was born three years later.

Mary described her memories of the house in which they lived during this period as "dark, gray, maybe because it was so depressing." She commented about her efforts to control her environment as unsuccessful attempts to stop the battering:

> I got to the point that I was only sleeping three or four hours a night. The rest of the time I was trying to figure out how to get the house and the kids perfect so that he wouldn't beat me again for something that was wrong at home. I was always on alert. . . . All my energy went into planning every little detail so it would be perfect. I thought I could stop it [the abuse] by myself.

She described the incident that led her to enter a shelter with her children:

> I heard the sound of his motorcycle. He had been drinking, and it was late. He came in and wanted to eat. Dinner was warming in the oven. All his clothes were clean and pressed. I could tell he was in a bad mood and looking for something to be wrong and I

would get beaten. He threw off his shirt. When I offered to get him a clean one, he said he wanted the blue one. That was the one he had just thrown on the floor. He got angry and began to hit me. My son was about seven. He took his sister into the bedroom and hid her under the bed. He tried to call the police, and my husband pulled the phone cord out of the wall. My son began to hit him to try to get him to stop hitting me. My husband hit him so hard . . . he threw him against the wall. Something just happened to me.

I suddenly thought . . . he could really hurt my children. I had never thought that before. I knew we had to get out. The next day after he left for work I took the kids and went to a shelter. I got group treatment.

I wonder why I didn't worry more about my kids. I worry they will always be scarred because of what they had to live through. I had a hard time even thinking about another relationship with a man. I didn't trust anyone.

Now that I'm remarried, I'm worried somehow the same thing will happen again. My husband gets angry, but he has never hit me or the kids. I'm just really worried, even though it doesn't make any sense.

As a result of the abusive relationship, Mary developed several symptoms. During her first marriage, as the battering increased in severity, so did her self-blame, depression, isolation, sleeping disturbance, and distorted cognitions about herself and her situation. Also, up until the final abusive episode involving her children, she had denied and minimized the possibility of risk of serious injury to herself or her children. Finally, symptoms persisted long after the end of the abusive relationship. One of the more salient symptoms was the mistrust of her current husband.

Using a cognitive-behavioral, problem-specific treatment regimen of eighteen sessions, Mary was able to establish a more trusting relationship with her current husband; more accurately evaluate her assumptions and fears regarding the potential for abuse and abuse-related cues in her current marriage; address the issue of chronic, moderately depressive cognitions; and communicate openly and honestly with her children regarding the previous abuse.

Evaluation of Clinical Interventions

If intervention services for battered women are to achieve their stated objectives, they must be based on a systematic plan and evaluation of the program's stated goals. Unfortunately, program planning, coordination with other disciplines, and program evaluation have not been given the necessary attention, despite what appears to be the provision of quality care in many programs.

There has been little research on the impact of the short- and long-term adjustment of battered women using mental health services. The clinical literature has suggested that cognitive-behaviorally oriented crisis and time-limited treatment models are the desired approaches in treating battered women. The adequacy of services (program evaluation) and information regarding the woman's adjustment should be obtained at the end of crisis interventions. The client's satisfaction with time-limited intervention should be obtained at the end of the brief treatment course, along with measures of the client's current psychological functioning. Both crisis and time-limited intervention should use client satisfaction questionnaires, in which women are asked to rate the usefulness of specific strategies, the overall perceived utility of the services, the adequacy of the educational information provided, the availability of services, and the clinician's skills. Clients could also make suggestions for program changes and additional services. This form could be provided in a packet along with self-help information. With a telephone follow-up, such information could also be obtained at the end of the contact.

Notes

1. Information about these options can be obtained by contacting Straus c/o Family Research Laboratory, University of New Hampshire, Durham, N.H. 03824.
2. Information about the scale is available from the authors.
3. The scale is available from Psychological Assessment Resources.

Appendix: Interview Guide

Jackson, Quevillon, and Petretic-Jackson (1985) wrote an interview guide designed to identify a range of concerns relevant to victims of abuse by modifying the original outline formulated by Jackson and associates to relate specifically to the concerns of battered women, we recommend that the following material be assessed in the interview.

    I. The Nature and Circumstances of the Assault
        A. Circumstances (who, what, when, where, how)
            Assess the woman's defensive violence, and determine her perceived threat of serious injury or death to her or others
        B. Attribution of blame (victim's perception of the "why" of assault: Is blame placed on self or batterer?)
        C. Assessment of other aspects of relationship with batterer, aside from the abuse
        D. Type and extent of coercion methods employed (verbal threats, use of intimidation, use of children, sexual assault, isolation; economic abuse, emotional withholding; psychological destabilization)
        E. Level and nature of violence (threats of death, use of a weapon, battering).
            Assess the last few battering incidents to determine potential escalation; use Campbell's measure or other information to determine risk of lethality from batterer
   II. Postassault Interactions
        A. Professional contacts (legal, medical, woman's shelter or center)
            Assess adequacy of response to woman
        B. Time between assault and help seeking (self-care: whom did she talk to; who determined that she would seek mental health services?)
        C. Social support system (friends, family of origin, children)
            1. Partner
            2. Family of origin or children (style of family coping, allowance for victim's control, dependency issues, levels of support and blame)
            3. Friends (levels of support and blame)

III. Victim's Initial Reaction
  A. Self-perceptions
     (In your own words, describe your thoughts and your feelings)
  B. Symptoms
     Refer to the categories of physical, cognitive, emotional, interpersonal,
     and relationship issues); assess fear and vulnerability associated with
     severity of PTSD symptoms; evaluate congruence between self-reported
     problems/symptoms and other assessment data; assess changes in vege-
     tative function—sleep, appetite, weight, menstruation, elimination as-
     sociated with depression, and/or anxiety; assess suicidal ideation, plan;
     assess any sexual trauma
  C. Initial changes in daily functioning
     Job performance, relationships, social life,
     change or maintenance of place and circumstances of residence,
     need to visit relatives, future plans, etc.
  D. Mental status changes
     Judgment, orientation to person, place, time; memory; affect; cognitive
     functions
  E. Changes in personality or behavior reported by others if collateral re-
     ports are available
        Obtain woman's prior consent for this
        Examine congruence between reports of victim and significant others
        other than batterer
        Evaluate anger and risk of homicide by partner; evaluate woman's
        anger expression and homicide risk to partner
IV. Current Status
  A. Evaluate mental status
  B. Coping efforts and strategies
     Identify defenses
     Assess strategies to escape, avoid, and survive
     Cognitive vs. affective coping:
        Intellectual insight with/without emotional working-through.
        For example, does the victim report that she knows "in her head" that
        it wasn't her fault, but still has problems "in her gut" believing she
        was not to blame?
  C. Symptom expressivity/issue of prolonged crisis
     Is there more to come?
     What other personal or social factors can exacerbate stress symptoms?
  D. Identify mediating variables
        Prior traumatic experiences
        Other current life stressors
        Level of social support
        Cognitive coping strategies
  E. Continue to chart current psychological response pattern
     1. Emotional
        PTSD-associated symptoms of avoidance (physical or emotional iso-
        lation) and intrusion (day: ruminations; night: nightmares)

    Depression
    Anxiety and fears
    Hostility and anger
    Guilt and shame

2. Cognitive
    Distortions
        Personal safety or invulnerability
        Self-blame
        Increased tolerance for abusive behavior and "normalizing" the violence
        Perceived limited options for self-protection
        Inability to identify inconsistency of abuse within an intimate relationship
    Problem-solving skills

3. Biological
    Increased health complaints and illness
    Physiological hyperarousal (startle response)
    Somatic disturbances (PTSD- or depression-associated)
        Eating (increased; decreased)
        Sleeping (increased; decreased)
        Physical symptoms specific to assault

4. Behavioral
    Aggressive behavior
    Suicidal or other self-destructive behaviors
    Substance abuse (alcohol; prescription drugs)
    Impaired social functioning
    Dysfunctional personality features (*DSM*-IV Axis II)

5. Interpersonal
    Sexual problems
        Sexual acting-out
        Sexual dysfunctions
        Lowered sexual satisfaction
    Heterosocial adjustment difficulties
        Mistrust
        Sexualized
    Social isolation
    Interpersonal problem solving difficulties
        Lack of appropriate assertiveness
        Problems setting personal boundaries
    Adequacy in the parental role
        Ability to protect children
        Abuse of children
        Parenting skills and discipline

V. Course
    A. Presence/absence of premorbid psychological history
        Prior psychiatric treatment,
        Prior psychiatric hospitalization,

Psychotropic medications,
Depression and suicide attempts
B. Social Functioning (partner, children and others)
Partner (dating/relationship status)
If staying in abusive relationship:
Victim violence directed at children
Personal revictimization
If involved in a new relationship:
Trust
Revictimization
Assertiveness
Trust level
C. Educational or occupational functioning
D. Symptom fluctuation
Use a graph to chart the symptom course
VI. Attributions
A. Attribution of blame (self, situation, offender)
B. Self-efficacy rating
How well do you feel you are doing?
Do you feel it is taking too long to get readjusted?
What had you anticipated?
Are you pleased or disappointed at where you are now in terms of gains?
C. Attributions to legal-medical-psychological community
(Were law enforcement and medical professionals supportive? Accusing? What could have been done to facilitate your coping?
VII. Future Orientation
A. Short-term plans and goals
B. Self-statements (ability to reinforce strategies used and gains made)
C. Realistic optimism regarding relationships and own recovery
(I can recognize that sometimes I am responding to my current partner not for what he is doing but because I'm thinking about my ex. If I keep that in mind, I will eventually be able to react to him given what I can judge from his behavior not from my fears to what happened in the past. I am a survivor. I have made gains. I will not tolerate violence from any man.)

References

American Psychiatric Association. 1994. *The Diagnostic and Statistical Manual of Mental Disorders (DSM-IV)*. Washington, D.C.: American Psychiatric Association.

Astin, M. C., K. Lawrence, G. Pincus, and D. Foy. 1990, October. "Moderator Variables for PTSD Among Battered Women." Paper presented at the convention of the International Society for Traumatic Stress Studies, New Orleans.

Ball, P. G., and E. Wyman. 1978. "Battered Women and Powerlessness: What Can Counselors Do?" *Victimology: An International Journal* 2: 545–52.

Beck, A., A. Rush, B. Shaw, and G. Emery. 1979. *Cognitive Therapy of Depression.* New York: Guilford Press.

Becker, J. V., and L. J. Skinner. 1983. "Assessment and Treatment of Rape-Related Sexual Dysfunctions." *Clinical Psychologist* 36: 102–4.

Becker, J. V., and L. J. Skinner. 1984. "Behavioral Treatment of Sexual Dysfunctions in Sexual Assault Survivors." In *Victims of Sexual Aggression: Treatment of Men, Women and Children,* ed. I. Stuart and J. Green, pp. 211–33. New York: Van Nostrand Reinhold.

Bowker, L. H. 1983. *Beating Wife-Beating.* Lexington, Mass.: Lexington Books.

Brekke, J. 1987. "Detecting Wife and Child Abuse in Clinical Settings." *Social Casework* 68: 332–38.

Briere, J. 1991. "The Trauma Symptom Inventory." Unpublished psychological test, University of Southern California School of Medicine, Los Angeles.

Briere, J., D. Elliott, and K. Smiljanich. 1994. "The Trauma Symptom Inventory: Reliability and Validity in Clinical and Nonclinical Groups." Unpublished manuscript.

Briere, J., and M. Runtz. 1988. "Multivariate Correlates of Childhood Psychological and Physical Maltreatment Among University Women." *Child Abuse and Neglect* 12: 331–41.

Briere, J., and M. Runtz. 1989. "The Trauma Symptom Checklist (TSC-33): Early Data on a New Scale." *Journal of Interpersonal Violence* 4: 151–63.

Broderick, J. 1980. "Attitudinal and Behavioral Components of Marital Satisfaction." Ph.D. diss., State University of New York at Stony Brook.

Brodsky, S. 1976. "Sexual Assault: Perspectives on Prevention and Assailants." In *Sexual Assault: The Victim and the Rapist,* ed. M. Walker and S. Brodsky, pp. 1–8. Lexington, Mass.: Lexington Books.

Burgess, A., and L. Holstrom. 1979. "Sexual Disruption and Recovery." *American Journal of Orthopsychiatry* 49: 648–57.

Butcher, J. N., W. G. Dahlstrom, J. R. Graham, A. M. Tellegen, and B. Kaemmer. 1989. *MMPI-2: Manual for Administration and Scoring.* Minneapolis: University of Minnesota Press.

Campbell, J. 1986. "Nursing Assessment for Risk of Homicide with Battered Women." *Advances in Nursing Science* 8: 36–51.

Campbell, J. 1989. "Women's Responses to Sexual Abuse in Intimate Relationships." *Health Care for Women International* 10: 335–46.

Carmen, E., P. Reiker, and T. Mills. 1984. "Victims of Violence and Psychiatric Illness." *American Journal of Psychiatry* 141: 378–83.

Constantine, M. 1992, August. "Treatment Considerations and Implications for Counseling African American Battered Women." Symposium presented at the annual meeting of the American Psychological Association, Washington, D.C.

Courtois, C. A. 1988. *Healing the Incest Wound: Adult Survivors in Therapy.* New York: Norton.

Davis, L. W. 1987. "Battered Women: The Transformation of a Social Problem." *Social Work* 32: 306–11.

de las Fuentes, C. 1992, August. "The Violent Latino Family: Implications for Treatment and Research." Symposium presented at the annual meeting of the American Psychological Association, Washington, D.C.

Derogatis, L. R. 1977. *SCL-90: Administration Scoring and Procedures Manual.* Baltimore: John Hopkins University Press.

Douglas, M., and J. Strom. 1988. "Cognitive Therapy with Battered Women." *Journal of Rational Emotive and Cognitive Behavior Therapy* 6: 33–49.

Dutton, M. 1992a. "Assessment and Treatment of Post-Traumatic Stress Disorder Among Battered Women." In *Treating PTSD: Cognitive–Behavioral Strategies,* ed. D. Foy, pp. 69–98. New York: Guilford Press.

Dutton, M. 1992b. *Empowering and Healing the Battered Woman.* New York: Springer.

Dutton, M., M. Freeman, and A. Stumpff. 1988. "Abusive Behavior Observation Checklist." Unpublished manuscript, Nova University.

Dutton, M., G. Hass, and L. Hohnecker. 1989. "Response to Violence Inventory." Unpublished manuscript, Nova University.

Dutton, M., S. Perrin, K. Chrestman, and P. Halle. 1990, August. "MMPI Trauma Profiles for Battered Women." Paper presented at the annual meeting of the American Psychological Association, Boston.

Dutton, M., S. Perrin, K. Chrestman, P. Halle, and K. Burghardt. 1991. "Post-Traumatic Stress Disorder in Women: Concurrent Validity." Poster presented at the annual meeting of the American Psychological Association, San Francisco.

Elliott, D. M., and J. Briere. 1992. "Sexual Abuse Trauma Among Professional Women: Validating the Trauma Symptom Checklist-40 (TSC-40)." *Child Abuse and Neglect* 16: 391–98.

Ewing, C. P., and M. Aubrey. 1987. "Battered Women and Public Opinion: Some Realities About the Myths." *Journal of Family Violence* 2: 257–64.

Ferguson, W., and T. L. Jackson. 1986, May. "Incest Victims' Attribution of Incest Blame and Symptom Severity." Paper presented at the Midwestern Psychological Association Convention, Chicago.

Ferraro, K., and J. Johnson. 1983. "How Women Experience Battering: The Process of Victimization." *Social Problems* 30: 325–39.

Foa, E., G. Steketee, and B. Rothbaum. 1989. "Behavioral/Cognitive Conceptualization of Post-Traumatic Stress Disorder." *Behavior Therapy* 20: 155–76.

Follingstad, D. 1980. "Reconceptualization of Issues in the Treatment of Abused Women: A Case Study." *Psychotherapy: Theory, Research and Practice* 17: 294–303.

Follingstad, D., A. Neckerman, and J. Vrombrock. 1988. "Reactions to Victimization and Coping Strategies of Battered Women: The Ties That Bind." *Clinical Psychology Review* 8: 373–90.

Follingstad, D., L. Rutledge, B. Berg, E. Hause, and D. Polek. 1990. "The Role of Emotional Abuse in Physically Abusive Relationships." *Journal of Family Violence* 5: 107–20.

Foy, D. W. 1992. "Introduction and Description of the Disorder." In *Treating PTSD: Cognitive–Behavioral Strategies,* ed. D. W. Foy, pp. 1–12. New York: Guilford Press.

Frieze, I. H. 1979. "Perceptions of Battered Women." In *New Approaches to Social Problems: Applications of Attribution Theory,* ed. I. H. Frieze, D. Bar-Tal, and J. Carroll, pp. 79–108. San Francisco: Jossey-Bass.

Gayford, J. J. 1975. "Wife Battering: A Preliminary Survey of 100 Cases." *British Medical Journal* 1: 194–97.

Harris, R. E., and J. D. Lingoes. 1968. "Subscales for the Minnesota Multiphasic Personality Inventory." Mimeograph, Langley Porter Clinic.

Hendricks-Matthews, M. 1982. "The Battered Woman: Is She Ready for Help?" *Social Casework: The Journal of Contemporary Social Work* 63: 131–37.

Hilberman, E. 1980. "Overview: The 'Wife-Beater's Wife' Reconsidered." *American Journal of Psychiatry* 137: 1336–47.

Hilberman, E., and K. Munson. 1977–1978. "Sixty Battered Women." *Victimology: An International Journal* 2: 460–70.

Horowitz, M. 1986. *Stress Response Syndromes,* 2nd ed. Northvale, N.J.: Jason Aronson.

Horowitz, M., N. Wilner, and W. Alvarez. 1979. "Impact of Events Scale: A Measure of Subjective Distress. *Psychosomatic Medicine* 41: 209–18.

Houskamp, B. M., and D. W. Foy. 1991. "The Assessment of Posttraumatic Stress Disorder in Battered Women." *Journal of Interpersonal Violence* 6: 367–75.

Hudson, W., and S. McIntosh. 1981. "The Assessment of Spouse Abuse: Two Quantifiable Dimensions." *Journal of Marriage and the Family* 43: 873–85.

Jackson, T. 1991. "A University Athletic Department's Rape and Assault Experiences." *Journal of College Student Development* 32: 77–78.

Jackson, T. L., and P. Eck. 1987, May. "Attribution of Assault Blame by Incarcerated Sex Offenders." Paper presented at the Midwestern Psychological Association Convention, Chicago.

Jackson, T. L., and W. Ferguson. 1983. "Attribution of Blame in Incest." *American Journal of Community Psychology* 11: 313–22.

Jackson, T. L. and S. M. Fischer. 1982, May. "Mental Health Professionals' Attitudes Towards Incest." Paper presented at the Midwestern Psychological Association Convention, Chicago.

Jackson, T. L. and T. Plane. 1987, May. "Attribution of Rape Blame Among Native Americans." Paper presented at the Midwestern Psychological Association Convention, Chicago.

Jackson, T. L., R. P. Quevillon, and P. A. Petretic-Jackson. 1985. "Assessment and Treatment of Sexual Assault Victims" In *Innovations in Clinical Practice: A Source Book,* vol. 4, ed. P. Keller and L. Ritt, pp. 51–78. Sarasota, Fla.: Professional Resource Exchange.

Jackson, T. L., and G. Sandberg. 1985. "Attribution of Incest Blame Among Rural Attorneys and Judges." *Women and Therapy* 4: 13–22.

Jaffe, P., D. Wolfe, S. Wilson, and L. Zak. 1986. "Emotional and Physical Health Problems of Battered Women." *Canadian Journal of Psychiatry* 31: 625–29.

Janoff-Bulman, R., and I. H. Frieze. 1983. "A Theoretical Perspective for Understanding Reactions to Victimization." *Journal of Social Issues* 39: 1–17.

Keane, T., P. Malloy, and J. Fairbank. 1984. "Empirical Development of an MMPI Subscale for the Assessment of Combat Related Post-Traumatic Stress Disorder." *Journal of Consulting and Clinical Psychology* 52: 888–91.

Kemp, A., E. Rawlings, and B. Green. 1991. "Post-Traumatic Stress Disorder (PTSD) in Battered Women: A Shelter Sample." *Journal of Traumatic Stress* 4: 137–48.

Kenning, M., and T. Jackson. 1984, May. "Attribution of Rape Among Rural and Urban College Women." Paper presented at the Midwestern Psychological Association Convention, Chicago.

Kilpatrick, D., L. Veronen, and P. A. Resick. 1980, November. "Brief Behavioral Intervention Procedure: A New Treatment for Recent Rape Victims." Paper presented at the annual meeting of the Association for Advancement of Behavior Therapy, New York.

Launius, M., and B. Jensen. 1987. "Interpersonal Problem-Solving Skills in Battered, Counseling, and Control Women." *Journal of Family Violence* 2: 151–62.

Levit, H. I. 1991. "Battered Women: Syndrome Versus Self-Defense." *American Journal of Forensic Psychology* 9: 29–35.

Marshall, L. L. 1992. "Development of the Severity of Violence Against Women Scales." *Journal of Family Violence* 7: 103–20.

McCann, I. L., and L. A. Perlman. 1990. "Vicarious Traumatization: A Framework for Understanding the Psychological Effects of Working with Victims." *Journal of Traumatic Stress* 3: 131–49.

McCann, I. L., D. Sakheim, and D. Abrahamson. 1988. "Trauma and Victimization: A Model of Psychological Adaptation." *Counseling Psychologist* 16: 531–94.

McKee, E. A. 1992, August. "Counseling South-East Asian Women: Culturally Sensitive Modifications of Treatment." Symposium presented at the annual meeting of the American Psychological Association, Washington, D.C.

Meichenbaum, D. 1977. *Cognitive-Behavior Modification.* New York: Plenum.

Miller, E. T., and C. A. Porter. 1983. "Self-Blame in Victims of Violence." *Journal of Social Issues* 39: 139–52.

Millon, T. 1983. *Millon Clinical Multiaxial Inventory Manual,* 3rd ed. Minneapolis: National Computer Systems.

Millon, T. 1987. *Millon Clinical Multiaxial Inventory-II Manual.* Minneapolis: National Computer Systems.

Mills, T. 1985. "The Assault on the Self: Stages in Coping with Battered Husbands." *Qualitative Sociology* 8: 103–23.

Mitchell, R. E., and C. A. Hodson. 1983. "Coping with Domestic Violence: Social Supports and Psychological Health Among Battered Women." *American Journal of Community Psychology* 11: 629–54.

Morris, Y., and T. Jackson. 1989, August. "Midwestern Attorneys' Blame Attribution and Sentencing Preferences in Rape." Paper presented at the American Psychological Association Convention, New Orleans.

Noonan, M. P. 1989. "Medical Students' Attributions of Blame in Cases of Domestic Violence." Master's thesis, University of South Dakota.

Pagelow, M. 1981. *Woman-Battering: Victims and Their Experiences.* Beverly Hills, Calif. Sage.

Pagelow, M. 1992. "Adult Victims of Domestic Violence: Battered Women." *Journal of Interpersonal Violence* 7: 87–120.

Parsons, L., B. Yutrzenka, and T. L. Jackson. 1987, May. "An Exploratory Study of an Expressive Versus Instrumental Violence Typology of Batterers." Paper presented at the Midwestern Psychological Association Convention, Chicago.

Pence, E., and M. Paymar. 1986. "The Domestic Abuse Intervention Project." Mimeograph.

Peterson, C., and M. Seligman. 1983. "Learned Helplessness and Victimization." *Journal of Social Issues* 2: 103–16.

Petretic-Jackson, P., and T. L. Jackson. 1990. "Crisis Intervention with Sexual Assault Victims." In *Crisis Intervention: Techniques and Issues,* ed. A. R. Roberts, pp. 124–52. Pacific Grove, Calif.: Wadsworth.

Pfouts, J. H. 1978. "Violent Families: Coping Responses of Abused Wives." *Child Welfare* 57: 101–11.

Porter, C. A. 1981. "The Interrelationships Among Causal Attribution, Affect and Coping in Battered Women." Paper presented at the annual meeting of the Canadian Psychological Association, Toronto.

Prentice, R., and T. Jackson. 1984. May. "Distribution of Incest Blame Rated by Metropolitan Police Applicants and Sworn Officers." Paper presented at the Midwestern Psychological Association Convention, Chicago.

Resick, P. A., and T. L. Jackson. 1981. "Attitudes Toward Rape Among Mental Health Professionals." *American Journal of Community Psychology* 4: 481–90.

Rhodes, N. R. 1992. "Comparison of MMPI Psychopathic Deviate Scores of Battered and Nonbattered Women." *Journal of Family Violence* 7: 297–307.

Roberts, A. R. 1984. "Crisis Intervention with Battered Women." In *Battered Women and Their Families: Intervention Strategies and Treatment Programs,* ed. A. R. Roberts, pp. 65–83. New York: Springer.

Rosal, M., M. Dutton-Douglas, and S. Perrin. 1990, August. "Anxiety in Battered Women." Paper presented at the annual meeting of the American Psychological Association, Boston.

Rosewater, L. B. 1982. "The Development of an MMPI Profile for Battered Women." Ph.D. diss., Union Graduate School.

Rosewater, L. B. 1985. "Schizophrenic, Borderline or Battered?" In *Handbook of Feminist Therapy: Women's Issues in Psychotherapy,* ed. L. B. Rosewater and L. Walker, pp. 142–61. New York: Springer.

Rosewater, L. B. 1987. "A Critical Analysis of the Proposed Self-Defeating Personality Disorder." *Journal of Personality Disorders* 1: 190–95.

Rosewater, L. B. 1988. "Battered or Schizophrenic? Psychologists Can't Tell." In *Feminist Perspectives on Wife Abuse,* ed. K. Yllo and C. Bograd. Beverly Hills, Calif.: Sage.

Rounsaville, B. J. 1978. "Battered Wives: Barriers to Identification and Treatment." *American Journal of Orthopsychiatry* 48: 487–94.

Sandberg, G. G., and T. L. Jackson. 1986a, May. "Psychologists' Blame Attribution in Domestic Violence." Paper presented at the Midwestern Psychological Association Convention, Chicago.

Sandberg, G. G., and T. L. Jackson. 1986b, May. "Psychologists' Perception of 'Duty to Warn' in Wife Abuse." Paper presented at the Midwestern Psychological Association Convention, Chicago.

Sandberg, G. G., P. Petretic-Jackson, and T. L. Jackson. 1985, May. "Definition and Attribution of Blame in Domestic Violence." Paper presented at the Midwestern Psychological Association Convention, Chicago.

Saunders, B. E., C. Arata, and D. Kilpatrick. 1990. "Development of a Crime-Related Post-Traumatic Stress Disorder Scale for Women Within the Symptom Checklist-90-Revised." *Journal of Traumatic Stress* 3: 439–48.

Saunders, D. 1990, June. "The Traumatic Aftermath of Violence Against Women." Paper presented at the Research Scientist Development Awardees Conference, Chevy Chase, Md.

Saunders, D., A. Lynch, M. Grayson, and D. Linz. 1987. "The Inventory of Beliefs About Wife Beating: The Construction and Initial Validation of a Measure of Beliefs and Attitudes." *Violence and Victims* 2: 39–57.

Schumm, W. R., and D. A. Bagarozzi. 1989. "The Conflict Tactics Scales." *American Journal of Family Therapy* 17: 165–68.

Schutte, N. S., L. Bouleige, J. L. Fix, and J. M. Malouff. 1986. "Returning to Partner After Leaving a Crisis Shelter: A Decision Faced by Battered Women." *Journal of Social Behavior and Personality* 1: 295–98.

Seligman, M. E. 1975. *Helplessness: On Depression, Development and Death.* San Francisco: Freeman.

Spitzer, R. L., and J. B. Williams. 1986. *Structured Clinical Interview for DSM III-R.* New York: New York State Psychiatric Institute.

Stark, E. 1984. "The Battered Syndrome: Social Knowledge, Social Therapy and the Abuse of Women." Ph.D. diss., State University of New York at Binghamton.

Stark, E., and A. Flitcraft. 1981. *Wife Abuse in the Medical Setting: An Introduction for Health Personnel.* Monograph No. 7. Washington, D.C.: Office of Domestic Violence.

Stark, E., and A. Flitcraft. 1988. "Personal Power and Institutional Victimization: Treating the Dual Trauma of Woman Battering." In *Post-Traumatic Therapy and Victims of Violence,* ed. F. M. Ochberg, pp. 115–51. New York: Brunner/Mazel.

Stark, E., A. Flitcraft, and W. Frazier. 1979. "Medicine and Patriarchial Violence: The Social Construction of a Private Event." *International Journal of Health Services* 9: 461–93.

Straus, M. 1979. "Measuring Intrafamilial Conflict and Violence: The Conflict Tactics (CT) Scales." *Journal of Marriage and the Family* 45: 75–88.

Symonds, A. 1979. "Violence Against Women: The Myth of Masochism." *American Journal of Psychotherapy* 33: 161–73.

Tarver, D., and T. Jackson. 1992, August. "Physician Blame Attribution in Domestic Violence Cases." Paper presented at the annual meeting of the American Psychological Association, Washington, D.C.

Tolman, R. M. 1989. "The Development of a Measure of Psychological Maltreatment of Women by Their Male Partners." *Violence and Victims* 4: 159–77.

Tolman, R. M. 1991. "Validation of the Psychological Maltreatment of Women Inventory: Preliminary Report." Unpublished paper, University of Illinois at Chicago.

Tolman, R. M. 1992. "Psychological Abuse of Women. In *Assessment of Family Violence: A Clinical and Legal Sourcebook,* ed. R. T. Ammerman and M. Hersen, pp. 291–310. New York: Wiley.

Veronen, L., and D. Kilpatrick. 1983. "Stress Management for Rape Victims." In *Stress Reduction and Prevention,* ed. D. Meichenbaum and M. Jaremko, pp. 341–74. New York: Plenum.

Walker, L. 1979. *The Battered Woman.* New York: Harper & Row.

Walker, L. 1984. *The Battered Woman Syndrome.* New York: Springer.

Walker, L. 1987. "Assessment and Intervention with Battered Women." In *Innovations in Clinical Practice: A Source Book,* Vol. 6, ed. L. Ritt and P. Keller, pp. 131–42. Sarasota, Fla: Professional Resource Exchange.

Ward, M., and P. Resick. 1980. "Attribution of Rape Blame Scale." Unpublished manuscript, University of South Dakota.

Webb, W. 1992. "Treatment Issues and Cognitive Behavior Techniques with Battered Women." *Journal of Family Violence* 7: 205–17.

White, P., and P. Petretic-Jackson. 1992, August. "Psychologists' Patterns of Blame Attribution for Wife Abuse." Paper presented at the annual meeting of the American Psychological Association, Washington, D.C.

13

The False Connection Between Adult Domestic Violence and Alcohol

Theresa M. Zubretsky and
Karla M. Digirolamo

Since the 1970s, significant efforts have been made to increase the public's understanding of domestic violence and to educate professionals and service providers about this problem. Through accounts from battered and formerly battered women, domestic violence is now understood to include a range of behaviors—physical, sexual, economic, emotional, and psychological abuse—directed toward establishing and maintaining power and control over an intimate partner. There is also an increased awareness that the societal tendency to blame domestic violence victims and excuse perpetrators is rooted in a history of cultural and legal traditions that have supported the domination and abuse of women by men in intimate relationships. Despite greater public awareness, however, myths and misconceptions about battered women's experiences persist. Interventions based on these myths can have a devastating effect on victims and their families.

Despite the significant correlation between domestic violence and chemical dependency, hardly any research has been conducted and little has been written about the need to develop intervention strategies that address both the domestic violence and the substance abuse problems of chemically dependent men who batter. Similarly, little has been done to assist battered women with chemical dependency problems to meet their needs for both safety and sobriety. Neither system currently is equipped to provide the range of services needed by battered women and batterers who are affected by chemical dependency.

In the addictions treatment system, misinformation often leads counselors to understand and respond to domestic violence through the use of an addictions framework, an approach that has particularly harmful consequences for battered women. Such an approach identifies battering either as a symptom of alcohol abuse or addiction or as an addiction itself. The interventions that follow are based on a number of *harmful, false assumptions:*

1. Alcohol use and/or alcoholism causes men to batter.
2. Alcoholism treatment alone will address the abuse adequately.
3. Battered women are "co-dependent" and thus contribute to the continuation of the abuse.
4. Addicted battered women must get sober before they can begin to address their victimization.

Batterers: Relationship of Alcohol Use to Violence

The belief that alcoholism causes domestic violence is a notion widely held both in and outside of the substance abuse field, despite a lack of information to support it. Although research indicates that among men who drink heavily, there is a higher rate of domestic violence and a higher rate of perpetrating assaults resulting in serious physical injury than exists among other men, the majority of batterers are not high-level drinkers and the majority of men classified as high-level or binge drinkers do not abuse their partners (Straus & Gelles, 1990).

Even for batterers who do drink, there is little evidence to suggest a clear pattern that relates the drinking to the abusive behavior. The majority (76 percent) of physically abusive incidents occur in the absence of alcohol use (Kantor & Straus, 1987), and there is no evidence to suggest that alcohol use or dependence is linked to the other forms of coercive behavior that are part of the pattern of domestic violence. Economic control, sexual violence, and intimidation, for example, are often part of a batterer's ongoing pattern of abuse, with little or no identifiable connection to his use of or dependence on alcohol.

The belief that alcoholism causes domestic violence evolves from a lack of information about the nature of battering and from adherence to the "disinhibition theory." This theory suggests that the physiological effects of alcohol include a state of lowered inhibitions in which an individual can no longer control his behavior. Research conducted within the alcoholism field, however, suggests that the most significant determinant of behavior after drinking is not the physiological effect of the alcohol itself, but the expectation that individuals place on the drinking experience (Marlatt & Rohsenow, 1980). When cultural norms and expectations about male behavior after drinking include boisterous or aggressive behaviors, for example, research shows that individual men are more likely to engage in such behaviors when under the influence than when sober.

Despite the research findings, the belief that alcohol lowers inhibitions persists and, along with it, a historical tradition of holding people who commit crimes while under the influence of alcohol or other drugs less accountable than those who commit crimes in a sober state (MacAndrew & Edgerton, 1969). Batterers, who have not been held accountable for their abusive behavior in general, find themselves even less accountable for battering perpetrated when they are under the influence of alcohol. The alcohol provides a ready and socially acceptable excuse for their violence.

Evolving from the belief that alcohol or substance abuse causes domestic violence is the belief that treatment for the chemical dependency will stop the violence. Battered women with drug-dependent partners, however, consistently report that during recovery the abuse not only continues, but often escalates, creating greater levels of danger than existed prior to their partners' abstinence. In the cases in which battered women report that the level of physical abuse decreases, they often report a corresponding increase in other forms of coercive control and abuse—the threats, manipulation, and isolation intensify (Minnesota Coalition for Battered Women, 1992).

Power and Control, Not "Loss of Control"

The provision of appropriate services for families affected by domestic violence and substance abuse is further complicated by the belief that battering itself is addictive behavior. This belief may arise in part from an attempt to explain why violence often increases in severity over time. The progressive nature of the violence is likened to the progressive nature of the disease of addiction, inviting the use of an addictions model for responding to the problem of battering.

An addictions framework assumes that there is a point at which a batterer can no longer control his abuse, just as an addict experiences loss of control over the substance use. The experiences of battered women, however, challenge this view. Battered women report that even when their partners appear "uncontrollably drunk" during a physical assault, they routinely exhibit the ability to "sober up" remarkably quickly if there is an outside interruption, such as police intervention.

Batterers also exhibit control over the nature and extent of the physical violence they perpetrate, often directing their assaults to parts of their partners' bodies that are covered by clothing. Conversely, some batterers purposefully target their partners' faces to compel isolation or to disfigure them so that "no one else will want them." Batterers can articulate their personal limits regarding physical abuse, reporting, for example, that while they have slapped their partners with an open hand, they would never punch them with their fists. Others admit to hitting and punching, but state that they would never use a weapon (Ptacek, 1987).

The escalation in the severity of violence over time does not represent a batterer's "loss of control" over the violence, as the analogy to addictions would suggest. Instead, violence may get worse over time because increasing the intensity of the abuse is an effective way for batterers to maintain control over their partners and prevent them from leaving. The violence may also escalate because most batterers experience few, if any, negative consequences for their abusive behavior. Social tolerance of domestic violence thus not only contributes to its existence, but may influence its progression and batterers' definitions of the acceptable limits of their abuse.

Interventions with Substance-Abusing Batterers

Batterers who are also alcohol or other drug involved need to address both problems separately and concurrently. This is critical not only to maximize the victim's safety, but also to prevent the battering from precipitating relapse or otherwise interfering with the recovery process. True recovery requires much more than abstinence. It includes adopting a lifestyle that enhances one's emotional and spiritual health, a goal that cannot be achieved if the battering continues.

Self-help programs such as Alcoholics Anonymous promote and support emotional and spiritual health and have helped countless numbers of alcoholics get sober. These programs, however, were not designed to address battering and are insufficient in motivating batterers to stop their abuse. Accordingly, a treatment plan for chemically dependent men who batter must include attendance at a program designed specifically to address the attitudes and beliefs that support batterers' behavior.

Impact of Co-dependency Treatment on Battered Women

Most often, the partners of batterers in chemical dependency treatment are themselves directed into self-help programs such as Al-Anon or co-dependency groups. Like other traditional treatment responses, however, these resources were not designed to meet the needs of victims of domestic violence and often inadvertently cause harm to battered women.

The goals of Al-Anon and co-dependency treatment typically include helping family members of alcoholics get "self-focused," practice emotional detachment from the substance abusers, and identify and stop their enabling or "co-dependent" behaviors. Group members are encouraged to define their personal boundaries, set limits on their partners' behaviors, and stop protecting their partners from the harmful consequences of the addiction. While these strategies and goals may be very useful for women whose partners are not batterers, for battered women such changes will likely result in an escalation of abuse, including physical violence.

Battered women often are very attuned to their partners' moods as a way to assess their level of danger. They may focus on their partners' needs and "cover up" for them as part of their survival strategy. Battered women's behaviors are not symptomatic of some underlying "dysfunction," but are the life-saving skills necessary to protect them and their children from further harm. When battered women are encouraged to stop these behaviors through self-focusing and detachment, they are, in essence, being asked to stop doing the things that may be keeping them and their children most safe.

Battered women whose partners are chemically dependent should be given accurate and complete information about available resources so that they can make informed choices and set realistic expectations about the potential benefits of these different sources of help. It is critical that they understand the purposes of Al-Anon and co-dependency groups and the limitations of these forums as sources of accurate information regarding safety-related concerns. They should also be advised of the availability of local domestic violence programs and referred to these services for assistance. Empowering women with accurate information will help them make decisions that best meet their individual needs.

Impact of Traditional Addictions Treatment on Chemically Dependent Battered Women

Although the vast majority of battered women are not alcohol or substance abusers, those who are confront a system that is ill-equipped to deal with their needs, particularly their need for safety. Often, intakes to treatment programs do not include an assessment for adult domestic violence. Even when domestic violence is identified, it is often assumed that treatment for the substance abuse must occur before the victimization can be addressed.

One of the concerns with the "sobriety-first" approach is that it does not consider the increased risk of violence that a woman's recovery may precipitate. Batterers often are resistant to their partners' attempts to seek help of any kind, including substance abuse treatment. In response, they may sabotage the recovery process by preventing victims from attending meetings or keeping appointments, or they may increase the violence or threats in order to reestablish control. Many chemically dependent battered women leave treatment in response to the increased danger or are otherwise unable to comply with treatment demands because of the obstacles constructed by their partners. Even if a battered women is able to complete a treatment program, being revictimized is predictive of relapse (Haver, 1987).

An additional concern with the "sobriety-first" approach is that it does not recognize the relationship between the substance use and a battered woman's victimization. Many battered women report that they began to use substances as a way to cope with unremitting danger and fear. Frequently, these women report that they had sought help repeatedly from the traditional social services and legal systems, but received inadequate or negative responses. In fact, many chemically dependent battered women are addicted to sedatives, tranquilizers, stimulants, and hypnotics, drugs that were prescribed by the health care providers from whom they sought help (Flitcraft & Stark, 1988).

Whatever the drug of choice, substance-using battered women often report that the substances helped them cope with their fear and manage the daily activities of their lives in the face of ongoing abuse and danger (Minnesota Coalition for Battered Women, 1992). These are women who may be particularly resistant to engaging in a recovery process until they are confident that they can achieve genuine safety from the violence. For these women, an intervention framework that requires "sobriety first" is an approach that is almost destined to fail.

Lack of Information in the Domestic Violence Field

Traditional addictions treatment approaches are insufficient to meet the needs of battered women, both those whose partners are addicted and those who themselves have a substance abuse problem. In many ways, the services typically provided by the domestic violence service system are equally inadequate to meet the needs of women affected by both problems.

Chemically dependent battered women often have very limited or no access to safe shelter through the emergency domestic violence shelter network because of their addiction. While admission and discharge policies must consider the safety needs of all shelter residents, policies that prohibit access by chemically dependent battered women and that often are based on misconceptions about addiction cut off many women from a vital resource. Even when admission criteria do not categorically exclude chemically dependent battered women from services, domestic violence programs do not conduct appropriate screenings for substance abuse and regularly fail even to minimally evaluate the addiction treatment needs of sheltered battered women (Bennett & Lawson, 1994).

Despite the fact that domestic violence programs do not adequately assess battered women for substance abuse problems, these programs do refer women to chemical dependency treatment agencies more frequently than the reverse occurs, suggesting to some that domestic violence programs have a greater desire to forge cooperative relationships with these providers of substance abuse treatment (Bennett & Lawson, 1994). There are, however, alternative explanations that may account for the high referral rates by domestic violence programs. The lack of information and training on chemical dependency among domestic violence program staff and/or the existence of harmful attitudes and beliefs about chemically dependent women may impede the direct provision of supportive and empowering interventions by domestic violence advocates. The subsequent referrals may then become a way to shift difficult cases to another agency or to someone else's caseload. Advocates often miss an important opportunity to interrupt the deadly progression of women's alcohol or other drug addictions, problems that may significantly impair battered women's efforts to get safe.

Creating an Effective Partnership

Meeting the needs of battered women who are affected by substance abuse requires an effective working relationship between the two service systems, a need consistently identified by workers in both fields, but an undertaking fraught with multiple obstacles to cooperation (Bennett & Lawson, 1994; Levy & Brekke, 1990; Rogan, 1985; Wright, 1985). The battered women's movement is a grassroots social change movement based on a socio-political analysis of domestic violence. The alcoholism field works from a medical model and provides treatment from a perspective that understands chemical dependency as a disease. The subsequent conflicts that emerge in attempts to coordinate services to individuals affected by both problems are predictable and legitimate. The differences in language and approach reflect the analyses and perspectives of two very different problems. They are differences, however, that can and must be reconciled.

Despite the disparities, both the substances abuse and domestic violence service systems are combating problems that each day threaten the lives and well-being of countless women, children, and men. Both systems are battling barriers rooted in social attitudes and traditions that interfere with the provision of effective services and that frequently lead to harmful responses to those seeking help. It is essential that providers work together to ensure that their respective responses promote victim safety, offender accountability, and recovery from addiction.

References

Bennett, L., and M. Lawson. 1994. "Barriers to Cooperation Between Domestic Violence and Substance Abuse Programs." *Families in Society: The Journal of Contemporary Human Services*, pp. 277–86.

Flitcraft, A., and E. Stark. 1988. "Violence Among Intimates, an Epidemiological Review." In *Handbook of Family Violence*, ed. V. D. Van Hasselt, R. L. Morrison, A. S. Bellack, and M. Hersen, pp. 159–99. New York: Plenum.

Haver, B. 1987. "Female Alcoholics: IV. The Relationship Between Family Violence and Outcome 3–10 Years After Treatment." *Acta Psychiatric Scandanavia* 57: 449–56.

Kantor, G. K., and M. A. Straus. 1987. "The 'Drunken Bum' Theory of Wife Beating." *Social Problems* 34: 213–30.

Levy, A. J., and J. S. Brekke. 1990. "Spouse Battering and Chemical Dependency: Dynamics, Treatment, and Service Delivery." In *Aggression, Family Violence and Chemical Dependency*, ed. D. Finnegan, pp. 81–97. Binghamton, N.Y.: Haworth.

MacAndrew, C., and R. B. Edgerton. 1969. *Drunken Comportment: A Social Explanation*. Chicago: Aldine.

Marlatt, G. A., and D. J. Rohsenow. 1980. "Cognitive Processes in Alcohol Use: Expectancy and the Balanced Placebo Design. In *Advances in Substance Abuse Behavioral and Biological Research*, ed. Nancy K. Mello, pp. 159–99. Greenwich, Conn.: Jai.

Minnesota Coalition for Battered Women. 1992. *Safety First: Battered Women Surviving Violence When Alcohol and Drugs Are Involved*. Minneapolis: Minnesota Coalition for Battered Women.

Ptacek, J. 1987. "Why Do Men Batter Their Wives?" In *Feminist Perspectives on Wife Abuse*, ed. K. Yllö and M. Bograd, pp. 133–57. Newbury Park, Calif.: Sage.

Rogan, A. 1985. "Domestic Violence and Alcohol—Barriers to Cooperation." *Alcohol Health and Research World*, pp. 22–27.

Straus, M. A., and R. J. Gelles. 1990. *Physical Violence in American Families*. New Brunswick, N.J.: Transaction Books.

Wright, J. 1985. "Domestic Violence and Substance Abuse: A Cooperative Approach Toward Working with Dually Affected Families." In *Social Work Practice with Clients Who Have Alcohol Problems*, ed. E. M. Freeman, pp. 26–39. Springfield, Ill.: Thomas.

14

Latina Battered Women: Barriers to Service Delivery and Cultural Considerations

Gloria Bonilla-Santiago

This chapter provides an overview of the cultural barriers, social service, and legal needs of Latina battered women. Latina women are women with parents, grandparents, or great grandparents from Latin America: Puerto Rico, Cuba, Mexico, the Dominican Republic, Central America and South America. As the prevalence of family violence has been recognized and shelter services, police proarrest laws, and orders of protection have become more readily available, the oppression and brutal assaults against Latina battered women are finally being acknowledged as well. For a variety of reasons, including cultural and religious beliefs, Latina battered women have not used existing community agencies to escape a violent home.

In my study of twenty-five incarcerated battered Latina women, I found that because of language and cultural barriers, most of the Latina women had received no assistance or protection from police, legal aid, welfare, family counseling agencies, or community mental health centers. This chapter concludes with policy and practice recommendations for legislators, community leaders, social work administrators, and battered women advocates for improving the correctional response to Latina battered women. The author recognizes that there is an urgent need for pro-bono legal services and client advocacy for the women in this study and that traditional law-enforcement and judicial agencies should provide culturally sensitive and bilingual services to this oppressed group.

Background

Domestic violence against women occurs in families from all cultural and ethnic groups (Straus, Gelles, & Steinmetz, 1980; Walker, 1984), and intervention policies and practices in treating battered women should accommodate the diverse cultural backgrounds of these women. Nevertheless, research or information on the cultural aspects of domestic violence against women and how they differ among ethnic groups is very limited. Most research on the abuse of women has focused on the Anglo-American population, and most of the literature has ignored cross-cultural differences or acknowledges that cross-cultural differences in women abuse have been minimally explored (Carrillo & Marrujo, 1984; Straus et al., 1980).

Ethnic heritage is a manifestation of values, attitudes, personality, and behavior. Different ethnic groups receive different societal opportunities and rewards, and they share certain attitudes and goals (Lystad, 1985). Although the United States is composed of many ethnic groups, the emphasis has been on assimilation—that is, conformity with Anglo-American values. Services offered to various ethnic groups are judged and categorized in accordance with their adherence to the dominant white values. Nonetheless, ethnic and cultural diversity constitutes the "fabric" of American society (Cafferty & Chestang, 1976), and cultural factors are relevant to all aspects of helping battered women.

Studies and statistics have established that the situation of Latinas is different from that of white and black women. Latinas face barriers of gender, national origin or race, and language that also affect the experiences of battered Latina women. Feelings of vulnerability and helplessness because of the lack of resources available to Latinas, the dearth of bilingual or bicultural services from social services, hospitals, and shelters, as well as the cultural isolation experienced by Latinas who do not speak English or whose cultural norms differ from those prevailing in the United States, converge and set certain boundaries on battered Latina women. The impact of these differences on Latinas' lives has led researchers to conclude that Latinas need support services that are targeted to their specific issues, to a greater extent than do other battered women (Gondolf, Fisher, & McFerron, 1988, pp. 34–44). These cultural factors are relevant as one understands the need to better serve the growing number of the undocumented battered Latina women. There is compelling evidence that America's new undocumented migrants are increasingly likely to be women and children. Many researchers have also indicated that more women will be migrating to the United States without their spouses because they are able to find jobs in the "hidden" service economy. However, while more immigrant women are coming to the United States seeking a better quality of life for themselves and their families, the barriers they face are tremendous. Fearing deportation and/or the loss of her children, an immigrant battered woman may be intimidated by her partner's threat to report her to the U.S. Immigration and Naturalization Service if she leaves him or calls the police. She may not realize that domestic violence is against the law, that she has legal options to stop the battering, and that there are agencies and community resources available to support her.

There may also be inhibitions based on cultural issues and ambiguities about domestic violence. Different countries and cultures may have different values and attitudes toward a "woman's place," family, marriage, sex roles, and divorce. Added to this is the fact that a major cause of domestic violence is rooted in society's tradition of the unequal power of men and women society. All these factors combine to make immigrant Latina women feel isolated and powerless to escape the cycle of violence. Therefore, criminal justice practitioners, social service providers, and immigrant assistance agencies can play a critical role in identifying domestic violence and giving immigrant battered women information about the help that is available in their communities.

People from Latin America often share a regional heritage that includes abuse from governmental officials, the military, and local law enforcement officials. Indeed, recent immigrants often are escaping police and military force, and so they bring with them memories of and suspicions about the assistance available from enforcement agencies. A Latina woman may be suspicious of the police, who have acted in a violent and repressive manner toward the community at large, and she must decide whether to ask for help from an outsider who does not share her language or any of her cultural values. She is therefore often left to fend for herself at a time of extreme danger and urgency.

Social workers and others providing services to Latina battered women thus should incorporate cultural factors into their care and intervention and their legislative policy. Law enforcement officials' education strategies also must be coordinated with community-based organizations and Latino advocates. Otherwise, the education programs will reflect ingrained stereotypes and merely intensify the same problems that the education efforts seek to remedy.

Descriptive Survey

Few research studies have investigated battering in the Latino community within the United States. This comparative study obtained information on the cross-cultural aspects of abuse of both Latina and Anglo-American battered women. Interviews were conducted with twenty-five Latina women and twenty-five white women residing at the Edna Mahan women's correctional facility in Clinton, New Jersey, and two resource centers for Latina women in Camden and Newark, New Jersey. The study focused on their attitudes toward wife abuse and their perception of what constitutes abuse and examined cross-cultural issues and aspects of abused Latina women and the implications for treatment and intervention.

Findings

Although domestic violence cuts across ethnic, religious, and economic lines, undocumented Latina women (undocumented immigrants are those persons whose authorized stay in the United States has expired and include temporary workers as well as those who have entered the country illegally) face serious difficulties because of both their abuse and their undocumented status.

The education of this group of respondents mirrors that of the general Latino population but is noticeably poorer compared with that of other females. Because of the high rate of teenage pregnancy among adolescent Latinas, these women are also less likely than other females are to finish high school or to complete an education or job-training program.

Interviews were conducted with twenty-five Latina women at the Clinton women's correctional facility. These women had been given long sentences because of (1) the possession of drugs (the largest reason for the rise of undocumented Latina inmates), (2) the distribution of drugs, (3) robbery and property crimes, and (4) murder as a result of domestic violence. The Latina women incarcerated at Clinton were mostly from poor urban areas and were poorly educated, with a fourth-grade reading level and even poorer occupational skills. The youngest woman we interviewed was fifteen, and the oldest was fifty-eight.

Many of the Latina women who participated in our focus group came from Central America, the Dominican Republic, and the Caribbean. Others came from poor urban areas. The majority were undocumented immigrants. Many of the women stated that they felt isolated in this country because they did not understand the language, culture, legal system, or social systems; consequently they often suffered the triple burden of discrimination based on sex, race, and their undocumented status.

The focus groups revealed that many immigrant Latina women were isolated and trapped in violent homes, afraid to turn to anyone for help. The results of the survey of Latina women revealed that 34 percent had experienced some form of domestic violence by their partners, in both their country of origin and the United States.

There were some significant differences among Latinas and Anglo-American battered women we studied. The Latina women were more tolerant of wife abuse and their perceptions of what constituted wife abuse differed from those of our Anglo-American subjects. For example, such acts as hitting or verbal abuse had to occur more frequently to be considered abusive by Latino women. Some acts perceived as abusive by the Anglo-American women were not considered as abusive by the Latina women, including verbal abuse and the failure to provide adequate food and shelter. Latina women were much more likely to consider an act as "physical abuse" because of their society's more frequent use of weapons such as knives, metals and guns, which was seen as a threat to their life. The following quotations reflect the feelings of anger, fear, and isolation of two Latinas:

The first time I went to the hospital [he] had broken my nose and cut my head open. He hit me on the head with metal, and I got seventeen stitches over my ear. I can't hear well on that side since that happened. The other time, I was pregnant with my third child . . . [he] hit me and kicked me with a weapon so that I almost miscarried in my sixth month. You know, [my son] has always been a slow learner, and I think it's because of the beating before he was born. (Interview with shelter participant, August 20, 1992)

One time the neighbors called the police. They heard screaming and yelling. He had been hitting me and throwing knives and threatening me around the house. A police officer came to the door and asked if everything was all right. You know, he stood right behind me, and I had to say that everything was fine. I was afraid he'd do something if I didn't. (Interview with shelter participant, August 10, 1992)

Their economic existence is often based on "underground" employment sources and markets. Many of these battered Latinas are not native English speakers and have limited English language comprehension. Thus they are unemployable due to the lack of skills and competencies, at higher rates than white or black women. The choices Latina women have in response to being abused and leaving her home, were few in comparison to white women. White women felt that they could go to a shelter or police and feel temporarily protected.

Latinas have a sense of futility in seeking police assistance:

> I never called the police here because [he] told me that they will deport us if I do. I've thought about learning some English, but between work and the kids there is hardly any time. So I've never really asked anybody for help. Anyway sometimes the police did came and never pay attention to my story, since he was there and always got to tell that it was a family misunderstanding. (Interview with inmate participant, Edna Mahan correctional facility, July 1992)

In this study with the Latina focus group, the women faced the precarious, often untenable, situation of the "double-blind" empowerment through the disempowerment of a male member of the community. The internal conflict and external pressure to cast police officials as outsiders, hostile to the community, frustrates the development of empowerment. There is evidence that officers have reacted to such arrest policies by arresting both the man and the woman, so called dual arrest. This occurred with Latinas in this study. Empowerment is unlikely when women are treated as if they have acted illegally, are as culpable as the batterer, or cannot be believed.

Recommendations

Consideration of and responsiveness to cultural and racial differences must be central to any strategies in the domestic violence movement. The issues, problems, and experiences of battered Latinas have not been taken into consideration in the social work community or by the social service providers in state government.

Extensive education efforts must be linked to mandatory arrest policies to inform the community of the policies and the duties of the police. Fears of deportation must be addressed through extensive education efforts and by the good-faith conduct of the appropriate agencies.

A great deal of what has been done with domestic violence has centered on the establishment and maintenance of shelters and increased social services. These are recognized as critical provisions for battered women. However, Latinas have not received sufficient resources and services to address their multiple needs. Latino and community-based organizations must be strengthened and provided with the financial and political flexibility to develop and implement domestic violence shelters and services. The Latino community must prioritize domestic violence initiatives.

References

Cafferty, P.S.J., and L. Chestang, eds. 1976. *The Diverse Society: Implications for Social Policy.* Washington, D.C.: NASW Press.

Carrillo, R. A., and R. Marrujo. 1984. "Aculturation and Domestic Violence in the Hispanic Community." Unpublished manuscript.

Gondolf, E. W., E. Fisher and J. R. McFerron. 1988. "Racial Differences Among Shelter Residents." *Journal of Family Violence*, no. 1.

Lystad, M. H. 1985. "Family Violence: A Mental Health Perspective. Emotional First Aid." Unpublished manuscript.

Straus, M., R. Gelles, and S. Steinmetz. 1980. *Behind Closed Doors.* Garden City, N.Y.: Anchor/Doubleday.

Walker, L. E. 1984. *The Battered Woman Syndrome.* New York: Springer.

Epilogue: Helping Battered Women

Ann A. Abbott

Violence against women has been a long-standing, pervasive problem, one not limited by age, race, class, or culture. Its existence has been perpetuated and minimized by a number of influential misconceptions and beliefs, the more prevalent of which include

- A man's home is his castle and what goes on there is sacrosanct, immune from public intervention.
- When a woman is abused, it is typically because she has done something to deserve it or in some way enjoys it (blaming the victim).
- The battering of women is primarily a lower-class phenomenon and is not worthy of major attention.
- It is more important to keep a family intact than to cause disruption by recognizing abuse.

Frequently, the intense shame and fear suffered by the abused have served as additional mechanisms for guaranteeing its protected status. The power of these beliefs in minimizing abuse has been of major concern. Of even greater concern is the fact that abuse against women may be indicative of other abuse within the family unit and may serve as a general barometer of society's overall acceptance or tolerance of violence.

Not only have these beliefs been challenged during the past quarter-century, but their beginning demise has been accompanied and facilitated by the significant emergence of the women's movement. As the feminist movement has gained in stature, so have the demands for empowerment and justice throughout society.

Recognition of the abuse of women has been heightened by the fact that more police officers have been killed intervening in domestic abuse situations than in the entire war on drugs. In addition, the impact of violence against women is frequently evident in the behavior of their children, many of whom, upon closer scrutiny, have been identified as victims of abuse themselves.

During the past twenty-five years, the shrouds protecting domestic violence, or violence against intimates, have been pulled aside, and service providers, community leaders, social work administrators, volunteers, and legislators alike have begun to recognize the problem as a cause for major concern and action. Communities have developed an array of emergency community-based services, volunteers have played a major role in funding and staffing these programs, providers have tested and refined a broad range of treatment approaches, and legislators have passed laws that give legal and financial support for programming for this specific population. Their collective efforts have resulted in some major legislative inroads. Early in his administration, President Carter established the Office of Domestic Violence in the Department of Health and Human Services; recently, Congress passed the Violence Against Women Act, a component of the 1994 crime bill.

Although national family violence surveys report comparable levels of abuse directed toward males, it is females who suffer the major effects of violence. Men by their very size wield the advantage, in addition to having mastery over the family purse strings.

An overview of relevant statistics reveals that more than one-quarter of all women have been victims of abuse by a spouse or an intimate partner. These statistics may well be underestimates. As we know, only the most severe cases are reported in the crime statistics, and shame and fear tend to restrict the victims' reports of abuse. In addition to the physical, sexual, or psychological abuse many female victims endure, many incarcerated women report physical or sexual abuse as a precursor or catalyst to their criminal acts, the result of which may be added abuse in the form of incarceration.

Throughout its history, social work has been a strong voice on behalf of women's rights, preaching the right to self-determination and advancing a strong commitment to social justice. For example, the Delegate Assembly, the policymaking body of the National Association of Social Workers (the largest professional social work association, with over 155,000 members), has developed a detailed public policy statement on family violence to guide the scope of the organization and the professional practice of its members. The initial statement was developed in the 1970s, approved by the 1979 Delegate Assembly, revised in 1987, and reconfirmed in 1993. In addition, NASW has declared "violence" to be the primary focus of its public-relations campaign efforts from 1993 to 1995 and has instituted a number of special initiatives to help children and families recognize, avert, and dispel all types of violence, including violence among intimates. In addition to providing lobbyists to play an active role in the legislative arena, NASW has focused on modifying the portrayal of violence in the media and informing the public of its dangers while providing avenues for corrective action.

Although social work has had an ongoing commitment to the protection of human rights and the prevention and treatment of family violence, social work practitioners, as do members of other human service professions, have much to learn in this arena. This book, *Helping Battered Women,* is an invaluable resource not only for increasing knowledge of direct practice/intervention skills and an understanding of program and policy development, but also for providing direction for essential social action. It reflects the joint thinking of a broad range of experts, including practitioners, researchers, educators, administrators, and policy analysts from the fields of social work, psychology, and criminal justice. The editor has guided the presentation of content to clearly illustrate the critical relationship among the various components involved in legislative efforts, policy development, the criminal justice system, and the broad service delivery system. In addition, it provides practical intervention steps and reminds the reader of the importance of such factors as culture and age in program development and intervention.

Although the book focuses on battered women, its principles go beyond this specific population, advancing the well-being of all vulnerable, abused populations. This comprehensive collection reinforces the necessity of the person-in-environment, or biopsychosocial, perspective, the importance of a diverse range of intervention strategies, and the necessity for broadly trained practitioners who are equally well versed in treatment skills, research capacities, and social change and policy development abilities. It should serve to raise the consciousness and skill level of a broad range of professionals, who as a result should ultimately play an enhanced role in heightening society's awareness of and support for battered women and their families. Familiarity with the content of this volume should prompt policy analysts, clinicians, and administrators to reaffirm their commitment to empowering the battered woman and advocating for her rights. This book should become a major reference, guiding their efforts to improve the plight of the battered woman and to decrease the incidents and effects of battering throughout our society.

Author Index

Abbott, A. A., xiv, xv, 235–37
Abelman, I., 53, 58
Abrahamson, D., 191
Achenbach, T., 174
Adelman, R., 49, 60
Ahrens, L., 18
Alexander, F., 113
Alvarez, W., 200
American Bar Association, 8
American Psychiatric Association, 176
Anderson, G., 172, 173, 178
Anderson, P. R., 111, 115
Anwar, R., 5
Arata, C., 200, 202
Astin, M. C., 7
Attorney General's Task Force on Family
    Violence, 117–18
Aubrey, M., 193
Austin, D., 17
Ayers, A., 163

Bachman, R., 103
Bacich, A., 90, 115, 128
Bagarozzi, D. A., 199
Baker v. *City of New York,* 113
Bandura, A., 72
Barling, J., 173, 176
Battered Women's Justice Project, 21–22
Beck, A. T., 167, 168, 201
Becker, J. V., 211
Beckett, J. O., 160
Beirne, P., 105
Bellack, A. S., 31

Bennett, B., 71
Bennet, L., 227
Berg, B., 192
Berk, R. A., 32, 91, 114, 115
Biden, J. R., 31
Bisno, H., 19
Blackstone, W., 104
Bograd, M., 68
Bolton, F., 161, 163, 164
Bolton, S., 161, 163, 164
Bonilla-Santiago, G., xiv, xv, 229–34
Breckman, R., 49, 60
Brekke, J., 198, 199, 227
Bricout, J. C., xiii, xv, 67–82
Briere, J., 202
Brink, J. C., 183, 184, 185
Brodsky, S., 193
Browne, A., 32, 34, 36
Brownell, P., xiii, xv, 44–66
Bruno v. *Codd,* 105, 112, 116
Buel, S. M., 112, 114
Bunch, C., 16, 27
Bureau of Justice Statistics, 5, 70, 118
Burman, B., 79
Butcher, J. N., 203
Buzawa, C. G., 90, 105
Buzawa, E. S., 90, 105

Cafferty, P. S. J., 230
Cahn, S., 71
Cameron, S., 183, 185
Campbell, J., 199
Cantor, M., 52, 53

Subject Index